COLERIDGE'S PLAY OF MIND

Painting by Joseph Wright of Derby, 1768: 'An Experiment on a Bird in an Air Pump'. Courtesy of the National Gallery.

Coleridge's Play
of Mind

JOHN BEER

OXFORD
UNIVERSITY PRESS

OXFORD

UNIVERSITY PRESS

Great Clarendon Street, Oxford OX2 6DP

Oxford University Press is a department of the University of Oxford.
It furthers the University's objective of excellence in research, scholarship,
and education by publishing worldwide in

Oxford New York

Auckland Cape Town Dar es Salaam Hong Kong Karachi
Kuala Lumpur Madrid Melbourne Mexico City Nairobi
New Delhi Shanghai Taipei Toronto

With offices in

Argentina Austria Brazil Chile Czech Republic France Greece
Guatemala Hungary Italy Japan Poland Portugal Singapore
South Korea Switzerland Thailand Turkey Ukraine Vietnam

Oxford is a registered trade mark of Oxford University Press
in the UK and in certain other countries

Published in the United States
by Oxford University Press Inc., New York

© John Beer 2010

The moral rights of the author have been asserted
Database right Oxford University Press (maker)

First published 2010

British Library Cataloguing in Publication Data

Data available

Library of Congress Cataloging in Publication Data

Data available

Typeset by SPI Publisher Services, Pondicherry, India
Printed in Great Britain
on acid-free paper by
the MPG Books Group

ISBN 978-0-19-957401-8

1 3 5 7 9 10 8 6 4 2

Contents

Abbreviations

BK	*Blake: Complete Writings, with variant readings*, ed. G. Keynes (Oxford: Clarendon Press, 1957; reprinted with additions and corrections in the Oxford Standard Authors series, 1966).
CAR	Coleridge, *Aids to Reflection* [1825], ed. John Beer, *CC* 9 (Princeton, N.J. and London, 1993).
CBL	Coleridge, *Biographia Literaria* [1817], eds. James Engell and Walter Jackson Bate, *CC* 7 (2 vols., Princeton, N.J. and London, 1983).
CBL (1907)	Coleridge, *Biographia Literaria* [1817], ed. John Shawcross (2 vols., Oxford: Clarendon Press, 1907).
CC	*The Collected Works of Samuel Taylor Coleridge*, general ed. Kathleen Coburn, associate ed. Bart Winer (16 vols., Princeton, N.J.: Princeton University Press, and London: Routledge & Kegan Paul, 1969–2002).
CCL	*The Collected Letters of Thomas and Jane Welsh Carlyle*, general ed. Charles Richard Sanders (Durham, N.C.: Duke University Press, 1970–).
CF (1809)	Coleridge, *The Friend* (28 parts, printed and published by J. Brown, and sold by Messrs. Longman and Co., 1809–10).
CFriend	Coleridge, *The Friend* [1809–18], ed. Barbara Rooke, *CC* 4 (2 vols., Princeton, N.J. and London, 1969).
CH	*Coleridge: The Critical Heritage*, ed. J. R. De J. Jackson (2 vols., London: Routledge & Kegan Paul, 1970–91).
CL	Coleridge, *Collected Letters*, ed. E.L. Griggs (6 vols., Oxford: Clarendon Press, 1956–71).
CLects (1795)	Coleridge, *Lectures 1795: On Politics and Religion*, ed. Lewis Patton and Peter Mann, *CC* 1 (Princeton, N.J. and London, 1971).
CLects (1808–19)	Coleridge, *Lectures 1808–1819: On Literature*, ed. R. A. Foakes, *CC* 5 (2 vols., Princeton, N.J. and London, 1987).

CLects (1818–19)   Coleridge, *Lectures 1818–1819: On the History of Philosophy*, ed. J. R. De J. Jackson, *CC* 8 (2 vols., Princeton, N.J. and London, 2000).

CLR   Coleridge, *Literary Remains*, ed. H. N. Coleridge (4 vols., London: Pickering, 1834–6).

CM   Coleridge, *Marginalia*, eds. George Whalley and H. J. Jackson, *CC* 12 (6 vols., Princeton, N.J. and London, 1980–2001).

CN   Coleridge, *Notebooks*, eds. Kathleen Coburn and Anthony John Harding (5 vols. in 10, Princeton, N.J.: Princeton University Press, and London: Routledge & Kegan Paul, 1959–2002).

CNB   Coleridge's MS Notebooks, in the British Library and elsewhere.

COM   Coleridge, *Opus Maximum*, ed. Thomas McFarland, assisted by Nicholas Halmi, *CC* 15 (Princeton, N.J. and London, 2002).

CPL (1949)   *The Philosophical Lectures, Hitherto Unpublished, of Samuel Taylor Coleridge*, ed. Kathleen Coburn (London: Pilot Press, 1949).

CPW (Beer)   Coleridge, *Poems*, ed. J. B. Beer, new edn., Everyman's Library (London: David Campbell Publishers Ltd. and Random House (UK), 2000).

CPW (CC)   Coleridge, *Poetical Works*, ed. J. C. C. Mays, *CC* 16 (2 (out of 6) vols., Princeton, N.J. and London, 2001).

CPW (EHC)   Coleridge, *Poetical Works*, ed. E. H. Coleridge (2 vols., Oxford: Clarendon Press, 1912).

CShC   *Coleridge's Shakespearean Criticism*, ed. T. M. Raysor [1936]; Everyman's Library 2nd edn. (2 vols., London: J. M. Dent and New York: E. P. Dutton, 1960).

CSWF   Coleridge, *Shorter Works and Fragments*, eds. H. J. Jackson and J. R. De J. Jackson, *CC* 11 (2 vols., Princeton, N.J. and London, 1995).

CTalker   *Coleridge the Talker: A Series of Contemporary Descriptions and Comments*, eds. Richard W. Armour and Raymond F. Howes (Ithaca, N.Y.: Cornell University Press, 1940).

CTT   Coleridge, *Table Talk* [1835], ed. Carl Woodring, *CC* 14 (2 vols., Princeton, N.J. and London, 1990).

CWatchman	Coleridge, *The Watchman* [1796], ed. Lewis Patton, *CC* 2 (Princeton, N.J. and London, 1970).
DQW	*The Collected Writings of Thomas De Quincey*, ed. D. Masson (14 vols., Edinburgh, 1889).
DWJ	*Journals of Dorothy Wordsworth*, ed. E. de Selincourt (2 vols., Oxford: Clarendon Press, 1941).
GEL	George Eliot, *Letters*, ed. G. S. Haight, Yale edn. (9 vols., New Haven, Conn.: Yale University Press, 1954–78).
HCR	*Henry Crabb Robinson on Books and Their Writers*, ed. E. J. Morley (3 vols., London: J. M. Dent and Sons, Ltd.,1938).
HW	*The Complete Works of William Hazlitt*, ed. P. P. Howe, after the edition of A. R. Waller and Arnold Glover (21 vols., London: J. M. Dent, 1930–4).
KL	*Letters of John Keats, 1814–1821*, ed. H. E. Rollins (2 vols., Cambridge, Mass.: Harvard University Press, 1958).
KP	*Poems of John Keats*, ed. M. Allott (London: Longman, 1970).
LL (Lucas)	*Letters of Charles and Mary Lamb*, ed. E. V. Lucas (3 vols., London: J. M. Dent & Sons Ltd., Methuen & Co. Ltd., 1935).
LL (Marrs)	*Letters of Charles and Mary Lamb*, ed. Edwin Marrs (3 vols. only, Ithaca, N.Y. and London: Cornell University Press, 1976).
PMLA	Publications of the Modern Language Association.
RX	John Livingston Lowes, *The Road to Xanadu* (London: Constable, 1927).
TLS	Times Literary Supplement.
WL (1787–1805)	*The Letters of William and Dorothy Wordsworth, The Early Years, 1787–1805,* ed. E. de Selincourt, 2nd edn., rev. C. L. Shaver (Oxford: Clarendon Press, 1967).
WL (1806–11)	*The Letters of William and Dorothy Wordsworth, The Middle Years, 1806–11,* ed. E. de Selincourt, 2nd edn., revd. Mary Moorman (2 vols., Oxford: Clarendon Press, 1969).
WL (1821–53)	*The Letters of William and Dorothy Wordsworth, The Later Years, 1821–53,* ed. E. de Selincourt; 2nd edn., revd. A. G. Hill (4 vols., Oxford: Clarendon Press, 1978–88).

WPrel	*The Prelude 1799, 1805, 1850*, eds. Jonathan Wordsworth, M. H. Abrams, and Stephen Gill (New York and London: W. W. Norton, 1979).
WPrW	Wordsworth, *Prose Works*, eds. W. J. B. Owen and J. W. Smyser (3 vols., Oxford: Clarendon Press, 1974).
WPW	Wordsworth, *Poetical Works*, eds. E. de Selincourt and Helen Darbishire (5 vols., Oxford: Clarendon Press, 1940–9).

Introduction

This study is the fruit of many years' study, and I owe more debts than I can begin to acknowledge. First and foremost I must thank the Trustees of the Leverhulme foundation for appointment to an Emeritus Fellowship for two years which enabled me to visit various libraries and embark on the main project. Previously, however, and for some years afterwards, I worked with the Bollingen Trust and Princeton University Press on the long work involved in producing the *Collected Works*, volumes of which continued to appear and are now, happily, complete. A distinctive feature of this work was to draw attention to the variousness of Coleridge's achievement, so that in every volume different kinds of expertise were called for. Over the years, therefore, I was able to benefit as each volume came into focus, from cooperation with the scholars concerned. Some, including Kathleen Coburn, Bart Winer, Earl Leslie Griggs, George Whalley, David Erdman, and Edward Bostetter, are no longer with us; others, happily, including Reg Foakes, Anthony Harding, Jim Mays, Thomas McFarland, and Heather and Robin Jackson lived to see the completion of a project which I. A. Richards termed 'one of the noblest, most arduous and most promising enterprises of our time'.

In the meantime I have been able to participate annually in the Wordsworth Summer Conference where Richard and Jonathan Wordsworth were notable organizers, along with Robert and Pamela Woof and, subsequently, Richard and Fiona Gravil. A more recent foundation—the biennial Coleridge Conference at Cannington—has enabled me to undertake exploration of more of the topics in these pages. Among late scholars who gave sterling help I must mention Owen Barfield, Bob Barth, Dorothy Emmet, Lionel Knights, Jack Owen, Herbert Piper, Hugh Sykes Davies, and Basil Willey; to whom I gladly add the names, past and present, of Mike Abrams, Rosemary Ashton, Lawrence Buell, Fred Burwick, Marilyn Butler, Stephen Bygrave, Paul Cheshire, Deirdre Coleman, John Colmer, John Cornwell, Graham Davidson, Josie Dixon, John Drew, Angela Esterhammer, Kelvin Everest, Tim Fulford, Marilyn Gaull, Andor Gomme, Nicholas Halmi, Paul Hamilton, Geoffrey Hartman, Samantha Harvey, Douglas Hedley, Geoffrey Hill, Richard Holmes, Mary Jacobus, Peter Kitson, Michael

John Kooy, Nigel Leask, Molly Lefebure, Paul Magnuson, Jim McCusick, Anne Mellor, Raimonda Modiano, Lucy Newlyn, Morton Paley, Reeve Parker, Mary Anne Perkins, Seamus Perry, Ralph Pite, Stephen Prickett, Tilottama Rajan, Donald Reiman, Nicholas Roe, Elinor Shaffer, Jane Stabler, Jack Stillinger, Donald Sultana, Anya Taylor, Edward Thompson, David Vallins, Mary Wedd, and Kathleen Wheeler.

1

The Missing Playground

In 1768, Joseph Wright of Derby completed a painting, 'Experiment on a Bird in an Air-Pump', which would in time hang in the British National Gallery. It showed a group of well-to-do people grouped by an air-pump while the effect of oxygen deprivation on a living being (in this case a bird) was being demonstrated. The people around displayed varying degrees of concern: a young girl was looking up in appalled wonder at the dying bird while her older companion covered her eyes to avoid the sight. A young man and woman to one side seemed only to have eyes for one another, while the centre was dominated by a figure looking directly toward the viewer, as if asking whether such inhumane behaviour in the name of science was really to be tolerated.

A few years later a scholarly clergyman in the west of England would welcome the latest addition to his large family, a baby to whom, when he grew up, questions about the end to which current rationalism pointed would all his life be a pressing concern. How far could the demands of scientific investigation and logical thinking be allowed to take precedence over the need for free play of mind and body? The baby, in question, Samuel Taylor Coleridge, would argue the matter back and forth, always acknowledging that many points of view were possible.

Though his birth and upbringing in a country vicarage looked to be of unusual conventionality and respectability, some questions hovered over his lineage, even, since according to a later statement of his own, a forebear on his father's side had been produced as the result of sexual play:

On my father's side I can rise no higher than my Grandfather, who was dropped when a Child, in the Hundred of Coleridge in the County of Devon; christened, educated, & apprenticed by the parish—he afterwards became a respectable Woolen-draper in the town of South Molton.[1]

---

[1] *CL* I 302. Griggs points out that South Molton was probably a mistake for Crediton. Professor J. C. C. Mays, who has kindly shown me his detailed unpublished study of Coleridge's parentage and background, agrees, suggesting that John Coleridge Senior may well have been a weaver.

Two years later Coleridge related the tradition again, this time taking it
a generation further back and telling Poole, after meeting a 'Mr Northmore, a pupil of Wakefield's' who lived near Exeter and had been at his
father's school, '*My* great-grandfather was *his* Great-great-grandfather's
Bastard'—though 'it was not this relationship however tender & interesting, which brought us together'.[2] This version is more detailed; it
is later and anchored to a particular person. In any case, the fact that
Coleridge believed his descent to be of doubtful legitimacy gives another
clue to the sense of insecurity that characterized many of his statements
about himself.

His childhood was not without its turbulences, the most central
involving a fight with his brother that he described in one of his
autobiographical letters to Poole:

I had asked my Mother one evening to cut my cheese entire, so that I might
toast it. This was no easy matter, it being a 'crumbly' cheese. My Mother
however did it. I went into the garden for something or other, and in the mean
time my brother Frank minced my cheese, 'to disappoint the favourite.'
I returned, saw the exploit, and in an agony of passion flew at Frank. He
pretended to have been seriously hurt by my blow, flung himself on the ground,
and there lay with outstretched limbs. I hung over him mourning and in a great
fright; he leaped up, and with a horse-laugh gave me a severe blow in the face.
I seized a knife, and was running at him, when my Mother came in and took me
by the arm. I expected a flogging, and, struggling from her, I ran away to a little
hill or slope, at the bottom of which the Otter flows, about a mile from Ottery.
There I staid; my rage died away, but my obstinacy vanquished my fears, and
taking out a shilling book, which had at the end morning and evening prayers,
I very devoutly repeated them—thinking at the same time with a gloomy
inward satisfaction—how miserable my Mother must be![3]

Two years later, in October 1781, Frank, then eleven years of age, left
home to go to sea. His father, who took him to Plymouth and found a
place for him under a religious captain, returned home on the 6th, only
to be taken ill and die suddenly during the night. (Coleridge later dated
the event on the 4th, the date of his own, and Wordsworth's marriage.)[4]

---

[2] Letter to Poole, 16 September 1799: *CL* I 528. Shortly before his death Earl Leslie
Griggs mentioned to me that he had discovered more about this connection with
Thomas Northmore (1766–1851), but he did not elaborate or publish his information.
Others have investigated further, including Professor Mays, mentioned above, whose
identification of Coleridge's grandmother is particularly persuasive.

[3] Ibid., I 352–3.

[4] Ibid., I 355. See also Coleridge: *The Early Family Letters*, ed. James Engell (Oxford:
Clarendon Press, 1994), pp. 6–8.

Frank was never to be seen by his family again, since in India, having accidentally met his brother John, who procured a commission for him in the army, he served as an officer and (to quote Coleridge's account) 'shot himself (having been left carelessly by his attendant) in a delirious fever brought on by his excessive exertions at the siege of Seringapatam'.[5]

In his 'Psychobiography' of Coleridge, entitled *His Brother's Keeper*,[6] Stephen Weissman argues that Coleridge must have seen in Frank's death fulfilment of the murderous impulse that had overtaken him in the childhood fight. He concludes that these events provide the key to an understanding of Coleridge's guilt feelings throughout his life, that they led him to identify himself with Cain in the biblical story and to believe that he was under the same curse, which would surface in times of stress. These, he argues, provided the driving impulse that led to the planning of 'The Wanderings of Cain' and the writing of *The Rime of The Ancient Mariner*.

Coleridge himself never gives any hint of having seen himself as a Cain-figure so far as his brother was concerned. When he attempted to write 'The Wanderings of Cain', interestingly, the only part that he succeeded in producing into verse was a passage describing Cain's innocent son Enos, wandering in the wilderness, which concluded, 'Has he no friend, no loving mother near?' If there was a self-identification here it was perhaps rather with the lost child that he had become during the night following the struggle with Frank. Any guilt he might have had concerning the fight itself seems to have been well buried.

A more likely biblical reference for himself is in another part of the Old Testament. When Coleridge ran away from home as a result of the fight with his brother he was eventually found and brought back next day after a night in the open. He was to carry a vivid memory of his father's response to his return:

[5] *CL* I 311. It is not clear that the suicide was as involuntary as Coleridge says and no doubt believed: see James Engell's study. Donald H. Reiman has seen Coleridge's mention of a portrayal of the battle of Seringapatam in the Notebooks (*CN* I 1494) as a fine emblem of his guilt over his fratricidal instincts, by which he interprets his tendency to satirize his brother poets ('Coleridge and the Art of Equivocation', *Studies in Romanticism*, 23 (1986), 350 and n). The picture, which Reiman refers to as 'the picture on his wall' as if Coleridge owned it, was actually described in notebook 7 during the Scottish Tour of 1803, and probably seen in a house that he visited there. It seems unwise to go beyond Kathleen Coburn's comment in her note that the picture 'would certainly have latent associations' for Coleridge (*CN* I 1494n).
[6] Madison, Conn.: International Universities Press, *c.*1989.

I remember, & never shall forget, my father's face, as he looked upon me while I lay in the servant's arms—so calm, and the tears stealing down his face: for I was the child of his old age.[7]

The final phrase carries an irresistible reminiscence of Genesis, where it is recorded that Jacob loved his son Joseph 'more than all his children, because he was the son of his old age'[8]—and it is hard to see how, as the youngest of his parents' ten children and a dreamer, Coleridge could have avoided comparing himself with this boy who had been persecuted by his brothers as the favourite of his father—or, indeed, not found satisfaction in the outcome of the tale, when Joseph prospered far more than they.

Despite his early sense of resentment, however, the evidence of the family letters is that the brothers were united in loyalty to each other and that they shared a concern for the future of young Sam, by then a scholar at Christ's Hospital.[9]

For further knowledge of his childhood we are largely dependent on his own record. The letters written to Poole in 1797 are well known, and have formed the basis of the biographies when they cover these years. Hardly known at all, on the other hand, and not published until 2002, are fragments of autobiographical record written just over two years before his death.[10] These cover a good deal of the same ground more briefly but also include records of his childhood and schooldays that do not appear elsewhere, his avowed emphasis lying in an attempt to understand his condition in medical terms. ('N. b. my purpose here is exclusively to give the retrospect of my *bodily* state & it's probable causes—')[11] He thought that because of his father's age he had possibly inherited his 'commencing decay of musculo-arterial Power', from which he inferred a possible further inheritance 'in part, from a constitutional overbalance of the Sensibility, the cerebronervous system, over the Irritability, better called the Instinctivity, or the Musculo-Arterial System—and a consequent predisposition of the Productivity, or Veno-glandular & capillary System, to the affections of sensitive Astheny, tho' it probably never put on the type of Scrophula—'.[12]

---

[7] *CL*, I 353–4.   [8] Genesis 37: 3.

[9] John Coleridge had some hope that General Goddard might be his patron, and made some efforts to have him made a cadet at the India House. A plan to enrol him in the military failed because of his young age. See e.g. the letters in *Coleridge: The Early Family Letters*, pp. 52, 54–5, 73, 80.

[10] CNB F°, ff 89ᵛ–91ᵛ (cf. *CN* V 6675). The passage was evidently known to, and used by, James Gillman in his 1838 *Life*.

[11] Ibid., f 91ᵛ.   [12] Ibid., f 89ᵛ.

The story of his hostile relationship with his brother Frank, and so by implication with his other brothers, then follows, with his lack of muscular strength being ascribed to the fact that as a child he was driven away from the other children's sports: 'I never played except by myself'. Yet this meant that he still learned to play—through the books he read; and in that area, it might be argued, he never stopped playing. Despite his continual countervailing drive to seriousness, a great deal is missed if this element in his nature is ignored: an important presence, leading to central insights such as his insistence on the need to carry on the feelings of Childhood into the powers of Manhood.

Despite this affirmation of continuing innocence, the next few years were not without their times of guilt—notably the crisis in his undergraduate affairs that led to his running away to London and enlisting for a time as a dragoon. Money problems were the avowed reason for this action, but he admitted to 'unchastities' at this time, and a veiled further reference suggests that he may have involved himself, however briefly, with one of the local prostitutes. It is even possible that a fear of having contracted a sexual disease contributed to the anxiety which led him to leave Cambridge precipitately. But whatever the reason the episode resulted in an upsurge of guilt as he relied on his brothers to rescue him. He confessed that at Cambridge he had 'fled to Debauchery', claiming that for the whole six weeks before the examination for the Greek prize he had been 'almost constantly intoxicated', and adding, with a touch of melodrama, 'My Brother, you shudder as you read—'.[13] In the autobiographical fragment written many years later, on the other hand, he repeated the story of his financial imprudence, but claimed nevertheless that he had taken credit for vices of which he was *not* guilty, and that he had been 'in heart & feeling as innocent as a child—& my imagination unstained'; yet he concluded, 'Whatever errors, or single acts of transgression I may have incurred from 20 to 23—in my 23rd year there was an end—and from my 23rd year I have not knowingly offended, in intemperance or unchastity—'.[14]

The effect of these statements is to emphasize the fact that between admissions of guilt and assertions of innocence there was little room for play of mind: the two were mutually exclusive, offering only the alternatives of bowing in humble penitence or indulging an unlimited further scope for speculation. These alternatives span the otherwise

---

[13] Letter to George Coleridge, 24 February 1794, *CL* I 67–8.
[14] CNB F°, f 91 (cf. *CN* V 6675).

puzzling contradiction of his poem 'The Eolian Harp', where he seems
to move effortlessly from the ranging thought play of projecting a
universe consisting entirely of organisms played on by an intellectual
breeze to a brisk rejection of such 'unhallowed' thoughts as products of
the 'unregenerate mind' of a man 'wilder'd and dark'. The conflicts
between the sportings of an innocent mind and the abysmal, cavernous
darkness of a guilty one were never to be resolved.

In childhood, meanwhile, any guilty feelings concerning his actions
towards his brother Frank had at least been offset a little by encourage-
ments to play from his sister Nancy, whom he recalled in *Frost at
Midnight* as

> My play-mate when we both were clothed alike!

But where else did he ever have later opportunities to develop such a
capacity? With the Evans family a little, perhaps; in Nether Stowey with
the Pooles, certainly, for there he was to remember evenings spent in

> Conundrum, Crambo, Rebus, or Charade:
> Enigmas, that had driven the Theban mad,
> And Puns then best when exquisitely bad:
> And I, if aught of archer vein I hit,
> With my own laughter stifled my own Wit!

With Wordsworth, similarly (though the fact is not always recognized),
he could play a jocular role. His friend, who had been willing to depict
himself as an object of interest to his neighbours for his strange appearance of melancholy, would recall how his frequent companion, 'A
noticeable Man with large grey eyes', exercised a different presence,
welcome partly for its lightening effect:

> Noisy he was, and gamesome as a boy;
> His limbs would toss about him with delight
> Like branches when strong winds the trees annoy.
> Nor lacked his calmer hours device or toy
> To banish listlessness and irksome care...[15]

If this is indeed a portrait of Coleridge it shows him in a light-hearted
mood not always evident in his writing. At this time, around 1802,
he had recently been exploring various scientific interests and even
making experiments of his own. Yet one detects a note of hesitancy in
Wordsworth's attitude, a failure to offer his friend total endorsement,

---

[15] *CPW* (CC) I (i) 247; *WPW* II 26.

that reflected the sense of a lack of grounding in his attitude, making
him like the infant prodigy of his implicit censure in *The Prelude*. It was
the misfortune of such a child, he would suggest, to lack what Wordsworth himself had been lucky enough to have enjoyed: contact with

> a race of young ones like to those
> With whom I herded!—(easily, indeed,
> We might have fed upon a fatter soil
> Of arts and letters—but be that forgiven)—
> A race of real children; not too wise,
> Too learned, or too good; but wanton, fresh,
> And bandied up and down by love and hate;
> Not unresentful where self-justified;
> Fierce, moody, patient, venturous, modest, shy;
> Mad at their sports like withered leaves in winds;
> Though doing wrong and suffering, and full oft
> Bending beneath our life's mysterious weight
> Of pain, and doubt, and fear, yet yielding not
> In happiness to the happiest upon earth.

Debarred from that resource, he felt, Coleridge, in spite of his

> learning, gorgeous eloquence,
> And all the strength and plumage of... youth...

in spite, also, of his

> subtle speculations, toils abstruse
> Among the schoolmen, and Platonic forms
> Of wild ideal pageantry, shaped out
> From things well-matched or ill, and words for things.

had been thrown back on

> The self-created sustenance of a mind
> Debarred from Nature's living images,
> Compelled to be a life unto herself,
> And unrelentingly possessed by thirst
> Of greatness, love, and beauty.[16]

For Wordsworth, what Coleridge had lacked as a result was a full
exposure in childhood to any buffeting against his fellow human beings
in the midst of nature, so that he was deprived of the ballast provided by
such experiences.

[16] *WPrel* (1805) vi, 306–7, 308–11, 312–16.

2

Fantastic Sportiveness

Looking back on his childhood, Coleridge shared Wordsworth's sense that an important element had been lacking from his childhood, blaming, at least in part,

the Jealousy of Old Nolly, my Brother Frank's dotingly-fond Nurse. And if ever Child by beauty & liveliness deserved to be doted on, my Brother Francis was that Child/ and by the infusions of her Jealousy into my Brother's mind, I was in earliest childhood lifted away from the enjoyments of muscular activity—from Play—to take refuge at my Mother's side on my little stool, to read my little books and to listen to the Talk of my Elders—I was driven from Life in Motion, to Life in thought and sensation—I never played except by myself, & then only acting over what I had been reading or fancying, or half one, half the other, with a stick, cutting down the Weeds & Nettles, as one of the Seven Champions of Christendom—Alas I had all the simplicity, all the docility of a little Child; but none of the Child's Habits—I never thought as a Child; never had the language of a Child.[1]

This did not mean that the instinct to play was altogether subdued, however; rather the opposite. From an early age it had presented itself in the form of his extraordinary powers of imagination—though Wordsworth believed that later, at school, that had resulted in developments less agreeable. On one occasion he discussed with Henry Crabb Robinson Coleridge's and Charles Lamb's fondness for verbal play of various kinds:

Talking of dear Charles Lamb's very strange habit of quizzing and of Coleridge's far more equivocal incorrectnesses in talk, Wordsworth said he thought much of this was owing to a *school habit*...Lamb...loved a quizzing lie—a fiction that amused him like a good joke or an exercise of wit. There was in Coleridge a sort of dreaminess which would not let him see things as they were.

---

[1] CNB F° ff 89ᵛ–90 (cf. *CN* V 6675).

He would talk about his own feelings and recollections and intentions in a way that deceived others, but he was first deceived himself.[2]

A proclivity that might intrigue and even distress his friends when they discovered the flimsy basis for something they had heard from his lips was also at its best the facility powering his poetic achievements. Among other things, once he became intimate with the Wordsworths, it informed his thinking about the 'one Life' and the manner in which it could reveal itself even through the activity of an essentially dead phenomenon such as hail. Before long, Wordsworth himself had also explored the idea:

> But see! where'er the hailstones drop
> The withered leaves all skip and hop;
> There's not a breeze—no breath of air—
> Yet here, and there, and everywhere
> Along the floor, beneath the shade
> By those embowering hollies made,
> The leaves in myriads jump and spring,
> As if with pipes and music rare
> Some Robin Good-fellow were there,
> And all those leaves, in festive glee,
> Were dancing to the minstrelsy.[3]

In his original published version the last two lines were still more apposite to the theme:

> And all the leaves, that jump and spring,
> Were each a joyous living thing...[4]

During this period there are few occasions when the term 'one life', which was to play an important part in the relationship during this period, is actually used. The most important, and indeed the only one, so far as Wordsworth was concerned, was a passage among his early versions of writing towards *The Excursion*. In the manuscript poem which came to be known as 'The Ruined Cottage', completed in the spring of 1798, long passages, describing the early experiences of the Pedlar who narrates the story, relate how nature educated him into a deeper sense of herself when he tended his father's sheep as a young boy:

[2] *HCR* II 486.
[3] 'A whirl-blast from behind the hill...' *WPW* II 128.
[4] Ibid., note.

> From Nature and her overflowing soul
> He had received so much, that all his thoughts
> Were steeped in feeling. He was only then
> Contented, when, with bliss ineffable
> He felt the sentiment of being, spread
> O'er all that moves, and all that seemeth still,
> O'er all which, lost beyond the reach of thought,
> And human knowledge, to the human eye
> Invisible, yet liveth to the heart,
> O'er all that leaps, and runs, and shouts, and sings,
> Or beats the gladsome air, o'er all that glides
> Beneath the wave, yea in the wave itself
> And mighty depth of waters. Wonder not
> If such his transports were; for in all things
> He saw one life, and felt that it was joy.

This was evidently an attempt by Wordsworth to describe his own experiences.[5] In work towards the Two-Part *Prelude*, where the idea of the 'one life' was being allowed to develop still further, he drafted a passage that dwelt notably on a sense of the whole:

> I seemed to learn
> That what we see of forms and images
> Which float along our minds, and what we feel
> Of active or recognizable thought,
> Prospectiveness, or intellect, or will,
> Not only is not worthy to be deemed
> Our being, to be prized as what we are,
> But is the very littleness of life.
> Such consciousness I deem but accidents,
> Relapses from that one interior life
> That lives in all things, sacred from the touch
> Of that false secondary power by which
> In weakness we create distinctions, then
> Believe that all our puny boundaries are things
> Which we perceive, and not which we have made—
> In which all beings live with God, themselves

---

[5] By the time that he had produced the first, two-part version of the poem that was to become *The Prelude*, he had in fact transposed the whole segment into the first person, so that the lines became

> Wonder not
> If such my transports were, for in all things
> I saw one life, and felt that it was joy... (*WPrel* (1799) II 458–60).

Are God, existing in one mighty whole,
As undistinguishable as the cloudless east
At noon is from the cloudless west, when all
The hemisphere is one cerulean blue.[6]

Such lines represent the closest Wordsworth came in these years to pantheism.[7] There is also another passage which gives signs of having been composed out of the current ferment:

Oh bounteous power,
In childhood, in rememberable days,
How often did thy love renew for me
Those naked feelings which when thou wouldst form
A living thing thou sendest like a breeze
Into its infant being.[8]

To read passages such as this, honouring 'the bond of union betwixt life and joy', is also to receive light on the emergence of the celebrated phrases in the 'Lines composed a few miles above Tintern Abbey' in July, concerning the mood in which

we are laid asleep
In body, and become a living soul;
While with an eye made quiet by the power
Of harmony, and the deep power of joy,
We see into the life of things.

On both the occasions when Wordsworth introduces versions of such beliefs they are immediately accompanied by a safeguarding clause. In *The Prelude* he continues 'If this be error, and another faith | Find easier

---

[6] *WPrel* p. 496. These lines were used for MS RV of the 1799 version, and some for lines 249–254 of the version itself.

[7] He may have drawn back from the pantheist implications, even in the excitement of that time, since they were only partly included in the fair copy of the 1799 *Prelude*. The lines in the previous passage he could continue generally to endorse, and they were allowed to pass directly into the 1805 version. By the time that the 1850 version was published, nevertheless, the phrase 'one life' also had disappeared; by then Wordsworth was perhaps still more cautious about expressing a belief that might be interpreted as pantheistic.
It may also be noted that the expression 'one life' had not appeared in the earlier draft of the passage that provided the first account of the Pedlar's upbringing, though most of the surrounding lines were there. That passage was produced, we are told, in 1797; examination of the various versions leads to the conclusion that it emerged only subsequently, as part of the intellectual ferment that also produced the various items in *Lyrical Ballads* during the spring and summer of the following year.

[8] Printed in *WPrel* 'Fragments', p. 489.

access to the pious mind...' In 'Tintern Abbey', similarly, he writes immediately afterwards 'If this be but a vain belief...' Nevertheless both passages were allowed to stand, at least for the time being. They are not both saying the same thing, obviously: in the earlier one, more fraught with boyish excitement, the life is continually associated with movement, while the later belongs essentially to the meditative, mature man. Yet the underlying sentiment is the same: in all life, if probed sufficiently, it is possible to trace a unity.

Although Coleridge, by comparison, did not use the phrase 'one life' in these years, his emphasis and emotional charge for the word 'life' betray a similar depth of interest. In the closing passage of 'This Lime-tree Bower my Prison', where he imagines his friend Charles Lamb delighting in a sunset scene not available to himself, the account culminates in an imagining of the homeward flight of a rook which

> Flew creeking o'er thy head, and had a charm
> For thee, my gentle-hearted Charles, to whom
> No sound is dissonant which tells of Life.

The placing of that last word is telling. And his concern at this time with all such manifestations emerges even more clearly in the opening to 'Frost at Midnight'. Silence, as most commonly understood, is a sign of death; a totally silent landscape would be sinister and deathly. Coleridge knows, however, that this is not necessarily always so: even if the effect of silence is disturbing it may also be masking a beneficent work that is not disclosing itself—or at least, not yet. After the description of the Frost's 'secret ministry' and the sinister cry of the owlet, he continues,

> 'Tis calm indeed! so calm, that it disturbs
> And vexes meditation with its strange
> And extreme silentness. Sea, hill, and wood,
> This populous village! Sea, and hill, and wood,
> With all the numberless goings-on of life,
> Inaudible as dreams!

An observation in Dorothy's *Journal* suggests that she too had been struck by the fact that life could betray its activity without presenting itself in identifiable sounds:

The sound of the sea distinctly heard on the tops of the hills, which we could never hear in summer. We attribute this partly to the bareness of the trees, but chiefly to the absence of the singing of birds, the hum of insects, that noiseless noise which lives in the summer air.[9]

If Coleridge did not use the exact expression 'one life' when he was writing about nature in his early poetry, it emerged some years later, when he revised a poem written shortly before he met William and Dorothy. In 'The Eolian Harp', he had shown for the first time his talents and deficiencies as a nature poet. Snatches of vivid description are nearly always modified in some way by moralizing. So his opening description of the flowers that cover the walls of their cottage, 'white-flower'd Jasmin and the broad-leav'd Myrtle', is immediately followed by a parenthesis: '(Meet emblems they of Innocence and Love!)'. As Coleridge and his young bride look to the scenes beyond there is a similar tendency to move beyond immediate sense-experience. They

> watch the clouds, that late were rich with light
> Slow sad'ning round, and mark the star of eve
> Serenely brilliant (such should Wisdom be!)
> Shine opposite! How exquisite the scents
> Snatch'd from yon bean-field! And the world so hush'd!
> The stilly murmur of the distant Sea
> Tells us of Silence.

The loss of brightness in the clouds provokes the need to describe them as 'saddening'; the sight of the evening star prompts the need to make it an emblem of wisdom; even the sound of the sea—though this is a subtler point—recalls to the observer the nature of silence. At this point however the use of metaphor has become more complex. Coleridge turns to the Aeolian harp that he has installed in the opening of his window to make music from the currents of air that pass through—a music that can fairly be described as the music of nature, since it is made without any subsequent human intervention. And as this music is described his imagination takes over until it becomes a music from fairyland,

> Where Melodies round honey-dropping flowers,
> Footless and wild, like birds of Paradise,
> Nor pause, nor perch, hovering on untam'd wing.

When Coleridge came to print these lines in his collection *Sibylline Leaves* twenty years later, he was moved to add a new passage, to be

---

[9] Journal for 23 January 1798. *DWJ* I 3–4.

included in an Errata slip. His reason, probably, was that he had recently been reading work, particularly from the Germans, on the relationship between sound and light that took him back to earlier speculations, including those on the nature of life.[10] So we find him writing

> O! the one Life within us and abroad,
> Which meets all motion and becomes its soul,
> A light in sound, a sound-like power in light,
> Rhythm in all thought and joyance every where...

This preoccupation with life had already originated when Coleridge went across from Somerset to Dorset two years after writing his first version of 'The Eolian Harp' and met the Wordsworths there. In 1797 he had already been thinking a good deal about its nature, following the great interest in the subject among the educated of the time.

One such was John Thelwall, who had recently published a pamphlet on Animal Vitality. At the end of 1796 Coleridge wrote a letter to him in which he boldly broached the subject, retailing the various current views: Beddoes and Erasmus Darwin thought that it was inexplicable, Monro believed in a plastic immaterial nature (which Coleridge thought rather like the view he had outlined in 'The Eolian Harp'), John Hunter asserted that the blood was the life, Ferriar, an orthodox Churchman, believed in a soul, and Plato thought it was harmony—which Coleridge regarded as part of his 'dear gorgeous nonsense'. As for himself, he wrote,

I do not know what to think about it—on the whole, I have rather made up my mind that I am a mere apparition—a naked spirit!—and that Life is I myself I! Which is a mighty clear account of it.[11]

The terms of this statement show Coleridge already thinking hard about something that was to concern him throughout his career: exactly what was involved in saying 'I am' that made it a different kind of statement from the third person 'it is'? By 1798, however, in the company of William and Dorothy Wordsworth, he was even more concerned with the nature of life as it manifested itself objectively in the scenes about him. His concern with its presence as displayed in the close of the poem 'This Lime-Tree Bower my Prison' has already been mentioned, but one may also notice a more intimate concern towards the beginning, where Coleridge's friends are imagined descending into a scene in which

---

[10] *CL* IV 750–1.   [11] Ibid., I 294–5.

the signs of life are minimal, but where the plants, though devoid of sunshine, are still memorable:

> —that branchless ash,
> Unsunn'd and damp, whose few poor yellow leaves
> Ne'er tremble in the gale, yet tremble still
> Fann'd by the water-fall! and there my friends
> Behold the dark green file of long lank weeds,
> That all at once (a most fantastic sight!)
> Still nod and drip beneath the dripping edge
> Of the blue clay-stone.

Although this is immediately striking as an acutely detailed piece of natural description, the present discussion shows it to be more—the work of a man who has looked at nature analytically, considering the powers that make for life and those that make against it. He is writing at a time when his fellows have been asking themselves for the first time about such questions, following the discovery of oxygen and its qualities. It had always been known that sun and water are necessary for the sustenance of vegetable life, clearly, but new discoveries in the electrical and chemical fields brought such considerations into newly sharpened focus. So what is presented in this scene is a view of life at its lowest ebb, when the power of sunlight is almost entirely withdrawn, and the only nourishment left for the plants that of water. The only breeze that reaches them, similarly, is created by the motion of the waterfall: the supply of oxygen is sharply restricted. Yet their poor yellow leaves still survive, together with the long lank weeds: a demonstration of what natural life is like at its minimal.

Perceptions such as this were developed further in *Lyrical Ballads*, as in the description of the hailstorm described earlier. In the subsequent period, the question of life became notably less straightforward. For Wordsworth the question of death, always a pressing one, came correspondingly to the fore; he may also have been impressed by Coleridge's reservations concerning any beliefs that might lead to pantheism. From this time onwards, at all events, he concentrated on the human heart and human affections—and most especially on the effects of experiencing loss through death; the positive charge to the conception of the 'one Life' would henceforward be transposed rather into the sense that 'We have all of us one human heart'. At the same time, he did not altogether let slip his belief in the existence of a universal joy: some of his greatest achievements, including the Immortality Ode, are constructed around that very awareness.

For Coleridge the perceptive powers displayed in poems such as 'This Lime-Tree Bower' crystallized in a further development: towards his formulaic saying 'every Thing has a Life of its own, and . . . we are all *one Life*'.[12] The twin affirmations of a communal sense of life, shared by all human beings, coupled with a delight in appreciating the distinctive identity of each of its separate manifestations, was providing a double keynote for his view of life generally, indicating why he was so deeply interested in mental phenomena—including the way in which ideas are associated in a state of excitement. And his speculations concerning the human mind and personality provided the reason for his coming to think that he might, after all, be more of a psychologist than a poet. To one of his friends he wrote

This I have done; but I trust, that I am about to do more—namely, that I shall be able to evolve all the five senses, that is, to deduce them from *one sense*, & to state their growth, & the causes of their difference—& in this evolvement to solve the process of Life and Consciousness.—I write this to you only; & I pray you, mention what I have written to no one.[13]

To evolve all the five senses from one sense would have been to provide further scientific backing for the idea of the 'one Life'. One suspects that it was a dream that in his subsequent speculations Coleridge never quite abandoned. But already in the letter-poem that became 'Dejection' he was forced to acknowledge that the very processes of subtle thought and analysis that would be needed to establish such a doctrine were preying on his psyche in a manner that could eat at the very fact of joy itself. He made a valiant effort towards the end of the poem to assert that his knowledge of the conjugal delight shared by William and Mary Wordsworth would bring a compensating, vicarious joy, but the assertion also had a touch of desperation. He was not again quite to recapture the intellectual delight of those months. Dorothy Wordsworth's eye for nature was sharpened by their collaboration to a fineness that makes her journals, like his notebooks of the subsequent period, a pleasure to read, but she too lost the particular *brio* that gave a particular liveliness to the Alfoxden notebook For a brief year all three had shared the common vision of a 'one Life' that had seemed to offer a new way of looking at nature, helping perhaps to restore a sense of unity to human beings as well. Their resulting work had the quality of a shared document.

[12] Ibid., II 864.   [13] *CL* II 706–7.

Meanwhile, Coleridge was able to pursue his own speculations, where the kind of musings that he had explored in 'The Eolian Harp' became for a time a constant presence. Was there some principle in human consciousness that responded immediately to any sign of life in nature? It was something he could think about in his own writing, such as his late night musings in *Frost at Midnight*, when he thought how

> the living spirit in our frame,
> That loves not to behold a lifeless thing
> Transfuses into all its own delights,
> Its own volition, sometimes with deep faith
> And sometimes with fantastic playfulness.

Developing this thought he could find it easy to regard even the soot-film on his grate as

> a companionable form,
> Whose puny flaps and freaks the idling Spirit
> By its own moods interprets, every where
> Echo or mirror seeking of itself,
> And makes a toy of Thought.

Still more impressive was the play of his own poetic practice, which could sometimes resolve the tensions of his own intellectual problems by a process of narrative dramatization. Instead of the orthodox theocratic world of his familiar background, his Mariner could be represented as delivered into the wide sea of a universe in which events belonged to multiple phenomena and were open to a wide range of possible interpretations. It was a world in which the killing of an albatross might or might not lead to effects in the elements; in which powerful figures might play dice for the fate of the seamen in their power; in which two other voices might discuss the bewildering events while only one of them claimed to know the truth about was going on; and in which that second voice could claim intimate knowledge of another spirit—who loved the albatross that the Mariner killed.

In all such instances the privilege of playing would have been transferred to the responsive imagination of the reader, with the prospect of setting up there a dance of intellect like that of the poet himself. His major interest continued to lie with the Wordsworths, but he increasingly felt that his own gifts were leading him in a different direction. To Francis Wrangham he wrote of Wordsworth at the end of the year 1800, 'he is a great, a true Poet—I am only a kind of a Metaphysician.'[14] The Lakeland climate did not suit his health, nor did his

---

[14] Ibid., I 658.

isolation; he needed the stimulus of a large community such as that to be found in the metropolis.

The power of Wordsworth's contributions during the *annus mirabilis* was still working in Coleridge's mind, nevertheless—most particularly, perhaps, his expression of the relationship between nature and the human mind in his 'Lines written . . . above Tintern Abbey' and his affirmation that it was possible to 'see into the life of things'. The phrase continued to resonate in Coleridge's mind, haunting his perceptions of nature. Words-worth in turn was able to address him in the first short two-book draft for *The Prelude* as 'one | The most intense of Nature's worshippers'.

His cultivation of the idea of 'one Life' suggested more work in the field of science, where his friendship with Humphry Davy pointed him in the most obvious direction One of the attractions of Davy's career and work was that it provided a continuity with the intellectual quests of his Bristol years. The researches in chemistry which had furnished a chief string for Priestley's bow (the 'Science' of his 'Science, Freedom and the Truth in Christ') had continued under his guidance, exciting interest among the literati—particularly when they were accompanied by the composition of verses good enough to attract Southey's attention.

Humphry Davy, also, was a young man of evident powers. His poem 'The Sons of Genius' spoke of the range of genius across different fields of knowledge in a manner bound to please the broadly inquiring Coleridge. His enthusiasm for science was linked to speculations that linked with Coleridge's idea that matter might be not dead but living—with the result that nothing could die. The concept of theism, also, worked through his whole thinking.[15]

---

[15] See e.g. a poem dated about 1816:

> If matter cannot be destroy'd
> The living mind can never die;
> If e'en creative when alloy'd
> How sure its immortality!

and his lines 'Written after recovery from a Dangerous Illness', which began,

> Lo! o'er the earth the kindling spirits pour
>   The flames of life that beauteous nature gives;
> The limpid dew becomes the rosy flower,
>   The insensate dust awakes, and moves, and lives.
>
> All speaks of change: the renovated forms
>   Of long-forgotten things arise again;
> The light of suns, the breath of angry storms,
>   The everlasting motions of the main.
>
> These are but engines of the Eternal will,
>   The One Intelligence, whose potent sway
> Has ever acted, and is acting still,
>   Whilst stars, and worlds, and systems all obey.

Some of Coleridge's most absorbing speculations at this time had to do with his ideas about the nature of human growth. In particular, he remained fascinated by the manner in which such development involved a separation between the vegetative element in the human and the development of energy. From the time when, in 'The Eolian Harp', he had connected the experience of a bean-field, played over by a wind that released the scents of its flowers, with the idea that all organic forms might be played on by a similar 'Intellectual breeze' he had been fascinated by the relationship between the organic and the vital. It directed his attention to the early growth of children as a source of knowledge about the human, since the process of birth and emotional development necessarily involved a disjunction between the state in which the growing foetus was in a totally organic relationship with the body of its mother and experiences from birth onwards when this state of unity was disturbed, interfered with, and eventually severed. He could see that this might prove the most fruitful means of acquiring knowledge about the manner in which human perception developed. A notebook entry of 1803 sets out in rough his ideas on the subject:

Contact—the womb—the amnion liquor—warmth + touch/—air cold + touch + sensation & action of breathing—contact of the mother's knees + all those contacts of the breast + taste & wet & sense of swallowing—

Sense of diminished Contact explains the falling asleep—/ this is Fear,... this produces Fear—

Eye contact, pressure infinitely diminished, organic Conness (con to ken) proportionally increased.[16]

The progress of his thought may have to be inferred from these notes, but is fairly clear, involving an analysis of the idea of 'contact' by way of isolating the elements of 'con' (knowing) and 'tact', or touch. The implication is that once the sense of total oneness between mother and child is destroyed after birth, that total 'con-tact' is also compromised, so that occasions of relationship which promise its restoration are unusually interesting to study. The most hopeful means of restoration and reassurance for the child is through touch from the mother, while a means of reconciliation with the situation is provided by the explora-

---

John Davy, *Memoirs of the Life of Sir Humphry Davy, Bart* (2 vols., London: Longman, Rees, Orme, Brown, Green, & Longman, 1836) II 96 and I 390. According to his brother, the second poem had been begun some years before his illness and completed in 1808 during his convalescence, when it was given its final title.

[16] CNB 4 f 28 (cf. *CN* I 1414).

tions of taste. 'Babies touch *by taste* at first,' he wrote in a notebook, 'then about 5 months old they go from the Palate to the hand.'[17]

Many years later, in his manuscript drafts for the *Opus Maximum*, he was still exploring the significance of touch as the central human sense, linking the baby first to its mother and then to other human beings.[18] The possibility of establishing a firm connection between that growth of sense experience and nurture of the human imagination, grounding both in the original I Am, the divine that was the source of all true creativity, was to provide the goal—the holy grail, even—the quest for which would be a haunting obsession for the rest of his life, newly exciting the play of his mind over and over again.

Towards the end of the decade, acknowledging lack of success in that ultimate aim (as he always would be forced to do) he retired briefly to a farmhouse near Porlock, where details of the history and culture of East and West that he had massively absorbed from his reading clashed in his mind so powerfully that when in a narcotic trance he found himself producing poetry about a far eastern potentate who tried to create a place of pleasure, guarded by walls and towers, only to find himself subjected to ancestral voices warning him against pending forces of violence, the setting seemed to be in Europe. He could hope that the danger to his own civilization (shortly to be realized in the threat posed by Napoleon) might be averted; as a writer, however, he could offer fellow-citizens only the 'miracle of rare device' glimpsed in his own images of reconciliation: a musical solution in which the warring impulses of mankind might transcend the contraries of nature, to resolve themselves into entranced harmony.

The underlying problem, though continuing, belonged still to the future, and must be left for his successors to grapple with. The hope must be that they would not tear themselves apart in fruitless battles between a Western strategy of the head, based on scientific and mathematical calculations, and an Eastern regard to the whole body and polity (despite its obstinate clinging to entrenched customs) but that they would learn how to reconcile technological exactitude with the imaginative attractions of romance; that they would reject the way of death and choose that of life.

At this point, however, the result of his reverie could be no more than a poetic 'fragment', ambivalent and complete in its own way, but not to be published until nearly twenty years later—when it would be offered as a 'psychological curiosity', and bear the title 'Kubla Khan, A Vision'.

[17] CNB 4 f 31ᵛ (cf. *CN* I 924).
[18] See especially *COM* 14 and n, 30 and n, 119–27, 131–3.

3

Dances of the Intellect and Emotions

Seeking an image for 'The figure of the Youth as Virile Poet'[1] Wallace Stevens lighted on that of Coleridge at a moment in late September 1798 when he set sail for Hamburg in a packet boat. As well as himself, there were some unusual people on its passenger list, including William and Dorothy Wordsworth. Six months earlier he had completed *The Rime of the Ancient Mariner*; now he was going to sea for the first time. William and Dorothy soon retired below decks to be hideously seasick, but he himself remained on deck in the best of spirits:

I talked and laughed with the Passengers—then went to sleep on the deck—was awaked about three o'clock in the Afternoon by the Danes, who insisted in very fluent but not very correct English, that I should sit down and drink with them—Accordingly I did—My name among them was Docteur Teology—(i.e. Theology)—& dressed as I was all in black with large shoes and black worsted stockings, they very naturally supposed me to be a Priest—I rectified their mistake—what then? said they—Simply I replied, un Philosophe.—Well, I drank some excellent wine & devoured Grapes & part of a pine-apple—

> Good things I said, good things I eat,
> I gave them wisdom for their meat.—

And in a short time became their Idol—Every now and then I entered into the feelings of my poor Friends below, who in all the agonies of sea-sickness heard us most distinctly, spouting, singing, laughing, fencing, dancing country dances—in a word being Bacchanals.[2]

For his illustration Wallace Stevens lighted on that moment of Coleridge's dancing. The image of the poet joining in the hilarity is indeed an attractive one; it should be remembered, however, that the version of the account that Stevens was drawing on was the later one, revised for

---

[1] 'The Figure of the Youth as Virile Poet', in *The Sewanee Review*, ed. Allen Tate, 52/4 (October–December, 1944).

[2] *CL* I 421.

the 1809 *Friend* and then for *Biographia Literaria*, which gave a rather more organized impression of what had happened:

Certes we were not of the Stoic School. For we drank and talked and sung, until we talked and sung all together; and then we rose and danced on the Deck a set of Dances.[3]

The 1809 *Friend* continues with the words '. . . which in one sense of the word at least were very intelligibly and appropriately entitled Reels'; the original, however, expressing sympathy with the Wordsworths, who from below could still hear them 'spouting, singing, laughing, fencing, dancing country dances—in a word being Bacchanals—', had a certain wild abandon; the quality of the revised version, on the other hand, by very reason of its statelier rhythm, reveals what was not so apparent in the original, that, whether doctor of theology or *philosophe*, the writer was a serious poet in life as well as art, trying to organize harmony from the chaos of ordinary experiences.

The switch towards a more organized—though equally spirited—dancing is not the only change made for the later version. Coleridge also revised the picture of himself a little, stating that it was his companions who had suggested he was a *philosophe*, and that although it was 'that time of my life, in which of all possible names and characters I had the greatest disgust to that of "*un philosophe*"' he had submitted to the description with a bow. His contemporaneous account had given no hint of reluctance, however, even if in the previous March he had complained to his brother of 'those men both in England & France, who have modestly assumed to themselves the exclusive title of Philosophers', declaring that his opinions were 'utterly untainted with French metaphysics, French Ethics, and French Theology';[4] there may have been some inward self-satire, but in his account at the time the word *philosophe* was in fact the one he himself volunteered.

What is more interesting is the obscurity of his identity to his fellow-passengers. This uncertainty—priest or *philosophe*?—divine or poet, for that matter?—was in fact all too relevant to his condition at the time. For some years he had been trying to resolve the issue through finding a middle way. Such a compromise was inherent even in the ambiguity of his literary endeavours.

---

[3] *CF* (1809) 214 (cf. *CFriend* II 188; *CBL* II 162).   [4] *CL* I 395.

It is natural to look to the period he spent in Germany for signs of how he then regarded himself. Here the evidences are disparate. We know that at Göttingen he attended and was impressed by the lectures in physiology by Blumenbach, and that Blumenbach was sufficiently taken by him to attend a farewell dinner when he left. We also know that he attended the lectures of Eichhorn, as a result of which he was at that time well ahead in biblical scholarship—knowledge of which was to be considerably useful to him in years to come. Records of his conversation have survived, mainly from Clement Carlyon, which show him expressing himself with his usual fecundity. We also know that he brought back from Germany a number of philosophical works, and notably writings of Immanuel Kant. In his study *Coleridge and the Pantheist Tradition*, Thomas McFarland showed that one inevitable result of his encounter with the Germany of the time was to awaken or strengthen his interest in Spinoza.[5]

On his return to England he evidently tried to take up the threads of his previous occupations, and notably the fascination by the phenomena of 'life' and 'death' which he had recently shared with the Wordsworths. Yet in some respects the time in Germany had been disruptive in effect without giving him any clear way forward. If he had hoped for further light on animal magnetism, this had been thwarted by the fact that Blumenbach did not at this time believe in the phenomenon at all. The conception of the 'one Life' remained similarly at a stand, though overtaken by his growing interest in Spinoza.

It is hard to know whether that had already begun before he left England. One possibility is raised by the incident in which, just before the two poets went to Germany, they were investigated by a government agent.[6] Coleridge claims that in spite of his trying to conceal himself the

---

[5] *Coleridge and the Pantheist Tradition* (Oxford: Clarendon Press, 1969), *passim*. For the German and European background, see especially Chapter 2, 'The Spinozistic Crescendo'. It may be noted that Humphry Davy, whose twin aspirations as poet and scientific philosopher were discussed in the previous chapter, wrote a poem entitled 'The Spinozist'.

[6] See A. J. Eagleston, 'Wordsworth, Coleridge and the Spy', *Nineteenth Century*, August 1908; reprinted in *Coleridge: Studies by Several Hands...*, ed. Blunden and Griggs (London: Constable, 1934), pp. 73–87. The story has been further discussed by Nicholas Roe in *Wordsworth and Coleridge: The Radical Years* (Oxford: Clarendon Press 1988), chapter 7, and Kenneth R. Johnston in *The Hidden Wordsworth: Poet, Lover, Rebel, Spy* (New York and London: W.W. Norton and Co., 1998), pp. 526–35. The 'Spy nosy' element in the story was regarded as 'hardly credible' by Mary Moorman: *William Wordsworth A Biography* (Oxford: Clarendon Press, 1957), I 331, and treated with suspicion by Thomas McFarland: see his *Coleridge and the Pantheist Tradition*,

agent thought his presence had been suspected because they kept referring to a 'Spy nosy', but that after listening further he realized they were talking not about him but about a man who had written a book a long time ago. It sounds too much like some of Coleridge's other anecdotes for one to be sure that this was not made up as an entertaining fiction; if, on the other hand, it did happen as related it would not only provide evidence that Coleridge was already discussing Spinoza's ideas in this period, but also offer an interesting sidelight on how Coleridge pronounced his name—which he would hardly have done in the same way once he had talked to the Spinozist philosophers in Germany a year or two later.

The attraction for him of Spinoza's philosophy was that it provided a possible means of bringing together his delight in nature with current political and social concerns. The more one could see human beings as a part of nature the more it became possible to envisage an answer to the failure of the French Revolution by advocating a new philosophy, in which human beings could be brought together through sharing an enlightened view of nature.

At all events, and despite his being a great expositor of God's impersonality, Spinoza, a saintly figure, enviably selfless in his pursuit of truth, dominated his view of nature for a few years. In Spinoza the phenomena of life are caught into a system and sealed into permanence. While Coleridge found it at one level most satisfying, he recognized that its attractions as a release from immediate anxiety might in the end be short-lived. In detecting the weakness of such a philosophy he elaborated his rock imagery:

Righteous and gentle Spirit, where should I find that iron Chain of Logic, which neither man or angel could break, but which falls of itself by dissolving the rock of Ice, to which it is stapled—and which thou in common with all thy contemporaries & predecessors didst mistake for a rock of adamant?[7]

If the permanent resource that he was looking for was not to be found even in Spinoza, the alternative prospect, that of diffusing his mind into endless proliferation, was (despite a certain attractiveness) equally delusive.

---

p. 165, where he draws attention to further such puns, including one on 'Spy nosy' in 1799 and one on 'live Nits' in 1801: CNB $3^{1/2}$ f 50 (cf. *CN* I 432.4); *CL* II 747.

    [7] *CL* IV 548.

Closer connection with his psychological speculations led on to further questions, such as how the mind manages to distinguish between seeing things sometimes as a unity, sometimes as particulars. This was so intimately related to basic issues raised by Spinoza that he was prompted to write in a notebook,

If I begin a poem of Spinoza, thus it should begin/
I would make a pilgrimage to the burning sands of Arabia, or &c &c to find the Man who could explain to me there can be oneness, there being infinite perceptions—yet there must be a oneness, not an intense Union but an Absolute Unity.[8]

Earlier in the same year Wordsworth praised Coleridge in terms which suggested that he might be well on the way to solving such problems:

> To thee, unblinded by these outward shows,
> The unity of all has been revealed.[9]

Nevertheless, Coleridge's puzzlement was elaborated, and partly elucidated, when he revised the note four years later:

Poem on Spirit—or on Spinoza—I would make a pilgrimage to the Deserts of Arabia to find the man who could make understand how the *one can be many!* Eternal universal mystery! It seems as if it were impossible; yet it is—& it is every where!—It is indeed a contradiction in *Terms*: and only in Terms!—It is the co presence of Feeling & Life, limitless by their very essence, with Form, by its very essence limited—determinate—definite.—[10]

The previous month he had been struck by related feelings when he first looked down on Edinburgh:

I cannot express what I felt—such a section of a wasp's nest, striking you with a sort of bastard Sublimity from the enormity & infinity of it's littleness—the infinity swelling out the mind, the enormity striking it with wonder.[11]

Later still the puzzling relationship between the one and the many would be accepted as a mystery that was involved with the question of the Trinity:

---

[8] CNB 5 f 12ᵛ (cf. *CN* I 556).
[9] *WPrel* (1799) II 255–6.
[10] CNB 21 f 51 (cf. *CN* I 1561).
[11] Letter to Southey, September 1803: *CL* II 988.

... the Idea of God involves that of a Tri-unity: and as that Unity or Indivisibility is the intensest, and the Archetype, yea, the very substance and element of all other Unity and Union, so is that distinction the most manifest, and indestructible of all distinctions—and Being, Intellect, and Action, which in their absoluteness are the Father, the Word, and the Spirit will and must for ever be and remain the 'genera generalissima' of all knowlege.[12]

The issues of Nature and Spinozism were not unconnected to his personal life. While he was in Germany he had remained deeply attached to his wife. From a humane point of view it might have been better if he had returned from Germany when he heard of the death of little Berkeley, but he was urged not to do so and Germany was a long way away: if he had returned it would have been difficult for him to go back and resume what he had been doing.

Once he was back in Nether Stowey, on the other hand, strains and tensions became evident. There was illness in the house, which a few months later was flooded. Having stoically described Sara's exhaustion and his child's restlessness he added 'I however, sunk in Spinoza, remain as undisturbed as a Toad in a Rock'.[13] (The question whether living things could survive indefinitely if totally surrounded by rock had been a matter of discussion recently in scientific journals.) The omens were not altogether good, since his detachment was eloquent of deeper and broader ambitions, including the desire to create a 'great work'.

His ranging curiosity about the possibilities of new developments resulted in the resumption of collaboration with his old friend Robert Southey. After his return from Germany it was not long before they undertook a joint walking tour and were soon planning a joint poem in hexameters, following a suggestion from William Taylor of Norwich. He was drawn not only by the possibility of experimentation in a different metrical form but by the attraction of Eastern themes. Some lines toward a joint project from both poets, a poem on Mohammed, still survive. Despite the existence of a plot scheme drawn up by the two, however, further lines from Coleridge were not forthcoming, and Southey's enthusiasm waned.

Coleridge recalled their plans many years later in a notebook entry which again dwelt on the possible links between naturalism and comparative religion:

---

[12] Letter to Clarkson, October 1806: ibid., II 1197.
[13] Letter to Southey, 30 September 1799: ibid., I 534.

Had I proceeded in concert with R. Southey with 'The Flight and Return of Mohammed' I had intended a Disputation between Mahomet, as the Representative of Unipersonal Theism with the Judaico-Christian Machinery of Angels, Genii, and Prophets; an Idolater with his Gods, Heroes & Spirits of the Departed Mighty; and a Fetisch-Worshipper, who adored the Sensible only, & held no Religion common to all Men or to any Number of men other than as they chanced at the same moment to be acted on by the same Influence—as when a hundred Ant-hills are in motion under the same Burst of Sun-shine. And still, chiefly, for the sake of the last Scheme, I should like to do something of this Kind. My enlightened Fetisch-Divine would have been an Okenist+Zoo-magn. with the Night-side of Nature.[14]

The one fragment of the poem that Southey left, calling it 'Mohammed—a Fragment', was of good quality: It began

> Cloak'd in the garment of green, who lies in the bed of Mohammed,
> Restless and full of fear; yet semblant of one that is sleeping?
> Every sound of the feet at his door he hears, and the breathing
> Low of inaudible words: he knows their meaning of murder,
> Knows what manner of men await his outgoing and listens
> All their tread, and their whisp'ring, till even the play of his pulses
> Disturbs him, so deep his attention.

Coleridge's own fragment was actually less dramatic than Southey's; though its distinguishing feature was a similar attempt to employ the resources of classical metre:

Utter the Song, O my Soul! the flight and return of Mohammed,
Prophet and Priest, who scatter'd abroad both Evil and Blessing,
Huge wasteful Empires founded and hallow'd slow Persecution,
Soul-withering, but crush'd the blasphemous Rites of the Pagan
And idolatrous Christians.—For veiling the Gospel of Jesus,
They, the best corrupting, had made it worse than the vilest.
Wherefore Heaven decreed th' enthusiast Warrior of Mecca,
Choosing Good from Iniquity rather than Evil from Goodness.

Loud the Tumult in Mecca surrounding the Fane of the Idol;
Naked and Prostrate the Priesthood were laid—the People with mad shouts
Thundering now, and now with saddest Ululation
Flew, as over the channel of rock-stone the ruinous River
Shatters its waters abreast, and in mazy uproar bewilder'd,
Rushes dividuous all—all rushing impetuous onward.[15]

---

[14] CNB 25 ff 2–1ᵛ(cf. *CN* IV 4973).   [15] *CPW* (CC) I (1) 568.

The closing lines show Coleridge's persisting interest in imagery of the natural. The image of the divided stream was one that would recur—notably to characterize the current state of religion.[16] This was not the only dividedness in his mind, moreover. As the note on his projected poem about Mohammed shows, he was torn between a Spinozist view of life, with its natural unity, and persisting devotion to a unipersonal theism that could include Islam as well as Christianity.

On one point, however, he was clear. The kind of thinking that had developed in preceding centuries was no longer acceptable, nor were its adherents. Whether he realized it or not, one effect of his voyage to Germany had been to change him from being a provincial intellectual to become a metropolitan one. To say this is not to imply any ultimate comparative valuation of the two conditions. In many respects the great provincial centres of England were at the time ahead of London. As a great trading centre, Bristol was open to influences not necessarily picked up in the metropolis, while its dealings with the growing industrial centres of England linked it to centres of progressive thought. Yet there remained a sense in which London, simply through the range of people gathered in it, as site of the court, centre of government and international relations, along with its European ties, provided more of a centre in which existing currents could be appraised and judged. When Coleridge returned it was not surprising that for a time his thoughts centred there—not least because it was the place in which his writing talents were most likely to be appreciated and rewarded. Despite the major interests developed with the Words-worths, his sense of his own gifts was leading him in a different direction. His self-deprecation to Francis Wrangham, 'I am only a kind of a Metaphysician,'[17] has already been quoted. His metaphysical speculations were nevertheless by no means nugatory: they involved him in exploring the nature and significance of human life, which meant that he could benefit from the stimulus of a large metropolis.

The power of Wordsworth's contributions during the *annus mirabilis* was still prominent in his mind, nevertheless—most particularly, perhaps, his expression of the relationship between nature and the human mind in his 'Lines written . . . above Tintern Abbey'. The phrase 'see into the life of things' continued to resonate in Coleridge's mind, haunting his perceptions of nature. Wordsworth in turn was able to address him in

[16] The *CC* editor points this out in a note.   [17] *CL* I 658.

the first short two-book draft for the poem on his own mind as 'one | The most intense of Nature's worshippers'. For such a devotee Lakeland might be as important as London.

Meanwhile, the 'metropolitan' element in Coleridge's thought had been further nourished by his increasing interest in the work of Humphry Davy, whom he had come across through acquaintance with him in Bristol and their common friendship with Thomas Beddoes at the Pneumatic Institution there. When Davy moved to London and the Royal Institution, Coleridge kept in touch, following some of his experiments eagerly. Davy's reports on his experiments with nitrous oxide, for instance, included statements from Coleridge himself, while the latter's cultivation of the idea of 'one Life', suggesting the need for more scientific work, meant that the friendship could prove very bene-ficial for both men. One of the attractions of Davy's career and work was that it provided continuity with the intellectual quests of his Bristol years. His poem 'The Sons of Genius' spoke of the range of genius across different fields of knowledge in a manner bound to please the broadly inquiring Coleridge—particularly since the concept of theism worked through his thinking—while his scientific work linked readily to the Coleridgean speculation that matter might be not dead but living—with the implication that ultimately nothing could die. It is also worth mentioning again, particularly in view of the earlier discus-sion, that he wrote a poem entitled 'The Spinozist'.

During these discussions, of course, questions that had been aroused during the great year in North Somerset remained unresolved. The writing of the meditative poems had set ideas in motion but without prospect of real development; *The Rime of the Ancient Mariner* had dramatized some of his intellectual conflicts without in any way resolv-ing them, while his attempt at a more successful sequel in 'Christabel' had only served to bring out the ambiguity of some of his ideas, so that the poem languished incomplete.

In his encounters with literary London, Coleridge also had opportu-nities to enjoy dalliance with intelligent women, entering into friend-ships of a sentimental, somewhat flirtatious nature—for instance, his exchange of poems with Mary ('Perdita') Robinson and his friendship with Charlotte Smith.

A more pressing concern for himself and his wife, however, was the need to find a suitable dwelling place for them both. She was ready to leave the small cottage at Nether Stowey, but wanted to be closer to town-life and the proximity of her Bristol family. In the end, it was neither Bristol nor London that was decided on. The problem was solved when Southey joined Coleridge in bringing both their families to Cumbria, where they shared the tenancy of Greta Hall, near Keswick. This meant that they could have the sublime advantage of living surrounded by superb mountains and that at nearby Grasmere Coleridge could resume contact with Wordsworth, whose work continued to impress him. Verses such as 'A slumber did my spirit seal...' and the early drafts for his autobiographical work had convinced him that as a poet Wordsworth had mastered the secret of true sublimity. He could not hope to emulate him; but he could still, through living close to his friend and working with him, hope to probe psychologically the nature and quality of his gifts. The fact that Wordsworth was more interested in exploring the basic humanity that was displayed by individuals living in the midst of nature had not yet fully struck him, perhaps.

As Coleridge's desire to experiment continued, he tried to link the two localities of his greatest interest. In February 1801 he planned to establish a small laboratory in Keswick and invited Humphry Davy to join him and work there together with Wordsworth and William Calvert.[18] A month later he wrote to Godwin, explaining how in his illness scientific and mathematical concerns had, at least temporarily, driven poetry—though not, one notes, imaginative creativity—out of his head: he had

compelled into hours of Delight many a sleepless, painful hour of Darkness by chasing down metaphysical Game—and since then I have continued the Hunt, till I found myself unaware at the Root of Pure Mathematics—and up that tall, smooth Tree, whose few poor Branches are all at it's very summit, am I climbing by pure adhesive strength of arms and thighs—still slipping down, still renewing my ascent.—You would not know me—! all sounds of similitude keep at such a distance from each other in my mind that I have forgotten how to make a rhyme. I look at the Mountains (that visible God Almighty that looks in at all my windows), I look at the Mountains only for the Curves of their outlines; the Stars, as I behold them, form themselves into Triangles; and my hands are scarred with scratches from a Cat, whose back I was rubbing in the Dark in order to see whether the sparks in it were refrangible by a Prism.[19]

Given his underlying fascination with the nature of life, some of Coleridge's most absorbing investigations at this time continued to concern the nature of human growth. In particular, he remained fascinated by

---

[18] Ibid., II 670–1.   [19] Ibid., II 714, 25 March 1801.

the relation between vegetative expansion and the interventions of energy. From the time when, in 'The Eolian Harp', he had connected the experience of a bean-field, played over by a wind that set free the scents of its flowers, with the idea that all organic forms might be played on by a similar 'Intellectual breeze' he had been fascinated by the relationship between the organic and the vital in all life-forms. It directed his attention to the early growth of children as a source of knowledge about the human, since, as has already been mentioned, birth and emotional development necessarily involved breaching the totally organic relationship between the growing foetus and the body of its mother by way of a process in which this unity was disturbed, interfered with, and eventually severed. He could see that this might prove the most fruitful means of acquiring knowledge about the manner in which human perception developed.

All such phenomena contributed to the sense, notably developed during these years, that the greatest conundrum for humanity—given its existence as part of a nature which was at every point mysterious—was the riddle of growth. He still remained absorbed by the difference of roles between the silent, growing vegetative element and the vigorous workings of energy. As mentioned above, he was particularly attentive to the early growth and behaviour of children as a source of knowledge about the human.

To all this Wordsworth's recollections of his own childhood could contribute—along with the fact that he seemed also to have discovered the sublimity of true love, as he had shown when he introduced Coleridge to the Hutchinson sisters. In November 1799 his friend had set off with Joseph Cottle for the North. After making a tour of the Lake District with Wordsworth, he had returned to Sockburn, where an incident took place that was to have far-reaching consequences:

Nov. 24th—the Sunday—Conundrums & Puns & Stories & Laughter—with Jack Hutchinson—Stood round the Fire, et Sarae manum a tergo longum in tempus prensabam, and tunc temporis, tunc primum, amor me levi spiculo, venenato, eheu! & insanabili, &c.[20]

This initiating event did not tell the whole story. With his strong moral beliefs, Coleridge was not likely to enter lightly on a love such as that

[20] 'and I held Sara's hand behind her back for a long time, and in that time, then first, love pierced me with its arrow—poisoned, and alas! incurable', CNB 21 f 53 (cf. *CN* I 1575), transcribing in 1803 brief extracts from CNB 5 ff 17ᵛ–18ᵛ (cf. *CN* 575–8) four years earlier, and expanding what little survives there.

which he developed for Sara Hutchinson. It is hard to believe that he became so enamoured of her simply because she allowed him to flirt with her on one or two occasions. The terse account just given can be supplemented by what seems to be family tradition. When his grandson edited the poetical works he wrote, concerning the poem 'Love':

It is probable that the greater part . . . was written either during or shortly after a visit which Coleridge made to the Wordsworths' friends, George and Mary, and Sara Hutchinson, at Sockburn, a farm-house on the banks of the Tees, in November, 1799. In the first draft, lines 13 to 16 . . . run thus:—

> She lean'd against a grey stone rudely carv'd,
> The statue of an armed Knight:
> She lean'd in melancholy mood
> 　　Amid the lingering light.

He commented

It is difficult to believe that the 'armed knight' and the 'grey stone' of the first draft were not suggested by the statue in Sockburn Church, and the 'Grey - Stone' in the adjoining field.

E. H. Coleridge evidently thought that the incident reflected an experi-ence of Coleridge's own, a supposition further supported by a stanza which Coleridge wrote at some point in the period, referring to it first in a notebook of 1804:[21]

> All Look or Likeness caught from Earth,
> 　　All accident of Kin or Birth,
> Had pass'd away: there was no trace
> Of aught upon her brighten'd face,
> Uprais'd beneath that rifted Stone
> But of one image—all her own!
> She, She alone, and only She
> Shone thro' her body visibly.—[22]

It was this experience, surely, that was the initiating one to be associated with Coleridge's 'Love'—the experience, we must suppose, of seeing Sara Hutchinson either by the recumbent statue in the church or by the Grey-stone in a manner that revealed to him an unusual beauty in her

---

[21] CNB 15 f 23 (cf. *CN* II 2055).
[22] In February 1805 the lines were quoted in prose form in CNB 17 f 17 (cf. *CN* II 2441); three years later they appeared again, in CNB 23 ff 3–3ᵛ, slightly differently and this time as verse (cf. *CN* III 3291).

face, suggesting the existence in her of an eternal self that could from time to time shine through her in a quite unearthly way.

The suggestion that both Hutchinson sisters possessed such an elusive beauty is reinforced by Wordsworth's tribute to Mary as having a dual quality, combining the beauty of a 'Phantom of delight' with 'household motions light and free';[23] what is less often remarked is that he wrote a sonnet to Sara after her death referring to 'that heaven-revealing smile of thine'.[24]

The growing love for Sara Hutchinson continued the fascination for the natural world that had been part of the lore that Coleridge shared with the Wordsworths. In herself, it seems, she was not strikingly beautiful—probably less attractive on a first impression than his own wife—but he was aware of qualities in her that Sara Coleridge lacked. In many ways his wife was evidently lively and attractive; she and he seem to have had a satisfactory sexual relationship. What he particularly valued in Sara Hutchinson, by contrast, was a different potentiality:

> ... being innocent and full of love,
> And nested with the Darlings of thy Love,
> And feeling in thy Soul, Heart, Lips & Arms
> Even what the conjugal and mother Dove
> That borrows genial Warmth, from those, she warms,
> Feels in her thrill'd wings, blessedly outspread...[25]

Sara, in other words, not only possessed an occasional unusual radiance but was warm and kindly in ways that his wife was not. Sara Coleridge evidently had many of the qualities of a good wife and mother, including an ability to make the most of the present moment, but lacked fineness of sensibility or the immediate sympathy which De Quincey noted in Dorothy Wordsworth: 'The pulses of light are not more quick or more inevitable in their flow and undulation, than were the answering and echoing movements of her sympathizing attention.'[26] Sara Hutchinson might not reach to the same intensity but there was an evident core of warmth and light, as in her sister, which impressed Dorothy, causing her to understand how Coleridge missed it in his own wife—on whom she commented 'She is to be sure a sad

[23] *WPW* II 213. [24] Ibid., III 17.
[25] *CPW* (Beer) 404. [26] *DQW* II 239.

fiddle-faddler'.[27] In his *Letter* Coleridge wrote that Sara Hutchinson
had no need to ask of him 'What this strong music in the soul may be',

> This Light, this Glory, this fair luminous Mist.
> This beautiful & beauty-making Power!

She need not ask, we are to assume, because she already possessed it in
herself.

He mused further on this phenomenon and its implications:

This abstract Self is indeed in its nature a Universal personified—as Life, Soul,
Spirit, &c. Will not this prove to be a deeper Feeling, & of such intimate
affinity with ideas, so to modify them & become one with them, whereas the
appetites and the feelings of Revenge and Anger co-exist with the Ideas, not
combine with them; and alter the apparent effect of the Forms not the Forms
themselves./ Certain modifications of Fear seem to approach nearest to this
Love-sense, in its manner of acting.

Behind all such events lurked a growing alienation from his wife. 'God
knows where we can go,' he wrote to Poole in January 1800 before
moving to Keswick, 'for that situation which suits my wife does not suit
me, and what suits me does not suit my wife'; a short time later he
described to Southey (in Latin) her lack of sympathy for his studies, his
temperament, and even his infirmities. What had earlier been disparity
masking a tolerable relationship had evidently transmuted into jarring
antipathy. When he was in the Wordsworth circle, it may be surmised,
he could form part of chain of intelligence nourished by ready sympathies; to return to Sara after such pleasures was to experience little but
dyspathy and harshness. Where was the immediacy of answering sympathy characteristic of Dorothy and the Hutchinsons, their physical
warmth?

As it happened, he could redeem the situation in a gratifying manner
through knowing that some of the works he needed were likely to be
found in the Cathedral Library at Durham, enabling him to stay on the
Hutchinsons' farm while visiting the city. The notebooks (and the
records of the Library) show that the books he borrowed were chosen
for their comments on the mind, and particularly on memory. A long
passage in the notebooks, taken from Aquinas's commentary on Aristotle,

---

[27] Letter of 29 April 1801 from Dorothy Wordsworth to Mary Hutchinson: *WL*
(1787–1805) 331.

contains observations on the means by which memory seems to work through association of ideas.[28]

It was an essential part of these investigations that they facilitated close contact with the Hutchinson sisters. It was not simply that their proximity created a pleasant feeling-tone around his investigations; the associations actually contributed to the nexus of ideas that he was exploring. His affection spread to the signs of life around them in the countryside, and notably the beehive, with its suggestions of a multiplicity combined with unity in life like that which had possessed his mind as a child. When he thought of Sara in the months to come particular images possessed him. On one occasion he and Sara had both leant on Mary's lap close enough for Coleridge to feel Sara's eyelash on his cheek. It was a scene that he was later to recreate in an imaginative poem—only to stop himself:

> But let me check this tender lay
>   Which none may hear but she and thou!
> Like the still hive at quiet midnight humming,
> Murmur it to yourselves, ye two beloved women!

A few nights later he would compose the letter to her that was to become 'Dejection: an Ode'. In the original version he again conjured up that scene:

> It was as calm as this, that happy night
> When Mary, thou, & I together were,
> The low decaying Fire our only light,
> And listen'd to the Stillness of the Air!
> O that affectionate & blameless Maid,
> Dear Mary! on her Lap my head she lay'd—
>   Her Hand was on my Brow,
>   Even as my own is now;
> And on my Cheek I felt thy eye-lash play.
> Such Joy I had, that I may truly say,
> My Spirit was awe-stricken with the Excess
> And trance-like Depth of it's brief Happiness.[29]

In the poem he imagined Sara looking at the same scene as himself—but with the subsequent preference that she should be situated more

---

[28] CNB 6 f 2–5 (cf. *CN* I 973A).
[29] *CPW* (Beer) 389 and 396.

peacefully at her home, where she could enjoy the scents and hear the
low voice of the bee-hive that spoke of omnipresent life.

> O Sara! in the weather-fended Wood,
> Thy lov'd haunt! where the Stock-doves coo at Noon,
> I guess, that thou hast stood
> And watch'd yon Crescent, & it's ghost-like Moon.
> And yet far rather, in my present mood,
> I would that thou'dst been sitting all this while
> Upon the sod-built seat of Camomile—
> And tho' thy Robin may have ceas'd to sing,
> Yet needs for my sake must thou love to hear
> The Bee-hive murmuring near.
> That ever-busy & most quiet Thing
> Which I have heard at Midnight murmuring.[30]

These minglings of trance and sensitivity, projecting the subconscious at
its best and most pleasurable, were closely linked to the 'metaphysical'
speculations that he was undertaking at the same time, integrating his
existence.

How far is it legitimate to trace continuity between such idyllic
alternations and the puzzles that had attended the making of his
previous poetry? In one (surprising) sense they were still responses to
the French Revolution and the events of the Terror. To anyone who had
lived through the breakdown of law and order in a violent revolution
the thought of returning to the banalities of ordinary life could come as
a blessed relief: a relief which, I suggest, can be sensed throughout the
collection. On this reading, placing *The Ancient Mariner* first is a shock
tactic, an attempt to arrest the casual reader into a fuller appreciation of
the rest of the volume.

What the true subject of that opening poem should then be taken to
be has proved controversial. Coleridge himself records discussion of the
issue: 'Mrs Barbauld told me that the only faults she found with the
Ancient Mariner were—that it was improbable, and had no moral. As
for the probability, to be sure that might admit some question— but,
I told her that in my judgment the chief fault of the poem was that it
had too much moral, and that too openly obtruded on the reader. It
ought to have had no more moral than the story of the merchant sitting
down to eat dates by the side of a well and throwing the shells aside, and

---

[30] *CPW* (Beer), 394.

the Genii starting up and saying he must kill the merchant, because a date shell had put out the eye of the Genii's son.'[31]

Mrs Barbauld's second objection is indeed a rather strange one, though at first sight the 'moral' might seem questionable, echoing Leslie Stephen's comment:

the moral, which would apparently be that people who sympathize with a man who shoots an albatross will die in prolonged torture of thirst, is open to obvious objections...[32]

There are still further puzzles when one tries to determine the universe in which the poem is taking place. The 'kirk' might possibly suggest a reformation background, though for the most part the action, with 'Mary Queen' and a guardian saint, seems to presuppose medieval Catholicism. But then the spectre-ship, where Death and Life-in-Death dice for possession of the Mariner, belongs to an amoral world where things happen purely by chance. Finally, of the Two Voices, one seems to understand the situation better than the other. How do they fit in?

This is bewildering enough; further layers are added to the problem when one takes account of the prose gloss, not added till later, but giving a more orthodox slant to the poem's meaning—after which one might note the night sound of the brook in the middle stanzas, along with the music of the Mariner's trance as he hears the 'sweet jargoning' of the birds, or the angel's song 'that makes the heaven be mute'.

Once one has considered these elements—not to mention the sun and moon—one sees the justice of Coleridge's comment that the poem had 'too much' moral. Although a rough kind of moral can easily be extracted, reflecting, for example, the unexpected convergence between fluent beauty and religious convention in the Hermit's actions, the poem as a whole seems riven with contradictions.

Insofar as these contradictions are to be reconciled, nevertheless, it is through the overwhelming power of love. Love, ministered through the kind of sensibility that can respond to nature, is for Coleridge the perpetual solution.

But while poetry of this kind was helping to establish his fame, readers might have noticed that his behaviour was not always single-minded.

---

[31] Table Talk of 31 March 1832: see *CTT* I 272–3, citing MS B 36: 214. A slightly more elaborate version, dated 31 May 1830, appeared in H. N. Coleridge's 1836 edition.

[32] Leslie Stephen, *Hours in a Library* (London: Smith, Elder & Co., 1892) III 359.

Even while he had been hymning sympathy in *The Rime of the Ancient Mariner* he had been writing another poem about a bird, this time a raven, with the 'moral', 'Revenge it was sweet'.[33] His political advocacy of human sympathy, similarly, was accompanied by evidences of occasional dyspathy—as when the most significant among his rivals turned out to be none other than James Mackintosh.

[33] 'The Raven': *CPW* (Beer) 147–8.

4

Coleridge and Mackintosh: Revisionary Poet and Simpering 'Dungfly'

About the turn of the century Coleridge wrote several poems in a mode which Morton Paley has characterized as the 'apocalyptic grotesque'.[1] Among them were verses he sent to Humphry Davy in October 1800 as a 'Skeltoniad (to be read in the Recitative Lilt)': they formed a satire in which he imagined the local graveyard awaiting the Last Trump, the coming of the Lord, and the resurrection of the dead, and projected a particular grave as one on which at times of snow two round spaces might be seen, marking the place where the Devil and his 'grannam' were waiting with exceptional confidence for the return of a certain 'counsellor Keen':

> From Aberdeen hither this Fellow did skip
> With a waxy Face and a blabber Lip,
> And a black Tooth in front to shew in part
> What was the Colour of his whole Heart!
> This Counsellor sweet! This Scotchman compleat!
> Apollyon scotch him for a Snake—
> I trust, he lies in his Grave awake![2]

To anyone in the know it was evident that the figure under the gravestone was a scurrilous caricature of James Mackintosh, with whom Coleridge had had various recent dealings.

Among the cases where Coleridge's behaviour could be contradictory—even two-faced, if it comes to that—this is an extreme example, though

---

[1] *Apocalypse & Millennium in English Romantic Poetry* (Oxford: Clarendon Press, 1999), pp. 140–53.

[2] *CL* I 632–3; *CPW* (EHC) I 353–5. I am grateful to J. C. C. Mays for having allowed me to see in advance a draft of his note on the poem for his *CC* edition of the *Poetical Works*.

his behaviour towards Mackintosh can partly be explained by the fact that it brought together different levels of his experience. Sympathizers with the calls for reform were likely to see the Scottish lawyer as a hero by reason of his early rejoinder to Burke's *Reflections on the late Revolution in France*, entitled *Vindiciae Gallicae*. His book ranked with Godwin's *Political Justice* as a major influence on the young of the time. Coleridge,[3] who shared the contemporary enthusiasm, but had not been able to join in the fashionable accolade for this volume, was appalled by the unanimity with which erstwhile adherents then turned against Godwin following the change of attitude towards France during the 1790s—particularly since in his view an author who had demonstrated such extraordinary capabilities in works such as *Caleb Williams* and *St Leon* was not lightly to be dismissed.

Mackintosh's abjuration, one of the most dramatic reversals, and publicly announced in a lecture of 1800 at which Godwin himself was present, was taken as a personal attack by the latter, who wrote demanding an explanation. Mackintosh's reply was courteous and polished, denying that criticism of Godwin himself could have been intended.

Having a few years before renounced former views of his own concerning the French Revolution,[4] Coleridge, who cannot have been altogether unsympathetic to Mackintosh's changed position, felt that this open and public avowal gave aid and comfort to the anti-Jacobin faction who had recently assumed a dominant voice in British culture, slandering in the process figures such as Southey, Lloyd, Lamb, and himself.[5] This disgust, felt not only by Godwin but by others such as Hazlitt, helps to explain the nature of Coleridge's attitude in subsequent years: the distaste, largely political in its basis, was shared with like-minded members of his immediate circle. Lamb wrote a bitter, tasteless epigram for the *Albion* on Godwin's apostasy, comparing him, to his disadvantage, with Judas.[6] Coleridge, in acrid comments intended for

---

[3] See his account, in an 1818 letter to James Perry, of his lasting sense of debt for having enabled him to meet such an illustrious figure in the 1790s: *CL* IV 830–1nn.

[4] See his 'France: An Ode', originally entitled 'The Recantation: an Ode': *CPW* (EHC) I 243–7; and cf. *CPW* (CC) I(1) 462–8 and nn; *CF* (1809) 161–2 (cf. *CFriend* II 146–7).

[5] See E. K. Chambers, *Samuel Taylor Coleridge* (Oxford: Clarendon Press, 1938), p. 93.

[6] Letter to Thomas Manning of August 1801: *LL* (Marrs) II 13. It has been claimed that the *Albion* had to cease publication as a result of including this poem.

the eyes of the aggrieved Godwin, spoke witheringly of 'the Animalcula, who live on the dung of the great Dung-fly Mackintosh',[7] and of his lectures and conversations as 'the Steam of an Excrement'.

Concerning the lawyer's attitude as a whole, on the other hand, some discrimination is called for. When he first knew him Mackintosh had shown him little but kindness, sending him a letter in November 1797[8] which was full of praise for a young and struggling writer whom he had heard of through Beddoes and 'my amiable Friend Miss Allen'; in it he reported that he had been able to persuade Daniel Stuart to offer him some money in return for contributions to the *Morning Post*. Coleridge's reply and his subsequent letter[9] showed delight at Mackintosh's recognition and gratitude for his help in finding journalistic work.

By the beginning of the following year, as Hazlitt recalled, Coleridge was describing him in a sharper vein as a 'mere logician', in comparison to Burke, the true 'metaphysician'.[10] This conversation took place at the beginning of 1798. Coleridge's more critical stance may have owed something even at this stage to Mackintosh's opinions concerning Wordsworth, and his unwillingness to show appreciation of poetry such as that being assembled for *Lyrical Ballads*.[11] It seems that they had met at Cote at about this time. In his memoir Clement Carlyon states that in Germany Coleridge was already speaking of the intellectual exchanges between them when they had met at the Wedgwoods' house, which points to a first encounter between the November exchange of letters and his departure for the continent in the following autumn; he also mentioned that Coleridge had 'no great liking' for

---

[7] Letter to Godwin, 21 May 1800: *CL* I 588. He put his views more soberly in a letter of 13 October: ibid., 636.

[8] *CL* I 359–60n; *CL* II 737 and *HW* XVII 111. By 1808, however, Mackintosh was expressing a favourable opinion of Wordsworth's poems. See *WL* (1806–1811) 265.

[9] See Edmund Garratt's article, 'Lime Blossom, Bees and Flies: Three Unpublished Letters of S. T. Coleridge to Sir James Mackintosh', in *Romanticism* VII (2001) 1–15.

[10] *HW* XVII 111.

[11] In her note to *CN* II 2468, Kathleen Coburn presents the evidence in favour of Shawcross's suggestion that Mackintosh was the 'Papilianus' addressed in the motto to *Lyrical Ballads* ('How absolutely not after your liking, O learned jurist!'), quoted in this notebook entry, about a dream—also in connection with Mackintosh's inability to appreciate subtle psychological thinking—which he would 'prove to be Nonsense by a Scotch Smile'). In a letter to Godwin of 23 June 1801, Coleridge hoped with satisfaction that Sharp and Rogers, who had been visiting the Lakes, would return 'with far other opinion respecting Wordsworth, than the Scotch Gentleman has been solicitous to impress his Listeners with' *CL* II 737. Cf. also his comment, reported by Hazlitt, to Mackintosh and Tom Wedgwood on their 'indifferent opinions' of Wordsworth: 'He strides on so far before you that he dwindles in the distance': *HW* XVII 111.

him.[12] Daniel Stuart recorded a memory of Coleridge being there 'during the Christmas holidays', monopolizing the attention of the company, particularly that of Tom Wedgwood, and so preventing general conversation:

> Mackintosh, at the instance of some of the inmates, attacked Coleridge on all subjects, politics, poetry, religion, ethics, &c. Mackintosh was by far the most dexterous disputer. Coleridge overwhelmed listeners in, as he said, with reference to Madame de Staël, a monologue;[13] but at sharp cut-and-thrust fencing, by a master like Mackintosh, he was speedily confused and subdued. He felt himself lowered in the eyes of the Wedgewoods: a salary, though small as it was, was provided for him; and Mackintosh drove him out of the house: an offence which Coleridge never forgave.

Stuart's memory was not by now very accurate, and his account must be treated with caution. That the inhabitants of the house-party should have resented this monopolizing young talker and applauded Mackintosh's debating strategy is quite plausible, but in what sense he 'drove him out' is not clear, and Coleridge's subsequent intimacy with Tom Wedgwood militates against the idea that the purpose of the pension (which was in fact a generous one) was to keep him away. Stuart himself reports Coleridge's subsequent comment on Mackintosh's skill in maintaining an argument about Locke—followed by a private confession to himself afterwards that he had never read that writer. His account of their duels recalls Lamb's memories of the 'wit-combats' at school between Coleridge and Le Grice, with Coleridge like a Spanish great galleon, slow and solid, against the faster manoeuvres of his opponent's English man-of-war.[14] Some covert hostility towards Coleridge survived, however, among the rest of the Wedgwood family. Catharine Wedgwood, in particular, when faced with the prospect of entertaining him with her brother at Cote in 1803, wrote that Coleridge would have to sleep in the 'tower', confessing that she had 'never seen enough of

---

[12] Clement Carlyon, *Early Years and Late Reflections* (4 vols., London: Whitaker and Co., 1836–58) I 68–70. He also, however, reported Coleridge's view that Mackintosh could only appreciate people of superior intellectual qualities; according to Carlyon he evidently included himself among the number.

[13] The case was precisely the opposite, of course: it was Madame de Staël who spoke of Coleridge as excellent in monologue, 'mais il ne savait pas le dialogue'. For a full discussion see Seamus Perry, *S. T. Coleridge: Interviews and Recollections* (London: Palgrave Macmillan, 2000), p. 148 and n. 40; p. 150.

[14] See 'Christ's Hospital Five and Thirty Years Ago', in *Elia*.

him to overcome the first disagreeable impression of his accent and exterior', finding in him 'too great a parade of superior feeling'.[15]

In 1798 Mackintosh was married for the second time, to Catherine Allen, sister of Josiah Wedgwood's wife, thus securing a permanent connection with the family. Coleridge, receiving in 1800 a ticket for his forthcoming lectures, was not impressed. He wrote to Poole that he thought them largely plagiarized from Condillac[16] and took issue on the question of priority in formulating the doctrine of innate ideas[17]— though he acknowledged that he had learned from him that the association of ideas had not been introduced by Locke until the fourth edition of his work.[18]

Elsewhere in the same notebook he was critical of Mackintosh's style:

Mackintosh intertrudes, not introduces his beauties. Nothing grows out of his main argument but much is shoved between—each digression occasions a move backward to find the road again—like a sick man he recoils after every affection. The Serpent by which the ancients emblem'd the Inventive faculty appears to me, in its mode of motion most exactly to emblem a writer of Genius. He varies his course yet still glides onwards—all lines of motion are his—all beautiful, & all propulsive—

> Circular base of rising folds that tower'd
> Fold above fold a surging maze, his Head
> Crested aloft, and Carbuncle his eyes
> With burnish'd Neck of verdant Gold, erect
> Amidst the circling spires that on the Grass
> Floted Redundant—
> So varied he & of his tortuous train
> Curls many a wanton wreath;

yet still he proceeds & is proceeding.—[19]

As a critique of Mackintosh's habit of mind this was radical and searching: true mental genius would express itself in a more organic fashion than his mechanical mode, so that the hearer would have a sense of growth. It is clear that there had been not only a further encounter

---

[15] R. B. Litchfield, *Tom Wedgwood, the First Photographer* (London: Duckworth and Co., 1903), pp. 139–40. She clearly felt strong reservations about his willingness to be dependent on the Wedgwood annuity, but declared herself to be not so 'rivetted to this opinion but that I can change, if upon seeing more of him he gives me sufficient grounds.'

[16] His notes on them can be found in *CN* I 634.

[17] *CL* II 681. [18] Ibid., 695. [19] CNB 4 ff 7ᵛ–8 (cf. *CN* I 609).

with Mackintosh but a development in his sense of what Coleridge believed him to lack (and—at least by implication—what he believed himself at his best to have). Reflecting, in addition, on his turncoat activity, he tried to understand psychologically the processes involved—how a man might turn hypocrite 'gradually & by ... little tiny atoms'.[20]

Whereas his remarks concerning Mackintosh had been scabrous in his letters to Godwin, in those addressed to Poole they were cuttingly precise— exacerbated, possibly, by knowing of Poole's dealings with Catharine, Josiah Wedgwood's sister. When Poole had earlier written to Tom Wedgwood in 1800 to ask if he might correspond with her, fairly clearly with a view to matrimony, he had received a reply containing a forceful refusal: 'I was stunned by it though I do not know why', he recalled, 'and I stood looking at it for an hour.' Tom expressed astonishment at Poole's 'presumption'—and Poole subsequently noted the assumption of a class difference between them.[21] If Coleridge knew of this event he might well have been surprised that while the Wedgwoods found Mackintosh acceptable as a member of their extended family they should have rejected an approach from his rough-speaking, radical-thinking, admirable friend: according to Carlyon he had explained to his companions in Germany his preference for Poole's directness over Mackintosh's logic. His references to the latter, whose interventions, as a firm adherent to associationism, and appeal to most in a general company through dexterity in debate were evidently powerful irritants, remained notably barbed.[22] His arguments with Mackintosh about Locke at Cote and the four long letters on the same subject that he sent to Josiah early in 1801[23] formed parts of a continuous underground warfare against the associationists, inviting Tom's support.

Coleridge's most searching criticism of Mackintosh came in an account of his visit to Keswick in 1801:

[20] CNB 21 ff 30–30ᵛ (cf. ibid., I 947).
[21] R. B. Litchfield, *Tom Wedgwood*, 100–1 and n.
[22] According to Mrs Sandford (*Thomas Poole and his Friends* [1888], new edn., Friarn Press, Over Stowey, Somerset, 1996) 204, Poole later met Mackintosh in unusual circumstances. While visiting the Louvre in Paris in 1802 he was looking at a picture of an albatross when he heard a stranger remark, 'He shot the albatross', and turned to see who had said this. When he introduced himself as a dear friend of Coleridge, he found the stranger to be Mackintosh.
[23] *CL* II 677–703.

We talked of all & every thing—on some very affecting subjects in which he represented himself by words as affected; on some subjects that called forth his verbal indignation—or exultation: but in no one moment did any particle of his face from the top of his forehead to the half of his neck, move. His face has no lines like that of a man—no softness, like that of a woman—it is smooth, hard, motionless—a flesh-mask!—As to his conversation, it was all uncommonly well-worded: but not a thought in it worthy of having been worded at all— He was however entertaining to me always; & to all around him then chiefly, when he talked of Parr, Fox, Addington, &c &c. When I asked him concerning Davy—he answered Oh!—little Davy—Dr Beddoes' Eleve, you mean?—This was an exquisite trait of character.[24]

Coleridge's response to the lifelessness of Mackintosh can be compared with D. H. Lawrence's towards Bertrand Russell, as projected fictionally in the account of Rupert Birkin and Sir Joshua Malleson in *Women in Love*.[25]

Catherine herself kept a journal of her Scottish tour as she and her husband travelled,[26] and set down her own impressions at Keswick when they 'found Mr Colleridge whom we had asked to dine with us waiting for us':

Thought Mr C improved altogether in appearance though he complained, or rather *boasted* of ill health. He was as usual very eloquent in conversation, apparently very happy with the idea of being able in his retirement to make out some grand discoveries through ye means of metaphysical speculations—His Vanity is probably unreasonable but at least it is not degrading. But his opinion of the importance of such Reveries as Godlinesses & his enthusiastic fondness for the writings of Spinosa puzzle one were it our purpose to make an estimate of his character when these are contrasted with the moral and religious feelings he seems to have—His conversation is a perpetual & seldom unsuccessful aim at finding something Recherchée, remote & uncommon resemblances; shades of difference, striking comparisons & illustrations of one part of nature to another in which he is often happy and never common. He staid till near ten...[27]

Next day, since the weather was poor, they stayed on in Keswick and spent a good deal of time with the Coleridges:

[24] Letter to Poole of 31 Oct 1801: *CL* II 770.
[25] See my *Romanticism, Revolution and Language* (Cambridge: Cambridge University Press, 2009), p. 127.
[26] The MS is now preserved among the Wedgwood papers.
[27] Ms Journal (Wedgwood ms E59/32631, f 13). Reproduced by courtesy of the Trustees of the Wedgwood Museum, Barlaston.

Mrs Colleridge I like very well & the day passed off pleasantly enough. The view from Greta Hall where Mr C— lives the most pleasing I have seen about the Lake.

After this, on Thursday,

Mr Colleridge called & mentioning his intention of going to Grasmere we took him so far with us & found no reason to say he was not 'a good companion in a Post Chaise'. He told us that Mr Fox had (which I before somewhat doubted) written a letter of commendation to Mr Wordsworth on his Lyrical Ballads sent him by the Bookseller, and had particularized as his favorite Poems 'Harry Gill' 'ye Mad Mother' We are Seven & ye poem entitled Love.

After some discussion of Fox, she continues,

Set Mr Colleridge down at Mr Wordsworth's Cottage on the banks of Winandermere—*Not* sorry to find that the Philosopher & his Sister were not within.[28]

Catherine's final comment suggests that she shared her husband's supposed attitude to the Wordsworths at this time.[29] There was apparent goodwill between all concerned, nevertheless: just as Catherine, for all her sharpness, gave a balanced picture of Coleridge, and clearly enjoyed the experience of his conversation, he in turn admitted her husband's verbal skill and his entertainingness. Yet all was not quite as it seemed. In a letter to Josiah of 1803 he was concerned to repair any damage that might have been caused by reports of an incident related to his visit to Cressely with Tom, early in December 1802.[30] This was evidently an event described by Kitty Wedgwood as 'the attack at Cresselly', in which she justified her own part on the grounds of her initial dislike, but about which little is otherwise known. Certainly Coleridge left such a pleasant impression on the Wedgwood family there that Fanny was soon afterwards disconcerted when her sister, Mackintosh's wife, responded hostilely to her praise:

---

[28] Wordsworth's cottage was not of course on the banks of Windermere, but above the lake at Grasmere; Catherine had evidently scrambled her memory of it with the situation of Lowwood, the inn by Windermere where they then went on to stay and with which they were pleased.

[29] Despite her love of nature she had a down-to-earth response which would have made her impatient with Wordsworth's further reflections. According to Coleridge, when he quoted to her Wordsworth's lines describing Peter Bell: 'A primrose by a river's brim | A yellow Primrose was to him, | And it was nothing more' as a possible illustration of her attitude, she commented 'Yes, that is precisely my feeling': see *HCR* I 97.

[30] *CL* III 21.

Her indignant feelings about our praise of Coleridge still more surprised me, as her letters to me did not prepare me to expect it & by her mentioning him gaily it flung me off my guard, & consequently there were many things in my letter to her, that I would gladly recall.[31]

At the same time, Coleridge had by no means abandoned criticism of Mackintosh in these years. In October 1803 he expressed agitation to Poole, believing that two paragraphs in the *Morning Post* would be attributed to him, though he thought them to be Mackintosh's, commenting 'O that they were! I would hunt him into Infamy',[32] and in January 1804 wrote again sarcastically that an offer which Mackintosh had made to find him a place when he went to India had been made assuring him 'on his Honor—on his Soul!!! (N.B. HIS Honor!!) (N.B. HIS Soul!!!) that he was sincere'. The memory of Mackintosh's apostasy evidently still rankled.[33]

That Coleridge retained a residual suspicion of Mackintosh is shown by a notebook entry of 1805, when, trying to distinguish between his use of the words 'Scotch' and 'Scottish' he gave as an example of the former 'the Scotch simper, or grin castrate of managed malignity in a Mackintosh'.[34] Although he made private criticisms, his public attitude softened notably, particularly when Mackintosh returned from Bombay in 1812 broken in health. In that year (and despite a virulent remark in a letter to Godwin of 1811)[35] he consulted with Stuart about the propriety of offering tickets for his forthcoming lectures to him and Lady Mackintosh without 'doing any thing that could be even interpreted into Servility'.[36] Mackintosh attended these and the lectures of 1818. In *Biographia Literaria*, meanwhile, Coleridge was flattering to the point of fulsomeness, introducing him as

Sir James Mackintosh (who amid the variety of his talents and attainments is not of less repute for the depth and accuracy of his philosophical enquiries, than for the eloquence with which he is said to render their most difficult results perspicuous, and the driest attractive).

He went on to dispute the claim, which he ascribed to Mackintosh, that Hobbes had been the original discoverer of the law of association

---

[31] The letter of Fanny, postmarked 14 March 1803 (Wedgwood ms 57/32012), is reproduced by courtesy of the Trustees of the Wedgwood Museum, Barlaston.
[32] *CL* II 1016. They have not, I think, been identified.
[33] Ibid., 1041. [34] CNB 17 f 109 (cf. *CN* II 2618).
[35] *CL* III 316. [36] Ibid., 403.

(having already claimed in private, in 1811, that he had convinced Mackintosh of the priority of Descartes and the schoolmen).[37] Mackintosh, who was, of course, all too ready to take issue with misrepresentations and elucidate his own views further, in due course did so.[38] By now, however, he was more prominent in English politics and so a convenient figure to whom Coleridge could apply when he was seeking support for a particular cause.[39]

Differences between the two men tended to dissolve, indeed, as Coleridge discovered how many political views they shared.[40] In the end, the main distinction between them boiled down to the sensed difference between their kinds of mind—a distinction which could rise to embrace the one he had made between talent and genius. As will be recalled, he had described Mackintosh to Hazlitt in 1798 as 'a master of the topics—or as the ready warehouseman of letters', his view having been emphasized further when he commented on Godwin's account of a dispute with Mackintosh, 'If there had been a man of genius in the room he would have settled the question in five minutes'.[41] The point recurs in his Table Talk of 1823, when he is reported as having distinguished between Mackintosh's mind as a '*hortus siccus*' and that of Humphry Davy, in the garden of which 'you could see his thoughts growing': as the chief of the men of talent, Mackintosh was 'very powerful; but he possessed not a ray of Genius'. On his forehead could be written 'Warehouse to Let'.[42]

---

[37]   *CTT* I 10.   [38]   *CBL* I 91–105 and nn.

[39]   See e.g. Edmund Garratt's newly discovered letter of 1822, p. 41, n. 9. above. Coleridge also wrote to more than one member of Parliament enlisting support for the Highgate bill: see *CL* V 236–8, 241–3. Since the letter reproduced on *CL* V 237, which is identified there only as 'To Unknown Correspondent', survives, like Catherine Mackintosh's journal, in the Wedgwood Collection, there is a prima facie case for supposing that it is in fact the one previously sent to Mackintosh.

[40]   See e.g. CNB 29 f 31ᵛ (cf. *CN* IV 4700)—though in another note soon after he still seems contemptuous of Mackintosh's ability to betray—even if only 'second hand truth': ibid., f 87 (cf. *CN* IV 4779).

[41]   See *HW* XVII 111 and text at n. 19 above.

[42]   Table Talk 27 April 1823: *CTT* I 40–2. In a review of the 1835 *Table Talk*, Francis Jeffrey took Coleridge to task for this metaphor, claiming 'If it was intended to insinuate that it was ready for the indiscriminate reception of any thing which any one might choose to put into it, there could not be a more gross misconception': *CH* II 56.

Jeffrey missed the subtlety of Coleridge's joke, however, which was contrasting the mechanical quality of Mackintosh's mental processes with a truly organic mode of thought. Some years later Coleridge's daughter Sara drew gratefully on some remarks by Mackintosh's 'intimate friend' Robert Hall as support for Coleridge's assessment: 'His mind is a spacious repository, hung round with beautiful images, and when he wants one he has

Coleridge did not often use his distinction between talent and genius publicly, one reason no doubt being that it could appear arrogant on his part to do so; nevertheless he was fully aware of the degree to which genius could be accompanied by impotence in practical affairs (a failure exemplified perhaps when he found himself thwarted by Mackintosh's debating skills at Cote). So far from identifying himself with the massive Spanish galleon of Lamb's metaphor he had a self-image of weakness and a lack of presence, in contrast with that of the men of the world among whom he was thrown. He considered the effects in a note of 1808:

My inner mind does not justify the Thought, that I possess a Genius—my Strength is so very small in proportion to my Power—I believe, that I first from internal feeling made, or gave light and impulse to this important distinction, between Strength and Power—the Oak, and the tropic Annual, or Biennial, which grows nearly as high and spreads as large, as the Oak—but the wood, the heart of Oak, is wanting—the vital works vehemently, but the Immortal is not with it—

And yet I think, I must have some analogon of Genius; because, among other things, when I am in company with Mr Sharp, Sir J. Mackintosh, Robert P. Smith and Sydney Smith, M' Scarlet, &c &c, I feel like a Child—nay, rather like an Inhabitant of another Planet—their very faces all act upon me, sometimes as if they were Ghosts, but more often as if I were a Ghost, among them—at all times, as if we were not consubstantial.[43]

Interestingly, in his essay on Mackintosh, Hazlitt applied Coleridge's distinction to the Scottish philosopher himself:

we cannot conceive of any two persons more different in colloquial talents, in which they both excel, than Sir James Mackintosh and Mr. Coleridge. They have nearly an equal range of reading and of topics of conversation: but in the mind of the one we see nothing but fixtures; in the other every thing is fluid. The ideas of the one are as formal and tangible, as those of the other are shadowy and

---

nothing to do but reach up his hand to a peg and take one down. But his images were not manufactured in his mind; they were imported' (quoted in Table Talk, *CTT* II 554).

When Mackintosh disparaged Coleridge a few years later, interestingly, he used the word 'ingenuity' rather than 'genius', thus in a sense reinforcing Coleridge's point: after reading Coleridge's refutation of the Doctrine of the Sovereignty of the People in *The Friend* in 1812 he wrote in his journal 'It is not without ideas of great value; but it is impossible to give a stronger example of a man whose talents are beneath his understanding, and who trusts to his ingenuity to atone for his ignorance.' R. J. Mackintosh, *Memoirs of the Life of Sir James Mackintosh* (2 vols., London: E. Moxon, 1835) II 195.

[43] *CN* III 3324.

evanescent. Sir James Mackintosh walks over the ground; Mr. Coleridge is always flying off from it. The first knows all that has been said upon a subject; the last has something to say that was never said before. If the one deals too much in learned common-places, the other teems with idle fancies. The one has a good deal of the caput mortuum of genius; the other is all volatile salt. The conversation of Sir James Mackintosh has the effect of reading a well-written book; that of his friend is like hearing a bewildered dream. The one is an Encyclopedia of knowledge; the other is a succession of Sybilline Leaves!

Coleridge's own attitude to Mackintosh was unstable. It shifted over time, as he moved from opposing him politically and philosophically to seeing him as a possible ally in some of the local battles he needed to fight. It changed also according to whether he was writing to Godwin, victim of Mackintosh's political tergiversation, or Poole the unsuccessful suitor of Catharine Wedgwood, or to the Wedgwoods themselves.

Mackintosh was aware of Coleridge's hostility.[44] If he bore any ill feeling towards him in return, however, he did not show it. There was probably no fixed attitude on Josiah Wedgwood's part, either. He could be impatient when Coleridge failed to make contact after his return from Malta, yet he also found him a perennial source of fascination. The fact that he had meant so much to Tom was an important factor, even if his failure to produce an adequate memoir disappointed him.

When in February 1833 'The Two Round Spaces' was republished in *Fraser's Magazine* with the lines describing Mackintosh's personal appearance included for the first time, the fact of Mackintosh's recent death made the gesture seem particularly insensitive and gave offence in the Wedgwood family. Coleridge himself had denied in the 1817 *Sybilline Leaves* that personal feeling on his part had been involved and had tried to explain the position:

This is the first time the author ever published these lines. He would have been glad, had they perished; but they have now been printed repeatedly in magazines, and he is told that the verses will not perish. Here, therefore, they are owned, with a hope that they will be taken—as assuredly they were composed—in mere sport.[45]

[44] R. J. Mackintosh, *Memoirs*, I 73.
[45] *CPW* (EHC) I 354n, II 1102.

After the republication in *Fraser's Magazine* he was forced to be more open:

I certainly did mean Mackintosh in the 'Two round spaces'—but as to meaning to lampoon him, as Fraser's Magazine says, from resentment I never had other than kind feelings towards Mackintosh all my life. He was taken slightly ill in passing through Grasmere—snow was deep, and I remember being tickled, as I looked on the humble churchyard, with the thought that if he, a great Scotch Lawyer, should die there, and have a great tombstone in the middle of the ground, how odd and funny it would be. When I repeated the verses to Wordsworth he smiled in his grave way—Southey roared at them, and wrote them down and gave copies.[46]

Coleridge's assertion that the lines had been written 'merely in sport' was rejected by Carlyon as 'special pleading' in the face of what in Germany had struck him as evident vindictiveness;[47] Poole, however, took another view, writing to Carlyon, 'This sort of feeling in C[oleridge] was never more than skin deep, of which being conscious he seemed to delight in sporting with it'.[48] That comment (which incidentally displays a psychological acumen that questions the judgment of the Wedgwoods in dismissing Poole's pretensions so readily) answers to an urge to enjoyment[49] and general volatility in him that many sensed, and which made it hard to be permanently angry with him. 'I cannot account satisfactorily for his apparent total neglect of my brother and myself for so long a time,' wrote Josiah Wedgwood in the summer of 1806, 'but I am neither piqued nor angry, for I consider him as privileged to dispense with the ordinary rules that govern the conduct of common men to each other in the less essential points of their intercourse. His genius excites my admiration, and his hypochondriacal affection, that too frequent attendant on genius, my pity.'[50] Over the next few months his attitude hardened when there was still no news,

---

[46] *CTT* I 352–3. The account is rather hard to understand as it stands. The references to 'being taken slightly ill' and, in the poem, to the 'House of Privity' may mean that Mackintosh was forced to use the Grasmere graveyard for his own, undignified purposes on this occasion. What is particularly puzzling about all this, however, is that Mackintosh is not known to have visited Grasmere before the 1801 visit recorded below. Either there was an earlier, unrecorded visit or Coleridge is romancing back, superimposing later thoughts on the already written poem.

[47] Carlyon, *Early Years and Late Reflections* I 69–70.   [48] Ibid., III 129.

[49] Cf. Lamb's remark to Leigh Hunt: 'You mustn't mind Coleridge, Hunt; he's so full of his fun'; E. V. Lucas, *Life of Charles Lamb* (London: Methuen, 1910), p. 667.

[50] Sandford, *Thomas Poole*, 248–9.

only to soften when George Coleridge urged that his brother was truly concerned and that it was his 'miserable hypochondriacal state' that was indeed to blame for his silence.[51]

The ambivalent feelings persisted, no doubt to be associated with Josiah's withdrawal of his part in the annuity in 1812.[52] But when he wrote to Fanny Allen shortly after Coleridge's death, seeking to elucidate certain details, including the 1802 'quarrel' at Cressely, she replied with a strongly favouring impression of the man, and his remembered play of mind:

I never had but one cause of quarrel with Coleridge—the fortnight that he and your brother past here are among some of the happiest of our lives.[53]

---

[51] Ibid., 249–50.

[52] For a balanced account of this event see Richard Holmes, *Coleridge: Darker Reflections* (London: Harper Collins, 1998), pp. 328–30.

[53] Wedgwood ms A11/ 9856, dated December 1834, reproduced by courtesy of the Trustees of the Wedgwood Museum, Barlaston. The 'cause of quarrel' may not, incidentally, have referred to Coleridge's opinion of Mackintosh but to the incident in which she incurred his displeasure by passing into convulsions of laughter when he read a passage from Wordsworth's poem describing how the Leech-gatherer's skin was so old and dry that the leeches would not stick to it. (The passage was later omitted and is now lost.)

5

Nature, Poetry, and the
Vicissitudes of Love

During the years following his first meeting with Sara Hutchinson the value of the relationship for Coleridge reached its peak. It must have seemed to him that his high-minded aspiration to combine Platonic entrancement in her company with acceptance of his marital responsibilities towards his wife might be offered as a prophetic model for his age. Such ideas are suggested by a later reference in which he likens his love to Jonah's prophesying under a gourd.[1]

It was a fervent hope, and for some years he allowed it to dominate his relationship with the Wordsworths. As William embarked on marriage with Mary Hutchinson, the knowledge that Sara would be accepted as part of the new ménage allowed him to pen a message of hope for their success—even if awareness of his own, necessary, physical exclusion meant that the title of that message would be, on further consideration, 'Dejection'.

Was he at all envious? A week after the marriage, an epigram based on one by Wernicke, referring to 'Annette, the *lovely Courtesan*' and entitled 'Spots in the Sun', appeared in the *Morning Post*. Some commentators have assumed the adoption of this name to have been designed to hurt Wordsworth publicly. But since few readers, if any, knew of Annette Vallon's existence, let alone her first name, it is safer to follow Jim Mays's verdict that 'there is no knowing whether the allusion was intended or was an unfortunate (perhaps 'Freudian') error'.[2] It is certainly true that Coleridge later showed restiveness at Wordsworth's enviable condition, but that was some years later; and even then he did

---

[1] CL V 250. Although the reference to Jonah iv is hard to interpret, it suggests that Coleridge saw his love for Sara Hutchinson as an equivalent to the sheltering gourd which the Lord raised over Jonah as a sign of his lovingkindness.

[2] *CPW* (CC) I (2) 733.

not describe his reaction (experienced in a dream) as other than 'involuntary jealousy'.

A more likely explanation of Coleridge's position during these years would take literally his tributes to Wordsworth's purity of purpose and his acceptance of the propriety of the decision to visit Annette, arranging both for her future and that of her daughter. It was only in the context of his alienation from his wife that he would come to feel more acutely the intensity of his love for Sara, or that his bitterness towards the Wordsworths would receive open expression. For the moment, he could delight in sharing the natural pleasures of their surroundings: birdsong, the sound of the bees in their nearby hive.

The sense that nature was on the side of their love extended to the phenomena of flowing. Coleridge's expressions of erotic love were often conveyed through imagery of springs and fountains, employed also for his symbolic bond with the Wordsworths.[3] A relevant brief notebook entry reads simply:

The spring with the little tiny cone of loose sand ever rising and sinking at the bottom, but its surface without a wrinkle.—W.W. M.H. D.W. S.H.[4]

While these initials signified the larger circle of his affectionate life, the core lay ineluctably in his intense love for Sara. Later on, he could still write a long notebook entry (dated by the editor in the spring of 1810) on the progress of true love, from the 'purpling Dawn of Love-truth' to the 'calm Even of confident Love', when the lovers can 'in mute recollection enjoy each other', and the peaceful silence that can then ensue:

So deeply do I now enjoy your presence, so totally possess you in myself, myself in you—The very sound would break the union, and separate *you-me* into you and me. We both, and this sweet room, its books, its pictures & the Shadows on the Wall Slumbering with the low quiet Fire are all *our* Thought, a harmonious Imagery of Forms distinct on the still substance of one Feeling, Love & Joy—a Lake—or if a stream, yet flowing so softly, so unwrinkled, that its flow is *Life* not Change— /—That state, in which all the individuous nature, the distinction without Division, of a vivid Thought is united with the sense and substance of Intensest Reality—.[5]

True as this may have been to one element in their relationship, it ignored the increasing degree to which Sara was wearied by the

---

[3] See Graham Davidson's article, 'Springs, Fountains and Volcanoes', in the *Coleridge Bulletin*, New Series 31, Summer 2008.

[4] CNB 21 f 32 (cf. *CN* I 980).   [5] CNB 17 ff 88ᵛ–9 (cf. *CN* III 3705).

emotional demands made upon her—to the point where she eventually found herself impelled to withdraw and join her brother Tom on his farm in Radnor. A few years before, Coleridge had made his decision to spend some time in Malta. On his return to England, the spirit of free inquiry, and the intellectual élan that had carried him along in the earlier part of the decade, were noticeably less active. Nor had the anticipated solutions to his personal problems come to pass: the recovery in health which he hoped for from staying in a hot climate had not happened; instead, the opium habit, now growingly reinforced by addiction to strong drink, had increased its hold. If he had hoped, also, that his relationship with Sara Hutchinson might be eased by the return of John Wordsworth from his last voyage, with the possibility of their marrying, such an outcome had been tragically prevented when he perished with his ship, precipitating instead a crisis of grief in the whole group. On hearing of his death Coleridge's immediate reaction was recorded in his notebook:

O William, O Dorothy, Dorothy!—Mary—& you loved him so!—and o blessed Sara, you whom in my imagination at one time I so often connected with him, by an effort of agonizing Virtue, willing it with cold sweat-drops on my Brow![6]

The echo of Christ's agony in the garden is particularly telling, the very effort needed to force such a wish on himself suggesting that the nobility of his gesture was in conflict with underlying feelings of natural jealousy, to which he could not own, but which must inevitably have been his immediate, subconscious reaction when news of John's death came. It is significant that his hearing the news occasioned a piece of confabulation—one of the clearest to be recorded, since the occasion was written about first in his notebook and later in a letter to his wife. The notebook entry was factual and dramatic:

...I went into the Drawing Room, which was full of visitors—Lady Ball addressed me, asking if I knew Capt[n] Wordsworth / I said a little—Is he not a Brother of the M[r] Wordsworth, you so often talk of?—No, I replied, still imagining she meant the Cousin / But you have heard his melancholy fate? What said I & the Ship? Here I turned pale & repeated the Question / Going from England, it sunk/ & 300 men are lost—& only but one hundred saved. But the Captain / he is lost—said Lady Ball, her voice faltering, for she saw my Emotion / I could just say—Yes! it is His Brother / & retired from the Room /

---

[6] CNB 17, f 47 (cf. *CN* II 2517).

Sir Alexander followed me—and D[r] Sewel to invite me to dine with him / I was nearly strangled—and at last just got out—I have just heard of the Death of a dear Friend, Sir! excuse me/—& got home led by the Sergeant & followed to the Door by Sir A. B. / O what an afternoon—[7]

The account in a letter to his wife, written over four months later and not sent until September,[8] differs noticeably, referring to a 'convulsive hysteric Fit'—which is, as Oswald Doughty pointed out,[9] an addition to the original account. In spite of what he told her, moreover, his notebook does not record exclusive confinement to his room during the subsequent fortnight. Perhaps significantly, this little piece of what appears to be bad faith was associated with a death about which he must have had ambivalent feelings. The same point may be made concerning another memory of the incident that came when he was explaining his failure to arrive to give a lecture in 1808 after hurting his head:

The pain however will soon subside, for it does not rise from so recent an Event as yesterday, but from a more distant period. It was when I was at Malta, Two years ago: a person rushed into my Apartment and abruptly announced to me the Death of a dear Friend, this occasioned my falling backwards and gave a contusion on my head which Brings back the pain occasionally upon any Exertion or Accident.[10]

This is another version. Instead of his hearing the news in a crowded room, as in both the other accounts, and instead of a precipitate exit, secured with the greatest difficulty, the narrative now is of a falling down and a contusion. While not totally impossible, it is certainly hard to reconcile the various elements in these accounts. It may not be without significance, also, that the failure recorded on this occasion should have been to give a literary lecture—presumably on Shakespeare.

Meanwhile, the loss of his brother brought about an increase in Wordsworth's own sense of his public responsibilities. The hope of cultivating private and local pleasures to assist the amelioration of public life lost its allure. If John Wordsworth was willing to die in his country's service it seemed less fitting for the Wordsworths and Southey to be

---

[7] Entry of 31 March 1805, CNB 17 ff 47[v]–45 (cf. *CN* II 2517).

[8] Letter of 21 July 1805, *CL* II 1170. Wartime activities made postal communication difficult.

[9] Oswald Doughty, *Perturbed Spirit: The Life and Personality of Samuel Taylor Coleridge* (Rutherford, N.J.: Fairleigh Dickinson University Press; East Brunswick, N.J.: Associated University Presses, *c.*1981).

[10] *CL* III 100–1.

enjoying a pleasurably retired life in Grasmere: there was, after all, a war in progress. Only a few years before England had been in danger of invasion; and that threat might recur.

But even if he only partly shared Wordsworth's shifting view, Coleridge must have felt at least willing to respect it. In the same manner he could also hope that Wordsworth understood how love was an essential part of what had been constructed around the Grasmere household, with Wordsworth, the undisputed head, gradually to be appreciated as a great poet, while Coleridge would rear, as complementary edifice, his understanding of the human mind.

In the period following the return from Malta his intimacy with the Wordsworths was no longer so prominent. To the opposition of his Devonshire relations he resolved to separate from his wife, while taking some responsibility for their children. His love for Sara meanwhile intensified. A turning point came on 27 December 1806 (singled out in his notebook as '**The Epoch**', in heavy letters) when at the Queen's Head near Coleorton he saw, or imagined, a scene which convinced him that Wordsworth and Sara Hutchinson were more intimate than he had realized. Just what this was (Wordsworth lying in bed, with both his wife and sister-in-law at hand, perhaps) never became clear, and Coleridge was subsequently convinced that he had been the victim of a delusion. (Molly Lefebure may be right in blaming the effects of opium.)[11] At all events, things were said that he swiftly came to regret; and when, a few days later, Wordsworth read aloud the current version of his autobiographical poem, he quickly composed an adulatory response, concluding with his own final reaction:

> Scarce conscious and yet conscious of it's Close,
> I sate, my Being blended in one Thought,
> (Thought was it? or aspiration? or Resolve?)
> Absorb'd, yet hanging still upon the sound:
> And when I rose, I found myself in Prayer![12]

Yet the scene at the inn remained imprinted on his memory—to revive when, during the following autumn at Nether Stowey, he reflected on his love for Sara in a long dithyrambic notebook passage:

[11] Molly Lefebure, *The Bondage of Love* (New York: Paragon House, 1989), pp. 180–1.
[12] *CPW* (EHC) I 408.

Loving her I intensely desire all that could make the greatest & (be it viceless) the weak, if they be amiable, love me—I am so feeble that I cannot yearn to be perfect, unrewarded by some distinct soul—yet still somewhat too noble to be satisfied or even pleased by the assent of the many—myself will not suffice—& a stranger is nothing/ It must be one who is & who is not myself—not myself, & yet so much more my Sense of Being . . . than myself that myself is therefore only not a feeling for reckless Despair, because she is its object.[13]

He reflected that without this connection of being he would be tempted to suicide, yet feared that she would despise him for such a thought or be urged by pity to withdraw herself from his affections, continuing,

O agony! O the vision of that Saturday Morning—of the Bed/—O cruel! is he not beloved, adored by two—& two such Beings—/ and must I not be beloved near him except as a Satellite?—But O mercy mercy! is he not better, greater, more manly, & altogether more attractive to any the purest Woman? And yet, and yet, methinks, love so intense might demand love—otherwise, who could be secure?[14]

This was followed by a near-hysterical outburst of envy:

W. is greater, better, manlier, more dear, by nature, to Woman, than I—I—miserable I!—but does he—O No! no! no! no! he does not—he does not pretend, he does not wish, to love you as I love you, Sara!—he does not love, he would not love, it is not the voice, not the duty of his nature, to love any being as I love you.[15]

The passage ends,

Awakened from a dream of Tears, & anguish of involuntary Jealousy, ½ past 2/ Sept: 13. 1807.

It was one of the mysteries of the unconscious for him that it could produce such unworthy emotions. Later, and particularly after he came to feel that the Wordsworths had in some way betrayed him by encouraging Sara Hutchinson's withdrawal, he resorted to a different tactic, writing a bitter little Latin poem entitled 'Ad Vilmum Axiologum' which reads, when translated into prose,

Do you command me to endure Asra's neglect? and to be able to see the eyes of my Asra averted? And to know her as false and cruel who always was, always will be dear to me? And me to suffer the daylight when, since I desperately love one who is false, the whole of my nature trembles and shudders? . . .[16]

---

[13] CNB 12 ff 43ᵛ–44 (cf. *CN* II 3148).   [14] Ibid., ff 45–46.
[15] Ibid., ff 46–46ᵛ.   [16] CNB 24 f 15ᵛ (cf. *CN* II 3231n).

Having pursued this bitter and reproachful thought to its conclusion, Coleridge entered into his notebook (whether immediately or later) another poem with the same Latin title, but this time addressing Wordsworth in English:

> This be the meed, that thy Song creates a thousandfold Echo!
> Sweet as the warble of woods that awake at the gale of the Morning!
> List! the hearts of the Pure, like Caves in the ancient Mountains,
> Deep, deep, *in* the Bosom, and *from* the Bosom resound it,
> Each with a different Tone, complete or in musical fragments,
> All have welcom'd thy Voice, and receive and retain and
> prolong it!...[17]

For Coleridge this was the voice of his true admiration for Wordsworth, whatever might have slipped out in the course of his night-thoughts. Transposed into stately hexameters, however, one notices that it loses spontaneity—even if it achieves originality by psychoscaping the effects of the poet on his audience in terms of a great mountain-voice, echoed alike from woods and caverns—sweetly in the one case, with deep profundity in the other.

In spite of such aspirations to nobility, it is apparent that the physical strain imposed by abstinence was beginning to tell. This would seem to be the import of a poem translated from Marino, 'Alla Sua Amica':

> Lady, to Death we're doom'd, our crime the same!
> Thou, that in me thou kindledst such fierce heat;
> I, that my Heart did of a Sun so sweet
> The Rays concenter to so hot a flame.
> I, fascinated by an Adders Eye,
> Deaf as an Adder thou to all my pain;
> Thou obstinate in Scorn, in passion I—
> I loved too much, too much didst thou disdain.
> Hear then our doom in Hell as just as stern,
> Our sentence equal as our crimes conspire
> Who living basked at Beauty's earthly Fire,
> In living flames eternal thou must burn/—
> Hell for us both fit places too supplies—
> In my Heart thou wilt burn, I roast before thine Eyes—[18]

---

[17] CNB 24 f 13ᵛ (cf. *CN* II 3231); *CPW* (EHC) I 391.
[18] CNB 13 ff 35–34ᵛ (cf. *CN* III 3377).

In the same notebook he produced a prose analysis of the same kind, this time using his old paradigm of the ideal image of true love as a sun uniting heat and light:

If love be the genial Sun of human nature, unkindly has he divided his rays in acting on me and [Aσρα]—on her poured all his Light and Splendor, & permeated my Being with his invisible Rays of Heat alone/ She shines and is cold, as the tropic firefly—I dark and uncomely would better resemble the Cricket in hot ashes—my Soul at least might be considered as a Cricket eradiating the heat which gradually cinerizing the Heart produced the embery ashes, from among which it chirps, out of its hiding-place.—[19]

In another self-analysis of the time (quoted by Graham Davidson) he allowed himself to envisage, however unbelievably, the possibility of his love being subdued in favour of lust—in which case the image of the peaceful fountain would be replaced by that of a volcano:

Could I feel for a moment the supremacy of Love suspended in my nature, by the accidents of temporary Desire; were I conscious for a moment of an Interregnum in the Heart, were the Rebel to sit on the *Throne* of my Being, even tho' it were only that the Rightful Lord of my bosom were sleeping, soon to awake & expel the Usurper, I should feel myself as much fallen & unworthy of her Love in any such tumult of Body indulged toward her, as if I had roamed, like a Hog in the rankest Lanes of a city, battening on the loathsome offals of Harlotry / yea, the guilt would seem greater to me / but when Love, like a Volcano beneath a sea always burning, tho' in silence, flames up in his strength at some new accession, o how can the waters but heave & roll in billows?— driven by no wind on the mere Surface, save that which their own tumult creates, but the mass is agitated from the depths, & the waves tower up as if to make room for the stormy Swelling.[20]

This is a counterpart to the easeful, spring-like nature of contented love, resembling rather the 'mighty fountain' of destructive power at the centre of *Kubla Khan*, and held in check only with great difficulty. Coleridge was increasingly torn apart at this time, divided between his lasting admiration for the Wordsworths and the intensity of his love for Sara; the workings of his passion could not in all honesty fail to be acknowledged, yet the possibility that some of his imaginings were the product of a disordered subconscious could not readily be dismissed, either. Molly Lefebure has argued forcefully that Coleridge—and in

[19] CNB 13 ff 34–33 (cf. *CN* III 3379).
[20] CNB 11 ff 21ᵛ–22ᵛ (cf. *CN* II 2984).

consequence, his wife also—should be regarded primarily as victims of drug addiction, everyone involved being participants in a pharmaceutically induced tragedy.[21] This is, however, to ignore certain other issues. Coleridge's own conviction that his addiction was the result of genuine attempts to deal with very present pain is hard to counter, particularly in view of the rudimentary state of medical knowledge at the time, and one is still faced with the problem of resolving the problem at the root of his intellectual quest: posed by his need both to understand the natural order and to offer a code that would satisfy humanity's moral needs and questionings. His own efforts at a solution, recognizing the indissolubility of his marriage while engaging Sara Hutchinson in a relationship of chaste love, were high-minded: if they had been successful they might, he hoped, have allowed for the propagation of truths beneficial to all mankind; the extract just quoted is, however, eloquent of the stresses and strains involved, particularly for Sara. Another notebook entry of the time, no doubt voicing a personal complaint, indicates the difficulties created for her by the need to offer him emotional support:

You never sate with or near me ten minutes in your life without shewing a restlessness, & thought of going, &c, for at least 5 minutes out of the 10.[22]

The undertow of his feeling for her, meanwhile, continued unabated. In 1807, when he had revisited places in Somerset where he had been accustomed to think of her, memories flooded back so vividly that he wrote a whole poem about them, entitled 'Recollections of Love', beginning

> How warm this woodland wild Recess!
> Love surely hath been breathing here;
> And this sweet bed of heath, my dear!
> Swells up, then sinks with faint caress,
> As if to have you yet more near.

As time went by, however, he was increasingly aware of the frustration created by Sara Hutchinson's unwillingness to allow any fuller return for his love so long as he remained faithful to his wife. The bitterness of his reflection on this was expressed in 'The Blossoming of the Solitary Date-Tree', a poem he did not complete in verse—perhaps because he

---

[21] See her *Samuel Taylor Coleridge: A Bondage of Opium* (London: Victor Gollancz, 1974).
[22] CNB 13 f 31 (cf. *CN* III 3383).

could not bear to. The part for which he did produce stanzas in verse
included the lines

> For never touch of gladness stirs my heart,
> But tim'rously beginning to rejoice
> Like a blind Arab, that from sleep doth start
> In lonesome tent, I listen for thy voice.
> Belovéd! 'tis not thine; thou art not there!
> Then melts the bubble into idle air,
> And wishing without hope I restlessly despair.

It then went on to conclude

> What then avail those songs, which sweet of yore
> Were only sweet for their sweet echo's sake?
> Dear maid! no prattler at a mother's knee
> Was e'er so dearly prized as I prize thee:
> Why was I made for Love and Love denied to me?[23]

The final, bitter question, which dogged Coleridge for the rest of his
days, inhibited him from producing much in the way of continuing love
poetry, apart from a few mourning his condition. Already, by the end of
1807, he was able to write a poem to two sisters, Mary Morgan and
Charlotte Brent, in which he praised their resemblance to the Hutchinson sisters—resemblance so close that he could find himself confusing
which pair was which, and directing to the Brent sisters the same
affection as to the Hutchinsons—yet insisting that the love he had
nursed towards Sara survived in some form. What could not be dismissed, at least for a few years, was a ghost of hope, still accompanying
his loss of love. So long as Sara was willing to act as his amanuensis for
the inception of further writing, there evidently survived the thought
that, even now, things might turn out better. But when she left in 1810
he had to face the realization that his love lacked a future. He might feel
that the Wordsworths had betrayed him by conniving in Sara's withdrawal, but behind, or beneath, such bitter reflections there must now
have persisted a recognition of inevitability.

    Her attitude, viewed from her own point of view, is understandable.
Coleridge had decided that he could not end his marriage, being

---

[23] *CPW* (EHC) I 395–7. It is not clear when the lines were composed. The poem was
first published in 1828, but Coleridge's quoting of the last lines in a letter to Allsop of
March 1822 (*CL* V 216) establishes that it was already in existence by then.

devoted to keeping his marriage vows.[24] (In this he was of course conforming with received opinion in his age, when divorce would have been virtually impossible and even separation a matter of scandal.)[25] In such a situation Sara evidently felt kindly but embarrassed, bound by the ties of family to the Wordsworths yet unable to give him the full affection he desired.

Her own silence is one of the most striking features of the affair. Although she wrote frequently to members of her family and others, the volume of her correspondence throws virtually no light on her own feelings. It is not even clear how far he ever expressed to her directly the full extent of the feelings that he expressed in his private notebooks. In view of this, one surviving piece of manuscript evidence, a letter from her to William contributed to a longer letter of Dorothy's and written after she had been staying in the district when he was away in London trying to resolve the quarrel, is particularly important:

My dearest William,
Dorothy has left me some blank paper to fill for you.
I have nothing to say but I love you dearly: am well and sorely grieved that this ugly affair should make your stay in London so uncomfortable—C's saying that he learned that I had given him up is just of a piece with the rest of his fancies— because till I came to Grasmere I did not know the merits of the case—and never did I breathe an opinion on it to any one or even mentioned the quarrel, or shyness, or whatever it may be call'd, to any living Soul—Mrs C. & I have many a battle—but we do not quarrel—She wonders how I could ever love any one of whom I think so ill; and thinks he ought to know what I do think of him—why I say every thing that I say to you have I said to himself—& all that I believe of him now I believed formerly (except that he should ever have behaved as he has done to you or believed that you could have said these things but in the Spirit of love)/ But if you were to repeat what I say of him it would appear very different—because she is angry & thinks I speak resentfully & in the spirit of resentment would she represent it to him—She is sure that we think far worse of him than ever she did & is now on his side quite. Montagu it appears had told him many trifling anecdotes as she calls them, which could only have come from us which confirmed his belief in the other things—such as his getting Spirits at the Public House &c &c—though I was sorry to find because it

---

[24] See his statement to Southey on 21 October, 1801: 'Carefully have I thought thro' the subject of marriage & deeply am I convinced of it's indissolubleness': *CL* II 767.

[25] For a summary account of contemporary attitudes see Lefebure, *Bondage of Love*, p. 172.

had nothing to do with the matter in question & appeared like complaint on your part.[26]

One point which emerges is that the two Saras remained on speaking, even cordial, terms. Indeed, as Molly Lefebure has pointed out, there seems often to have been more concord between the families at Greta Hall and at Grasmere when Coleridge was out of the way. The failure of the relationship with Sara was therefore much more to Coleridge than the ending of a particular love for a particular woman. For him she was representative, the nature of her illumination offering a key to human existence. But with her inability to sustain her role as the object of his love, the larger enterprise failed also. Within a few years he would be seeing this central key, and its collapse, in just such a darkened light as he wrote in his notebook:

Seven years ago, but oh! In what happier times—then only deluding, not deluded & believing the echo of my own voice in an empty vault to be the substantial voice of its indwelling Spirit—I wrote thus—

> O ye Hopes! that stir within me!
> Health comes with you from above!
> God is *with* me! God is *in* me!
> I *cannot* die: for Life is Love!

And now, that I am alone, & utterly hopeless for myself—yet still *I love*—& more strongly than ever feel that Conscience, or the Duty of Love, is the Proof of continuing, as is the Cause & Condition of existing, Consciousness.[27]

The debacle left him in deep depression. He wrote further eloquent expressions of his despair, coupled with verses querying the validity of visionary experiences in the context of affection. The poetry of love could not easily be resumed. Instead, he experimented with a kind of poetry of negativity, inspired partly by Donne's explorations of the loss of love in poems such as 'A Nocturnal upon St. Lucy's Day'. It was a genre with only limited range, for obvious reasons, but the sequence around his poem 'Limbo' showed what could be done. In particular, he sought what could be discerned in the colourless hinterland around utter negativity, trying to imagine a country where time and space were

---

[26] Dove Cottage, Wordsworth MS G1/1/4. Reproduced by courtesy of the Wordsworth Trust, and tentatively dated 13 May 1812. Cited in part, Lefebure, *Bondage of Love*, p. 202.

[27] CNB 24 f14ᵛ–15 (cf. *CN* II 3231).

almost, though not quite, non-existent—where 'Lank Space, and scytheless Time with branny hands'

> Fettered from flight, with night-mair sense of fleeing,
> Strive for their last crepuscular half-being;—
> Barren and soundless as the measuring sands,
> Not mark'd by flit of Shades,—unmeaning they
> As Moonlight on the dial of the day!
> But that is lovely—looks like Human Time,—
> An Old Man with a steady Look sublime,
> That stops his earthly Task to watch the skies;
> But he is blind—a Statue hath such Eyes;—
> Yet having moon-ward turn'd his face by chance,
> Gazes the orb with moon-like countenance,
> With scant white hairs, with foretop bald & high,
> He gazes still,—his eyeless Face all Eye;—
> As 'twere an organ full of silent Sight,
> His whole Face seemeth to rejoice in Light!
> Lip touching lip, all moveless, bust and limb,
> He seems to gaze at that which seems to gaze on him![28]

This was a direct obverse of the poetry some years before in which he had written of the moon as an immediate, magnetic power. Without the physical assurance of Sara's love he was banished into a sphere where he could see the heavens, with all their bodies, 'excellently fair', but, as in his 'Dejection' letter, could only see, not feel, their beauty. The poetry he could still write, likewise, would be a poetry of seeing, not feeling.

His desolation was not absolute, nor was he banished into a condition where vision, and its loss, were mutually exclusive. Loss of love could still alternate with vivid memory of what had been gained from its presence. Six years after Sara's withdrawal, in December 1816, he found himself compulsively writing her name in a notebook:

ΣΑΡΑ. Written as of yore. Christmas 1816, Coleridge
ΣΑΡΑ. Does the Past live with me alone? Coleridge.[29]

When it came to expressing his feelings, or loss of them, his main expedient had to be not poetry but dramatic writing. A striking instance of what could be achieved, a piece combining prose and poetry, entitled 'The Improvisatore', began with a prose dialogue inquiring into the

---

[28] CNB 18 ff 146–146ᵛ (cf. *CN* III 4073).
[29] CNB 17 ff 126ᵛ, 128 (cf. *CN* III 4320).

possibility of true love, in which two protagonists, named Eliza and Katharine, engaged with a poet, labelled the 'Friend', who spoke of

the too general insensibility to a very important truth... namely, that the MISERY of human life is made up of large masses, each separated from the other by certain intervals,

whereas

The HAPPINESS of life, on the contrary, is made up of minute fractions—the little, soon-forgotten charities of a kiss, a smile, a kind look, a heartfelt compliment in the disguise of a playful raillery, and the countless other infinitesimals of pleasurable thought and genial feeling...

whereupon Katharine commented

Well, Sir; you have said quite enough to make me despair of finding a 'John Anderson, my Jo, John', with whom to totter down the hill of life.

The Friend replied

Not so! Good men are not, I trust, so much scarcer than good women, but that what another would find in you, you may hope to find in another. But well, however, may that boon be rare, the possession of which would be more than an adequate reward for the rarest virtue.

Eliza commented, 'Surely, he, who has described it so well, must have possessed it?'—to be greeted by the Friend's, 'If he were worthy to have possessed it, and had believingly anticipated and not found it, how bitter the disappointment!'—followed, after a pause of a few minutes, by the improvisation itself, which, after recounting the course of disappointed love, concluded with a passage of reconciliation:

> O bliss of blissful hours!
> The boon of Heaven's decreeing,
> While yet in Eden's bowers
> Dwelt the first husband and his sinless mate!
> The one sweet plant, which, piteous Heaven agreeing,
> They bore with them thro' Eden's closing gate!
> Of life's gay summer tide the sovran Rose!
> Late autumn's Amaranth, that more fragrant blows
> When Passion's flowers all fall or fade;
> If this were ever his, in outward being,
> Or but his own true love's projected shade,
> Now that at length by certain proof he knows,
> That whether real or a magic show,

Whate'er it *was*, it *is* no longer so;
Though heart be lonesome, Hope laid low,
Yet, Lady! deem him not unblest:
The certainty that struck Hope dead,
Hath left Contentment in her stead:
And that is next to Best![30]

Coleridge's trials of love had led in his last years to a final *aporia*, a state which was not without its limited satisfactions. In his own life, meanwhile, he had tried to remedy some of his disappointment along the way by exploring what could be gained from forfeiting the literary delight to be derived from mingling the sensibilities of nature and love in favour of poetic achievements of a starker, more realistic kind.

[30] *CPW* (Beer) 509–15 (cf. *CPW* (EHC) I 462–8).

6

Coleridge, Tom Wedgwood, and Conceptions of the Mind

While Coleridge acknowledged the debt occasioned by the Wedgwood brothers' munificence in granting him a pension, he felt a particular sense of gratitude to Tom, whom he first met in 1797. The provincial radicalism of Tom Wedgwood's background is evident from John Cornwell's account:

This brilliant 'independent child of the enlightenment', who has gone down in history as the father of photography, had been raised in the laboratories of his father's potteries in Etruria.

Cornwell goes on to describe his dominating enterprise at this juncture. Now that he was twenty-six he was searching for assistance in a scheme for the amelioration of mankind, following the current fashion for educational experiments: a 'master-stroke' which would take the form of financing the education of a 'genius'. Writing to Godwin on 31 July, he had expressed his ambition to 'anticipate a century or two upon the large-paced progress of human improvement':

Let us suppose ourselves in possession of a detailed statement of the first twenty years of the life of some extraordinary genius; what a chaos of perceptions!... How many opposing tendencies which have negatived each other.... How many hours, days, months have been prodigally wasted in unproductive occupation! How many false and contradictory ideas imprinted by authority!

Wedgwood went on to explain his theories further:

The practice should be to simplify and render intense the first affections of Sense, and secondly to excite those affections under every possible favourable circumstance of pleasure.

Since the most important of the senses were 'Sight and Touch', special care should be taken with appropriate features of the construction:

Should not the nursery, then, have plain, grey walls with one or two vivid objects for sight and touch? Could not the children be made to acquire manipulation sooner? Let hard bodies be hung about them so as continually to irritate their palms.

The child, moreover, 'must never go out of doors or leave his own apartment'. Wedgwood further proposed that there should be none of the usual frivolity of 'romping, tickling and fooling':

The child should be held strictly to 'rational objects' with no time allowed for daydreaming. In the best regulated mind of the present day, has not there been, and is not there some hours every day passed in reverie, thought ungoverned, undirected? How astonishingly the powers and produce of the mind would be increased by a fixed habit of earnest thought. This is to be given.

The project was to be overseen by a committee of 'philosophers', including Godwin, the Bristol physician Thomas Beddoes, Holcroft, Horne Tooke and Wedgwood himself. Practical superintendents, however, might be more difficult to find: 'the only persons that I know of as at all likely for this purpose', wrote Wedgwood, 'are Wordsworth and Coleridge.' Coleridge, however, who, he thought, might be 'too much of a poet and religionist to suit our views' had different preoccupations at this time, anyway. In October 1796 he had told Charles Lloyd's father of his anxiety to bring up his own children from earliest infancy 'in the simplicity of peasants, their food, dress and habits completely rustic'.[1] Early in 1798 he wrote, of his own child:

> But thou, my babe! shalt wander like a breeze
> By lakes and sandy shores, beneath the crags
> Of ancient mountain, and beneath the clouds.[2]

The need to produce an effective answer to Tom Wedgwood's theory must have been a further important element in his autobiographical letters to Poole during the period following—when he stressed the importance of imaginative education—and in prompting Words-worth's similar reflections in *The Prelude*.[3] Tom, Coleridge's benefac-tor, obviously needed to be reasoned into a subtler view of the human

---

[1] *CL* I 240.

[2] The whole of the preceding account follows closely John Cornwell's, in his *Coleridge: Poet and Revolutionary 1772–1804, A Critical Biography* (London: Allen Lane, 1973), pp. 178–9; this in turn draws on D. V. Erdman's article, 'Coleridge, Wordsworth and the Wedgwood Fund', *Bulletin of the New York Public Library*, LX (1956).

[3] *CL* I 302–3, 310–12, 346–8, 352–5; *WPrel* (1805) V 290–369.

mind, no longer taking for granted the fashionable belief that its work-ings could be explained simply through association of ideas.

Meanwhile the nearest to a clear record of 'metaphysical speculation' by Tom himself, bearing in mind that 'metaphysical' at the time was often close to 'psychological', came in a note just after he had been staying with the Wordsworths at Alfoxden House in 1797:

Time, entering the garden at Langford September 15, 1797. Went down to Wordsworth's with John. Spent 5 days there. Remarked to John on the 5th day at Alfoxden that the time had gone like lightning. He agreed with me. Entering the garden at Langford, it struck me as being very long since I had entered it before, though I knew it was only five days. Might not this be owing to my having never 'intermediately' thought of the garden? Its recollection was faint, and suggested remoteness of time, as faint objects do distance in sight.[4]

Despite this attempt to explain a mental phenomenon by way of associationism, Tom's note also betrays an inquiring attitude: contact with the stimulus of Coleridge's conversation may already have sharp-ened his observations. The following June Coleridge wrote to Poole of his visit to the brothers at Stoke D'Abernon, 'I have been metaphysiciz-ing so long & so closely with T Wedgwood, that I am a caput mortuum, mere lees & residuum.'[5] Apart from this, however, evidence of Tom Wedgwood's 'metaphysical' interests exists only in unexamined form. In his biographical study R. B. Litchfield devoted a last chapter to 'His Metaphysics and Psychology', speaking of 'a chaotic heap of rough MSS., dealing wholly with one group of subjects, namely metaphysical and psychological speculation, with excursions into educational and social questions', but giving little account of their contents—though a page of the manuscript of the kind he describes is for the most part devoted to psychological observations which also raise interesting ques-tions. The position is further complicated by the fact that in 1800 Tom had discussions with James Mackintosh, concerning which Poole reported to Coleridge Josiah Wedgwood's comments:

When Tom was here he enjoyed a high satisfaction in explaining to Mackintosh the result of his metaphisical speculations, and in finding M. concur with him

    [4] Notebook of Wedgwood, quoted by R. B. Litchfield, *Tom Wedgwood, the first photographer; an account of his life, his discovery and his friendship with Samuel Taylor Coleridge, including the letters of Coleridge to the Wedgwoods and an examination of accounts of alleged earlier photographic discoveries.* (London: Duckworth and Co., 1903), p. 51.
    [5] *CL* I 413.

in his opinions, after discussing the points, though not at first disposed to do so. He has also convinced Sharpe, as far as he has opened the business to him. The subjects he has cleared are no less than Time, Space, and Motion; and Mackintosh and Sharpe think a metaphisical revolution likely to follow. It has given him great pleasure to be confirmed in the result of several years' meditation, and to acquire confidence to pursue what he has, I believe, so well begun, as far as his miserable health will permit...[6]

Coleridge was cautious about accepting this statement, replying that he had 'many reasons for being exceedingly suspicious of *supposed discoveries* in Metaphysics';[7] but that although he had a poor view of Sharpe's and Mackintosh's opinions on the subject,

...*I* take T. Wedgewood's own opinion, his own convictions, as STRONG presumptions that he has fallen upon some very valuable Truths—some he stated but only in short hints to me / & I *guess* from these, that they have been noticed before, & set forth by Kant in part & in part by Lambert.—I *guess*, that it will be so / yet I wish, they may not be, both for the sake of the Truth, & because if they should be, it would damp his spirits.—I have been myself *thinking* with the most intense energy on similar subjects...[8]

He seems subsequently, however, to have taken a more friendly view of the project, and of Mackintosh's proposed part in it—perhaps as a result of contact with the latter during his Keswick visit that summer. In the following January he and Mackintosh dined together[9] and a month later, on 19 February 1802, he told Poole that he was completing 'the history of the opinions concerning Space & Time' for Mackintosh.[10] On the sixth of the same month Southey had informed William Taylor that a great metaphysical book was conceived and about to be born, 'with Tom Wedgwood the parturient god and Mackintosh the man midwife' and a preface on the history of metaphysical opinions promised by Coleridge: 'This will perhaps prove an abortion, and be bottled up among other rarities in the moon. It has, however proceeded so far as to disturb the spiders, whose hereditary claim to Thomas Aquinas and Duns Scotus had not been disputed for many a year before. Time and Space are the main subjects of speculation.'[11] In February 1803 William Taylor told Southey that he had heard that Coleridge and Tom

---

[6] Sandford, *Thomas Poole*, 180n; *CL* II 675n.
[7] Ibid., II 675.
[8] Ibid., II 675.
[9] *CL* II 783.
[10] Letter of 19 February 1802, ibid., 787.
[11] Ibid., 787 n, citing J. W. Robberds (ed.), *A memoir of the life and writings of the late William Taylor of Norwich* (2 vols., London, 1843), I 398–9.

Wedgwood were 'going to publish conjointly some metaphysics of the Berkeleyan sort'.[12] The project languished, however, prompting a letter from Coleridge to Tom in the same month concerning the plan:

> As to Mackintosh, I never doubted that he means to fulfil his engagements with you; but he is one of those weak-moraled men, with whom the meaning to do a thing means nothing. He promises with 99% of his whole Heart; but there is always a little speck of cold felt at the core, that transubstantiates the whole Resolve into a Lie, even in his own consciousness.—But what I most fear is that he will in some way or other embroider himself upon your Thoughts; but you, no doubt, will see the Proof Sheets, & will prevent this from extending to the injury of your meaning.[13]

In April, Poole wrote to Josiah Wedgwood about Tom, 'I have been expecting to hear something of his metaphysical work: I hope it is in a progressive state.'[14] He said nothing about a possible collaborator, but Mackintosh was continuing to promise that he would help produce Wedgwood's work. Coleridge had, it seems, become reconciled, if with misgivings, to Mackintosh's being accepted as Tom's collaborator, particularly in view of his promises of help with publication. On 17 October 1803 Mackintosh was hoping to begin 'Time and Space' the next day, and on 26 December when he was about to sail for Bombay, where he was to become Recorder and planned to spend what he thought of as the 'long and undisturbed leisure' of his new post working on it, he apologized for having made no headway, declaring that as soon as his books were on their shelves he would devote himself to 'Time and Space'.[15] After Thomas's death in 1805 Poole wrote to Josiah in August that he hoped Mackintosh would now bring forward the metaphysical essays.

[12] Robberds, *Memoir*, I 451–2.

[13] *CL* II 931. A similar image of a 'cold hollow spot' was used also later by him in connection with his own early religious feelings: CNB F° f7ᵛ (cf. *CN* IV 5275).

[14] Eliza Meteyard, *A group of Englishmen (1795 to 1815): being records of the younger Wedgwoods and their friends, embracing the history of the discovery of photography, and a facsimile of the first photograph* (London: Longmans, Green, 1871), p. 129. After Thomas's death Poole wrote to Josiah in August 1805 that he hoped Mackintosh would now bring forward the metaphysical essays: ibid., 289; cf. pp. 293 and 300–1. Eliza Meteyard reports (p. 294) that the metaphysical essays appear to have been lost sight of or destroyed, commenting that 'habits of procrastination were through life as much an enemy to Mackintosh as they were to Coleridge'.

[15] R. B. Litchfield, *Tom Wedgwood*, 155, 159.

In the event neither produced their promised works.[16] Perhaps Coleridge thought that his own hope of displacing Newton's work on Optics might be following a false trail. In a letter urging Poole to destroy his letter on that subject, he referred to it as having been written 'in the ebulliency of indistinct Conceptions'; in another, 'with dream-like imagination respecting Sir Isaac Newton, & my hope of optico-meta-physical discovery'.[17] He may also have concluded that Mackintosh would be more suitable for the production of his friend's theories, the cast of Tom's mind being after all suited to the analytic, while he thought further how to elaborate his own—which might be better.

The most important clue to what was happening to him at this time is an entry in the diary of De Quincey, who was living far away and had not yet met either Wordsworth or Coleridge. On 1 June 1803 he wrote that he had heard that evening for the first time from a Mr Bree—and with surprise—that Coleridge intended to 'astonish the world with a Metaphysical work. on which he intends to found his fame.'[18] He also reported that Mrs Coleridge was very enthusiastic about the prospects for this work. Mr Bree was a neighbour of the Coleridges at Keswick, and if he had not been in touch with them for some time his informa-tion may have been a little out of date, but it suggests something of the excitement that Coleridge's conversation could generate—an excite-ment conveyed also by letters he wrote in the same summer. In the first (also in June) he wrote to Godwin about a work he was planning on Logic, beginning with accounts of the previous forms that had been set out by previous philosophers, from Plato and Aristotle to Condillac, and followed by his own system, arranging all possible systems of logic philosophically.[19] This plan was itself to be the forerunner to his great system of thought, which still awaited 'the experiments, which are to ascertain whether the Hopes of those, who have hoped proudly of me, have been auspicious Omens, or mere Delusions'. The very next month found him proposing to Southey the writing of a 'Bibliotheca Britan-nica, or an History of British Literature, bibliographical, biographical, and critical' which would begin in three volumes, being followed by 'a history of the dark ages in Britain' in the fourth, an account of meta-physics and ethics followed by a section on theology in the Roman

---

[16] Meteyard, *Englishmen*, 303. [17] *CL* II 1013–14 and 1046–7.

[18] H. A. Eaton (ed.), *A Diary of Thomas De Quincey, 1803; reproduced in replica as well as in print from the original manuscript* (London: N. Douglas, 1927), pp. 191–2.

[19] *CL* II 947–9.

Catholic church and 'all the other parts of Christianity' and a sixth and seventh containing an account of all the arts and sciences since the Reformation. Though it may have been little more than an opiate-inspired pipe dream, the remarkable feature of Coleridge's design is the detail with which it is worked out. Either he had an extraordinarily detailed memory of what he had read on the subject or enjoyed access at Keswick to works from which he had been able to construct his plan in a manner that showed his organizing power.[20]

Already Southey, although frequently critical of Coleridge during these years, had written vehemently to William Taylor after meeting Coleridge again in Bristol in June of that year about the way in which any sense of his friend's failings must be matched by consciousness of his extraordinary powers:

Coleridge and I have often talked of making a great work upon English literature; but Coleridge only talks, and poor fellow! he will not do that long, I fear; and then I shall begin in my turn to feel an old man,—to talk of the age of little men, and complain like Ossian. It provokes me when I hear a set of puppies yelping at him; upon whom he, a great good-natured mastiff, if he came up to them would just lift up his leg and pass on. It vexes and grieves me to the heart, that when he is gone, as go he will, nobody will believe what a mind goes with him,—how infinitely and ten thousand-thousand-fold the mightiest of his generation.[21]

Coleridge meanwhile went on enjoying the abundance of his thoughts without producing tangible results. In 1807, still silent about his planned collaborator, he wrote to Josiah:

Among my papers I had a mss. in which I had reduced into form all I had understood of my Benefactor's opinions in psychology—written partly from my sense of the possibility of Sir J. Mackintosh's Death or loss of the only authentic materials in his possession from other accidents, & partly too, I own, in justification of an assertion, I had once made to Mr Sharp & Sir James respecting the main principle of the System. But while shewing that it was only in the main principle, and not in the proofs or in the manner of coming at it, that it agreed with some philosophers of another country, I had drawn at full a portrait of my friend's mind & character.[22]

---

[20] *CL* II, 955–6.   [21] J. W. Robberds, *Memoir*, I 461–2.
[22] *CL* III 20. Coleridge included a tribute to the Wedgwood brothers in a substantial note to the 1809 *Friend: CF* (1809) 18–20nn (cf. *CFriend* II 22–26nn).

A few years later, he included a tribute to Tom in an extended note to *The Friend*, again making clear his hope to have explored psychological researches with him. Recalling his well known response to a lady who asked him if he believed in ghosts and apparitions ('No, Madam! I have seen far too many myself'), he continued,

I have indeed a whole memorandum Book filled with records of these Phae-nomena, many of them interesting as facts and data for Psychology, and affording some valuable materials for a Theory of Perception and its depen-dence on the memory and Imagination. 'In omnem actum Perceptionis imagi-natio influit efficienter.' WOLFE. But HE is no more, who would have realized this idea: who had already established the foundations and the law of the Theory; and for whom I had so often found a pleasure and a comfort, even during the wretched and restless nights of sickness, in watching and instantly recording these experiences of the world within us, of the 'gemina natura, quae fit et facit, et creat et creatur!'

After this the paragraph opened out into a eulogy of Tom Wedgwood's qualities (still without naming him) as

my Friend! my munificent co-Patron, and not less the benefactor of my Intellect!—He, who beyond all other men known to me, added a fine and ever-wakeful sense of Beauty, to the most patient Accuracy in experimental Philosophy and the profounder researches of metaphysical Science; he who united all the play and spring of Fancy with the subtlest Discrimination and an inexorable Judgment; and who controlled an almost painful exquisiteness of Taste by a Warmth of Heart, which in all the relations of Life made allowances for faults as quick as the moral taste detected them; a Warmth of Heart, which was indeed noble and pre-eminent, for alas! the genial feelings of Health contributed no spark toward it![23]

Wedgwood's ideas did make at least one appearance in print, in an article entitled 'An Enquiry into the Origin of our Notion of Distance', published more than a decade after his death and described as 'Drawn up from Notes' left by him.[24] This is of some interest for its time in its attempt to see the perception of distance as an ability drawing upon experience, by comparison with the perception of the linear, which is regarded as something all children have from the moment when they first use their eyes. The aim is to find a basis for the perception of

---

[23] A further, more extended, footnote in *CF* (1809) 184–5nn (cf. *CFriend* II 118–19nn).
[24] Published in the *Journal of Science and the Arts* III (1817) 1–12.

distance by repeated experiences of the visual, and not, as Berkeley had believed, by the experience of touch. But there is nothing in the article that seems to correspond to the claims made for his and Coleridge's researches by William Taylor. It is not known who edited the notes for publication; whoever it was may have missed the points that Tom Wedgwood would have thought crucial. Although Wedgwood deals with the well-known illusion that if a pencil is placed between two crossed fingers while the eyes are closed, it will be perceived as two pencils, any attempt to see this in connection with Coleridge's theory of 'double touch' is likely to fail: in particular, nothing is said here about a warmth sense. Nor did Mackintosh ever succeed in conveying his grounds for believing that 'a metaphysical revolution must follow'.[25] He did, however, discuss elements that had been important in Tom's theories. In his essay 'On the Philosophical Genius of Lord Bacon and Mr Locke', he at one point put forward the idea that the idea of time could not be innate, since it always arose in connection with some other perception, continuing,

Various modes of expressing these facts have been adopted by different philosophers, according to the variety of their technical language. By Kant space is to be the *form* of our perceptive faculty, as applied to outward objects; and time is called the form of the same faculty as it regards our mental operations. By Mr Stewart, these ideas are considered '*as suggested to the understanding*' by sensation or reflection, though according to him, 'the mind is not directly and immediately *furnished*' with such ideas, either by sensation or reflection: and, by a late eminent metaphysician, they were regarded as *perceptions*, in the nature of those arising from the senses, of which the one is attendant on the idea of every outward object, and the other concomitant with the consciousness of every mental operation. Each of these modes of expression has its own advantages.[26]

Coleridge meanwhile, needing to develop his own views, did so several years later in contributions to the volume known as *Omniana*, where he explored, if only tentatively, some of the paradoxical workings of the human mind. He was fascinated for example, by the phenomenon of the 'Bull'. In *Omniana* he proposed as his definition that a Bull

[25] In his account R. B. Litchfield suggests that the editor might have been James Mackintosh, He presumably had in mind Mackintosh's promises to Tom during his lifetime that he would produce his work; he gives no further evidence, however.

[26] *Miscellaneous Works* (London: Longman, Brown, Green and Longman, 1854), p. 333, referring to Stewart's *Philosophical Essays*, essay I chapter 2, and to Tom Wedgwood ('see *Life of Mackintosh* I 289').

consisted in 'a mental juxtaposition of incongruous ideas with the sensation, but without the sense, of connection', continuing,

The psychological conditions of the possibility of a Bull, it would not be difficult to determine; but it would require a larger space than can be afforded in the Omniana, at least more attention, than our readers would be likely to afford.[27]

One suspects, however, that a reason for not proceeding was his recognition that the enterprise was not quite as easy as he was suggesting. When he returned to the subject in 1815 in the *Biographia* (characteristically in a long footnote), it was to extend his earlier hint:

The psychological condition, or that which constitutes the possibility of this state, being such disproportionate vividness of two distinct thoughts, as extinguishes or obscures the consciousness of the intermediate images or conceptions, or wholly abstracts the attention from them.[28]

How far he ever fully elucidated the nature of bulls is open to question, but he was evidently attempting to understand them in terms of something more than simple association theory; at the same time the inquiry formed another aspect of his obsession—which lasted all his life—with the phenomenon of ambiguity.

Another long section was entitled 'The Soul and its Organs of Sense':

It is a strong presumptive proof against materialism, that there does not exist a language on earth, from the rudest to the most refined, in which a materialist can talk for five minutes together, without involving some contradiction in terms to his own system. *Objection.* Will not this apply equally to the astronomer? Newton, no doubt, talked of the sun's rising and setting, just like other men. What should we think of the coxcomb who should have objected to him, that he contradicted his own system? *Answer.*—No! it does not apply equally; say rather, it is utterly inapplicable to the astronomer and natural philosopher. For his philosophic, and his ordinary language speak of two quite different things, both of which are equally true. In his ordinary language he refers to a *fact* of appearance, to a phenomenon common and necessary to all persons in a given situation: in his scientific language he determines that one position or figure, &c, which being supposed, the appearance in question would be the necessary result, and all appearances in all situations may be demonstrably foretold. Let a body be suspended in the air, and strongly illuminated. What

---

[27] Southey and Coleridge, *Omniana, or Horae Otiosiores* (1812) I 220–1 (cf. *CSWF* I 307–8).
[28] *CBL* I 72fn.

figure is here? A triangle. But what here? A trapezium . . . ;—and so on. The
same question put to twenty men, in twenty different positions and distances,
would receive twenty different answers: and each would be a true answer. But
what is that one figure, which, being so placed, all these facts of appearance
must result, according to the law of perspective? . . . Aye! this is a different
question . . . this is a new subject. The words, which answer this, would be
absurd, if used in reply to the former.

Thus, the language of the scriptures on natural objects is as strictly philosophical as that of the Newtonian system. Perhaps, more so. For it is not only
equally true, but it is universal among mankind, and unchangeable. It describes
facts of *appearance*. And what other language would have been consistent with
the divine wisdom? The inspired writers must have borrowed their terminology,
either from the crude and mistaken philosophy of their own times, and so have
sanctified and perpetuated falsehood, unintelligible meantime to all but one in
ten thousand; or they must have anticipated the terminology of the true system,
without any revelation of the system itself, and so have become unintelligible to
all men; or lastly, they must have revealed the system itself, and thus have left
nothing for the exercise, developement, or reward of the human understanding,
instead of teaching that moral knowledge, and enforcing those social and civic
virtues, out of which the arts and sciences will spring up in due time, and of their
own accord. But nothing of this applies to the materialist; he refers to the very
same facts, which the common language of mankind speaks of: and these too are
facts, that have their sole and entire being in our own consciousness; facts, as to
which *esse* and *conscire* are identical. Now, whatever is common to all languages,
in all climates, at all times, and in all stages of civilization, must be the Exponent
and Consequent of the common consciousness of man, as man. Whatever
contradicts this universal language, therefore, contradicts the universal consciousness, and the facts in question subsisting exclusively in consciousness,
whatever contradicts the consciousness, contradicts the fact. Q.E.D.

At this point he continued:

I have been seduced into a dry discussion where I had intended only a few
amusing facts in proof, that the mind makes the sense, far more than the senses
make the mind. If I have life, and health, and leisure, I purpose to compile from
the works, memoirs, transactions &c of the different philosophical societies in
Europe, from magazines, and the rich store of medical and psychological
publications furnished by the English, French, and German press, all the essays
and cases, that relate to the human faculties under unusual circumstances (for
pathology is the crucible of physiology); excluding such only as are not intelligible without the symbols or terminology of science. These I would arrange
under the different senses and powers: as the eye, the ear, the imitative power,
voluntary and automatic; the imagination, or shaping and modifying power;
the fancy or the aggregative and associative power; the understanding, or the

regulative, substantiating, and realizing power; the speculative reason . . . *vis theoretica et scientifica*, or the power, by which we produce, or aim to produce, unity, necessity, and universality in all our knowledge by means of principles, *a priori*;[29] the will, or practical reason; the faculty of choice, (Germanice, *Will-kühr*), and (distinct both from the moral will, and the choice), the sensation of volition, which I have found reason to include under the head of single and double touch. Thence I propose to make a new arrangement of madness, whether as defect, or as excess of any of these senses or faculties; and thus by appropriate cases to shew the difference between, I. a man, having lost his reason, but not his senses or understanding—that is, he sees things as other men see them:—he adapts means to ends as other men would adapt them, and not seldom, with more sagacity; but his final end is altogether irrational: II. His having lost his wits, i. e. his understanding or judicial power; but not his reason, or the use of his senses. Such was Don Quixote; and, therefore, we love and reverence him, while we despise Hudibras. III. His being out of his senses, as is the case of a hypochondrist, to whom his limbs appear to be of glass. Granting that, all his conduct is both rational (or moral) and prudent: IV, or the case may be a combination of all three, though I doubt the existence of such a case, or of any two of them; V. or lastly, it may be merely such an excess of sensation, as overpowers and suspends all; which is frenzy or raving madness.

A diseased state of an organ of sense, or of the inner organs connected with it, will perpetually tamper with the understanding, and unless there be an energetic and watchful counteraction of the judgment (of which I have known more than one instance, in which the comparing and reflecting judgment has obstinately, though painfully rejected the full testimony of the senses) will finally over-power it. But when the organ is obliterated, or totally suspended, then the mind applies some other organ to a double use. Passing through Temple Sowerby, in Westmoreland, some ten years back, I was shewn a man perfectly blind; and blind from his infancy; Fowell was his name. This man's chief amusement was fishing on the wild and uneven banks of the River Eden, and up the different streams and tarns among the mountains. He had an intimate friend, likewise stone blind, a dexterous card-player, who knows every gate and stile far and near throughout the country. These two often coursed together, and the people here, as every where, fond of the marvellous, affirm that they were the best beaters up of game in the whole country. The every way amiable

---

[29] 'This phrase, *a priori*, is, in common, most grossly misunderstood, and an absurdity burthened on it which it does not deserve. By knowledge *a priori*, we do not mean that we can know any thing previously to experience, which would be a contradiction in terms; but having once known it by occasion of experience (that is, something acting upon us from without) we then know, that it must have pre-existed, or the experience itself would have been impossible. By experience only I know, that I have eyes; but then my reason convinces me, that I must have had eyes in order to the experience.' (Coleridge's note to section 174 of *Omniana*, II: cf. *CSWF* I 334n).

and estimable, John Gough of Kendal, is not only an excellent mathematician; but an infallible botanist and zoologist. He has frequently at the first feel corrected the mistakes of the most experienced sportsman, with regard to the birds or vermin which they had killed, when it chanced to be a variety or rare species, so completely resembling the common one that it required great steadiness of observation to detect the difference, even after it had been pointed out. As to plants and flowers, the rapidity of his touch appears fully equal to that of sight; and the accuracy greater. Good heavens! it needs only to look at him! . . . Why, his face sees all over! It is all one eye! I almost envied him; for the purity and excellence of his own nature, never broken in upon by those evil looks, (or features, which are looks become fixtures), with which low cunning, habitual cupidity, presumptuous sciolism, and heart-hardening vanity, *caledonianize* the human face,—it is the mere stamp, the undisturbed *ectypon*, of his own soul! Add to this that he is a quaker, with all the blest *negatives*, without any of the silly and factious *positives*, of that sect, which with all its bogs and hollows is still the prime sun-shine spot of Christendom in the eye of the true philosopher. When I was in Germany in the year 1798, I read at Hanover, and met with two respectable persons, one a clergyman, the other a physician, who confirmed to me, the account of the upper-stall master at Hanover, written by himself, and countersigned by all his medical attendants. As far as I recollect, he had fallen from his horse on his head, and in consequence of the blow lost both his sight and hearing for nearly three years, and continued for the greater part of this period in a state of nervous fever. His understanding, however, remained unimpaired and unaffected, and his entire consciousness, as to outward impressions, being confined to the sense of touch, he at length became capable of reading any book (if printed, as most German books are, on coarse paper) with his fingers, in much the same manner in which the piano-forte is played, and latterly with an almost incredible rapidity. Likewise by placing his hand, with the fingers all extended, at a small distance from the lips of any person that spoke slowly and distinctly to him, he learnt to recognize each letter by its different effects on his nerves, and thus *spelt* the words as they were uttered: and then returned the requisite answers, either by signs of finger-language to those of his own family, or to strangers by writing. It was particularly noticed both by himself from his sensations, and by his medical attendants from observation, that the letter R, if pronounced full and strong, and recurring once or more in the same word, produced a small spasm, or *twitch* in his hand and fingers. At the end of three years he recovered both his health and senses, and with the necessity soon lost the power, which he had thus acquired.[30]

This long disquisition represents one of Coleridge's most striking efforts to bring together the main points of his psychological beliefs at that

[30] *Omniana* (1812) II 9–29 (cf. *CSWF* I 332–6).

stage of his career. Most notable was his attempt to distinguish, as against the Will, 'the sensation of volition, which I have found reason to include under the head of single and double touch'. This reference to his old theory[31] formed part of a larger plan, that of discriminating between levels of human consciousness, which, he trusted, would inevitably lead to a distinguishing between what was *a priori*, and therefore ungrounded; what was infinite, and so primary; and all that was essentially subordinate. The hope that he might do so was taking him well into a sphere more difficult than any that Tom Wedgwood had dreamed of entering.

---

[31] For a full discussion of his 'old old theory' of single and double touch, including its appearance in Keats's 1818 record of his talk, see my study *Coleridge's Poetic Intelligence* (London: Macmillan, 1977), especially chapter 4 and pp. 280–2.

7

Wordsworthian Naturalism and the Coleridgean Sublime

Few writers begin their careers with the intention of making literary criticism their profession, and Coleridge was no exception. At first, when he intended to take holy orders, any plans to write would have been comprised within that vocation, following an honourable tradition that had included figures as diverse as John Donne, George Herbert, Jonathan Swift, and Edward Young. In the 1790s, when, under the stimulus of the French Revolution, his ambitions changed direction, his most pressing need was evidently to find a progressive but non-violent social programme, an alternative to what had been initiated in France. For a time he followed the lead of Joseph Priestley, who had succeeded in being at one and the same time religious dissenter, political radical, and innovative scientist: an early hope, traceable particularly in his poem 'Religious Musings', was to become a prophet for the age: perhaps to follow the tradition of Milton while taking into account all the developments in knowledge since the seventeenth century.

If that stance could authorize many activities in the 1790s, literary criticism was not prominent among them. His critical position, so far as he had one, can be found in a letter he wrote in 1796 to Thelwall, the political activist, where it emerges directly from an attempt to justify the kind of poetry he was currently writing:

I feel strongly, and I think strongly; but I seldom feel without thinking, or think without feeling. Hence tho' my poetry has in general a *hue* of tenderness, or Passion over it, yet it seldom exhibits unmixed & simple tenderness or Passion. My philosophical opinions are blended with, or deduced from, my feelings: & this, I think, peculiarizes my style of Writing. And like every thing else, it is sometimes a beauty, and sometimes a fault. But do not let us introduce an act of Uniformity against Poets—I have room enough in *my* brain to admire, aye & almost equally, the *head* and fancy of Akenside, and the *heart* and fancy of

Bowles, the solemn Lordliness of Milton, & the divine Chit chat of Cowper: and whatever a man's excellence is, that will be likewise his fault.[1]

When Coleridge's career began to complicate itself in the following year, two factors were prominently involved. One was a growing disillusionment concerning the possibilities of political action, as he contemplated the hardening of social attitudes in Britain, along with the very marginal impact made by his periodical *The Watchman*: even in the limited progressive circles where he could best hope for a sympathetic response the demand had proved small and vacillating. And at the same time he was turning increasingly to the one man who seemed to him to be indisputably possessed of major poetic powers: William Wordsworth.

If Coleridge had not met Wordsworth at this time it is hard to guess how his career might have developed. He would no doubt have continued to devote himself for longer than he did to the cause of radical thinking, replacing political activity by intellectual, and trying to relate the latest developments in science to what had come to be known of ancient tradition through the mythological and religious researches of his contemporaries and predecessors.[2] In his attempt to educe a living tradition which could form the core of a revitalized Christianity he might well have continued to look to Unitarianism, along with various contemporary figures who were pursuing scientific investigations. A good deal of documentation was now available concerning ancient philosophies and other religions, while the new scientific research that was being carried out in Bristol by Thomas Beddoes, shortly to be joined by Humphry Davy, offered further scope for such free enquiry.

There are signs, indeed, that Coleridge continued to think in this manner for a time. But the most important factor in giving direction to his thought, the relationship with Wordsworth, was shaping his career differently. Wordsworth, who had suffered a political disillusionment deeper, even, than his own, was turning his thoughts less to science than to the significance of nature, and particularly the influences on humanity provided by living close to it. Coleridge, in turn, was fired by this way of giving concrete expression to his preceding intellectual concerns. For a time, indeed, both men were evidently exchanging ideas so rapidly and

---

[1] *CL* I 279.
[2] The scope of theorizing that was possible has been well indicated by Ian Wylie in *Young Coleridge and the Philosophers of Nature* (Oxford: Clarendon Press, 1989).

intensely that some of them could be said to emerge from the relationship, rather than from either of the participants.

One major effect on Coleridge's writing soon became evident: his
favourite habit of thinking about nature in terms of vivid mental images
derived from his reading gave way to concentration rather on Nature's
sensuous detail—which meant he was considering the nature of life in a
more direct way, looking at nature and asking himself just what in it,
viewed directly, rather than through the eye of the scientific experiment-
er, could be thought to constitute the sense of its vitalism.

At the same time, he was conscious of a decline in his own ability to
initiate new poetry, so that instead of continuing to write alongside his
friend he had to note that he was falling behind. As he put it in a letter to
Godwin of 1801,

If I die, and the Booksellers will give you any thing for my Life, be sure and
say—'Wordsworth descended on him, like the Γνῶθι σεαυτόν [Know Thyself]
from Heaven; by shewing to him what true Poetry was, he made him know,
that he himself was no Poet.'[3]

It would be all too easy to conclude from this that it constituted a
farewell to verse-making, and that from henceforth Coleridge devoted
himself entirely to philosophical and scientific prose. Such an assumption would be mistaken, however. Coleridge was accepting that any plan
to write a great poem should be abandoned, but he would by no means
give up writing in verse.

The description of living things, a major feature of Coleridge's
meditative poetry, began to enter his criticism as well, prompting him
to look at the literary works of others for their signs of organic life. He
further explained what was in his mind by criticizing the great available
model for thinking about nature generally that had been offered by
Newton. In this case, he believed, the attitude of the observer had been
conceived wrongly:

Mind in his system is always passive—a lazy Looker-on on an external World. If
the mind be not *passive*, if it be indeed made in God's Image, & that too in the
sublimest sense—the Image of the *Creator*—there is ground for suspicion, that
any system built on the passiveness of the mind must be false, as a system.[4]

Alongside this his favourite sentence (which, as already mentioned, he
may even have been employing when he was in Germany in 1798–9),

<hr>

[3] *CL* II 714.   [4] Ibid., 709.

'Every Thing has a Life of it's own, and . . . we are all one Life',[5] provided a telling brief statement of his own particular philosophy. The two formulations help to catch something of an idea that had been impressing itself more and more on Coleridge's thinking in the previous years: that there appeared to be two levels to the consciousness of human beings: the attentive waking concentration, on the one hand, in which they focus upon outward objects and try to understand them through observation; on the other, the passive subconscious processes by which they relate the life processes in themselves to those of other people—and indeed of all living beings. The one level of consciousness is realized most extremely in cold analysis of the external world, the other in a warm empathy with other organisms. Somewhere between the two, there occurs that mediating state of consciousness in which, to quote Wordsworth's words in 'Tintern Abbey', 'We see into the life of things'.

To learn to think in this complex fashion did not simply reflect Coleridge's view of nature; inevitably it affected his literary criticism, also. Some of his subsequent thinking on these lines evidently went into the Preface to *Lyrical Ballads* in the edition of 1800, where a notebook phrase of his, 'recalling of passion in tranquillity', is half-echoed in Wordsworth's famous 'emotion recollected in tranquillity'.[6] There are signs that in thinking more and more in terms of psychological investigation and its relationship to poetry he was still clinging to his affirmation that the age needed a joint working of head and heart—of intellect and the emotions. One of his aims in writing *Christabel,* he said later, was to try a new metric principle, 'counting in each line the accents, not the syllables'. 'Nevertheless,' he went on, 'this occasional variation . . . is not introduced wantonly, or for the mere ends of convenience, but in correspondence with some transition in the nature of the imagery or passion.'[7]

In 1802, when he had already reached some limits in his journalistic work and scientific speculation and withdrawn to the Lake District,

---

[5] See the letter to Sotheby quoted below at note 12. For his possible use in Germany see Clement Carlyon, *Early Years and Late Reflections* (4 vols., London: Whittaker, 1856–58), I 193, where it appears as 'the concentrated definition of Spinozaism'; although this is presented in the context of Coleridge's stay in Germany, the following pages, with their reference to Giordano Bruno, make it more likely that Coleridge gave it to Carlyon at a later meeting in London, probably in 1803.

[6] CNB $5^{1/2}$ f 65 (cf. *CN* I 787); *WPrW* I 148. Cf. Coleridge's comment (*CL* II 811): '. . . the first passages were indeed partly taken from notes of mine'.

[7] Preface to the first edition of 1816: *CPW* (EHC) I 215.

where he hoped he could devote himself to the development of his own ideas, his thinking in this manner became still more complex and pervasive. As he approached his marriage to Mary Hutchinson, Wordsworth was writing, in an extraordinary burst of productivity, 'The Rainbow', the Immortality Ode and many other poems celebrating his life with Dorothy in Grasmere. Coleridge's participation in that feeling was darkened not only by the negative recognition that such a way forward was not available to him but by a suspicion that the beneficent working of nature was not as straightforward a matter as Wordsworth maintained. The writing of 'Dejection: An Ode' was one response. Although he might in that poem lament the fact that his 'shaping spirit of imagination' appeared to have deserted him—at least for the time being—the very writing of the poem showed other elements in his poetic powers to be strongly active. This was reflected in his comments on poetry during the summer. In a letter to Sotheby of 13 July he wrote about the need for every phrase, every metaphor, every personification to have its justification in 'some *passion* either of the Poet's mind, or of the Characters described by the Poet'. 'But *metre itself*,' he continued, 'implies a *passion*, i.e. a state of excitement, both in the Poet's mind, & is expected in that of the Reader.'[8] At the end of the same month he quoted to Southey Milton's praise of poetry that was 'simple, sensuous and passionate'.[9]

Elsewhere in the July letter to Sotheby he criticized the continental poetry of the time, proceeding into one of his finest pieces of general criticism. The full implications of the 'one Life' as a criterion for poetic making emerged to the full as he explained what he thought made a great poet, locating it in an ability to live in the lives of others:

It is easy to cloathe Imaginary Beings with our own Thoughts & Feelings; but to send ourselves out of ourselves, to *think* ourselves in to the Thoughts and Feelings of Beings in circumstances wholly & strangely different from our own/ hoc labor, hoc opus/ and who has atchieved it? Perhaps only Shakespere. Metaphisics is a word, that you, my dear Sir! are no great Friend to/ but yet you will agree, that a great Poet must be, implicité if not explicité, a profound Metaphysician. He may not have it in logical coherence, in his Brain & Tongue; but he must have it by *Tact* / for all sounds, & forms of human nature he must have the ear of a wild Arab listening in the silent Desart, the eye of a North American Indian tracing the footsteps of an Enemy upon the Leaves that strew the Forest—; the *Touch* of a Blind Man feeling the face of a darling

---

[8] *CL* II 812.   [9] Letter to Southey, 29 July 1802, ibid., II 830.

Child—/ and do not think me a Bigot, if I say, that I have read no French or German Writer, who appears to me to have had a heart sufficiently pure & simple to be capable of this or any thing like it./[10]

Those sentences offered one programme for a kind of writing that would to some degree be fulfilled by his successors. At the same time they ran counter to some of the most dearly held positions of later criticism. A New Critic would have been deeply disturbed by the suggestion of an ability to get inside other minds—which was later to be regarded as impossible, and in any case inappropriate to the purposes of literary judgment. Coleridge, concerned both to escape the tyranny of a rule-bound poetry and to bring about the unification of head and heart that was persistently his ideal, entertained no such reservations, while the kind of poetry he was proposing had for him the further virtue of guarding against self-enclosure and self-regard. He returned to the theme in another letter to Sotheby in September of the same year, in which he expressed his disappointment at the contents of the latest volume published by his former poetic hero, William Lisle Bowles:

There reigns thro' all the blank verse poems such a perpetual trick of *moralizing* every thing—which is very well, occasionally—but never to see or describe any interesting appearance in nature, without connecting it by dim analogies with the moral world, proves faintness of Impression. Nature has her proper interest; & he will know what it is, who believes & feels, that every Thing has a Life of it's own, & that we are all *one Life*. A Poet's *Heart* & *Intellect* should be *combined, intimately* combined & *unified*, with the great appearances in Nature—& not merely held in solution & loose mixture with them, in the shape of formal Similies.[11]

This did not, of course, signal a retreat from moral considerations. On the contrary, Coleridge was facing the fact that his own moral principles would not permit him to abandon his marriage. And in spite of his high valuation of poetry in which we 'send ourselves out of ourselves', he could not allow his penchant for entering into the lives of others to proceed so far as to indulge a free flow of thought without self-restraint. In view of its naturalism one might have thought that he would have been drawn at this time to Greek art and poetry; on the contrary, however, when he returned to these questions months later, in

[10] Letter to Sotheby, 13 July 1802: ibid., II 810.
[11] Letter to Sotheby, 10 Sept 1802: ibid., II 864.

another letter to Sotheby, a different literature was found exemplary of the sublime:

It has struck [me] with great force lately, that the Psalms afford a most compleat answer to those, who state the Jehovah of the Jews, as a personal & national God—& the Jews, as differing from the Greeks, only in calling the minor Gods, Cherubim & Seraphim—& confining the word God to their Jupiter. It must occur to every Reader that the Greeks in their religious poems address always the Numina Loci, the Genii, the Dryads, the Naiads, &c &c—All natural Objects were *dead*—mere hollow Statues—but there was a Godkin or Goddessling *included* in each— In the Hebrew Poetry you find nothing of this poor Stuff—as poor in genuine Imagination, as it is mean in Intellect—/ At best, it is but Fancy, or the aggregating Faculty of the mind—not *Imagination*, or the *modifying*, and *co-adunating* Faculty. This the Hebrew Poets appear to me to have possessed beyond all others—& next to them the English. In the Hebrew Poets each Thing has a Life of it's own, & yet they are all one Life. In God they move & live, & <u>have</u> their Being—not *had*, as the cold System of Newtonian Theology represents/ but *have*.[12]

In this passage one senses a straining of discourses between the natural and the moral. No concessions were to be made to Hellenism, but his attempt to run together an appeal to Hebrew righteousness and to the imaginative foreshadowed Arnold's. From one point of view the two traditions clearly pull apart, since the linking of imaginative experience with sensuous attraction might seem Hellenic in quality. What holds the two together in Coleridge's mind, on the other hand, is his belief in a continuity between the inward being of the human psyche and the inward being of God, with nature as intermediary. And this, of course, he expected to find reflected in the work of the creative imagination, which he suspected could represent, in however limited and imperfect a fashion, the creative power of the divine. While the introduction of Hebrew poetry as an ideal might seem to be constraining the range of Coleridge's thought within the domain of 'righteousness', this other, secret bonding between the levels of his thought kept him from having to draw that conclusion.

During these years, when there was a struggle between his creative imagination and the demands of his moral sense, the creative imagination was always likely to gain a subterranean victory. Once a statement had been made blending imaginative and moral discourses it would

---

[12] Letter to Sotheby, 10 Sept 1802: Ibid., 865–6.

continue working, producing the germ of the next statement. In the letter of September 1802, for example, there is an important distinction half-buried in the run of the argument, as he describes the Greek use of mythology: 'At best, it is but Fancy, or the aggregating Faculty of the mind—not Imagination, or the modifying, and co-adunating Faculty.' The thoughtful phrasing suggests that it is not the first occasion of its use; in any case it emerges still more strongly a year or two later in a commendation of Wordsworth:

Wordsworth is a Poet, a most original Poet—he no more resembles Milton than Milton resembles Shakespere—no more resembles Shakespere than Shakespere resembles Milton—he is himself: and I dare affirm that he will hereafter be admitted as the first & greatest philosophical Poet—the only man who has effected a compleat and constant synthesis of Thought & Feeling and combined them with Poetic Forms, with the music of pleasurable passion and with Imagination or the *modifying* Power in that highest sense of the word in which I have ventured to oppose it to Fancy, or the *aggregating* power—in that sense in which it is a dim Analogue of Creation, not all that we can *believe* but all that we can *conceive* of creation.[13]

Coleridge's thinking in the early years of the century was nevertheless increasingly dominated by a growing respect for established attitudes. This new appreciation, evident also as he honoured his resolution to deal with his love for Sara Hutchinson morally, was accompanied by a fresh recognition of the solidity and permanence of the natural world, as he strove to become 'manlier' and set his mind to the achievement of positive tasks.

Heidi Thomson's assertion that Coleridge's contributions to the *Morning Post* during these years reflected his developing poetic concerns[14] deserves serious consideration. In particular, she draws attention to the mannered form of the announcement of Wordsworth's marriage:

Monday last, W. Wordsworth, Esq. was married to Miss Hutchinson of Wykeham, near Scarborough, and proceeded immediately, with his wife and his sister, for his charming cottage in the little Paradise of Grasmere. His neighbour, Mr. Coleridge, resides in the vale of Keswick, 13 miles from Grasmere. His house (situated on a low hill at the foot of Skiddaw, with the Derwent Lake in front, and the romantic River Greta winding round the hill)

---

[13] Letter to Richard Sharp, 15 Dec 1804, ibid., II 1034.
[14] See her article, '"Merely the Emptying out of my Desk": Coleridge about Wordsworth in the Morning Post of 1802', *The Coleridge Bulletin*, Summer 2008, n.s. 31, pp. 82–3.

commands, perhaps, the most various and interesting prospects of any house in the island. It is a perfect *panorama* of that wonderful vale, with its two lakes, and its complete circle, or rather ellipse, of mountains.

This insertion, with a disproportionate amount of space devoted to Coleridge's house, was not received altogether kindly by the Wordsworths, Dorothy assuming that it was simply a case of Daniel Stuart being 'ridiculous'; but, since the description corresponds almost word for word with one in a letter from Coleridge himself, Thomson plausibly suspects some collusion, at least. She also points out that it might be related to his growing sense of a radical disagreement between their respective poetic theories. The account of Wordsworth's abode in Grasmere would correspond to his friend's recent acceptance of the local and domestic as providing the most appropriate sites for a naturalistic poetry, while that of Coleridge's own house tallied with his current aspirations towards the sublime.

To see Coleridge's poetry at the start of the new century in those terms makes sense of various items, including his growing belief that examples of the true sublime were more likely to be found outside English shores. Thus the voice of the 'Mad Monk', (in a poem admittedly written 'in Mrs Radcliff's manner') was heard 'on Etna's side'; while other poems benefited from Coleridge's acquaintance with the German mountains. The idea was strengthened in him when he undertook a number of walks across the Lake District during the summer of 1802—though it is perhaps indicative of his new frame of mind that (as A. P. Rossiter pointed out) he should at this time have been particularly interested in waterfalls and torrents, and the way in which they could exhibit a reconciliation between power and permanence. These great emblems had already fascinated him in their own right, as in his poem 'The Old Man of the Alps', set in a landscape dominated by a convent 'Where the huge rocks with sounds of torrents rang', or in 'A Thought suggested by a View...', where the 'tyrannous and strong' force of winds and thronging torrents is contrasted with the quietness of the sky and its forms.[15]

However logical in terms of his own experience, his renewed aspiration to the sublime was problematic. The natural and conversational mode which he had developed in meditative poems such as 'Frost at Midnight', and even the 'Letter to Sara', could not be invoked in aid of

---

[15] *CPW* (EHC) I 250, 347. Cf. e.g. ibid., 35–6.

his new project. So on Scafell, he wrote to William Sotheby in September, he

poured forth a Hymn in the manner of the *Psalms*, tho' afterwards I thought the Ideas &c disproportionate to our humble mountains—& accidentally lighting on a short Note in some swiss Poems concerning the Vale of Chamouny, & it's Mountain, I transferred myself thither, in the Spirit,& adapted my former feelings to these grander objects.[16]

His 'Hymn before Sun-rise, in the Vale of Chamouny' was to achieve a considerable popular reputation, particularly in America. It was also in accord with the 'radical difference of opinion' that Wordsworth should have disliked this attempt from his friend at the sublime. As Coleridge later recalled,

Mr Wordsworth, I remember...condemn'd the Hymn in toto...as a specimen of the Mock Sublime. It may be so for others; but it is impossible that I should find it unnatural, being conscious that it was the image and utterance of Thoughts and Emotions in which there was no Mockery.[17]

Wordsworth was evidently put out at Coleridge's claim to have actually experienced what he was describing: Coleridge, he asserted, 'was never at Chamouni, or near it, in his life'.[18] He may well also have been registering a sense of falsity. After the subtle rhythms and emotional expressiveness of the 'Letter to Sara' the language here has a touch of bombast. Despite the vivid touches throughout, the reader feels the power of the poem to be a shade forced—all the more so since the name of God, invoked throughout, does not, in English, carry a power of sound quite equivalent to that conveyed by 'Jehovah'.

Most of all, however, Wordsworth's criticism indicated the manner in which his own sense of the sublime had been developing. When he had written his own *Descriptive Sketches* many years before, the 'sublime' had been a quality to be regarded as a straightforward feature in his accounts of mountain scenery. He had been able to write, for example, 'The ideas excited by the stormy sunset I am here describing owed their sublimity to the deluge of light, or rather of fire, in which nature had wrapped the immense forms around me...'[19] After the advent of Coleridge, however, he had come to concentrate primarily less on

[16] *CL* II 864–5.   [17] Ibid., IV 974.
[18] *Prose Works*, ed. Alexander Grosart (3 vols., London: E. Moxon, 1876), III 442.
[19] *WPW* I 62n.

nature itself than on the mind that was perceiving it, or the writing produced by such a mind. His friend had, for example, found it quite correct to describe the poem beginning 'A slumber did my spirit seal' as a 'most sublime epitaph'.[20] It was a logical consequence that Wordsworth should at that time have embarked on the autobiographical poetry, recording 'sublime' experiences in natural surroundings during his boyhood, that would become the poem to be known as *The Prelude*. But he would always insist that truth to sublime feelings must be accompanied by truth to nature in all its particulars. Such attention to detail (which in its extreme form Coleridge sometimes criticized as his 'matter-of-factness')[21] was a permanent feature of his poetic aspiration; hence his uneasiness when Coleridge seemed to be neglecting any aspect of 'the factual': he might seem to be favouring sublime feelings at the expense of the natural.

Wordsworth's sense of falsity may have been justified in at least one respect. It is perhaps a sign of Coleridge's new frame of mind that he should have begun to indulge further the practice of borrowing without acknowledgement for his literary work. He had occasionally done this before.[22] In the new case, however, where he was admittedly expanding an existing poem by Friederike Brun, including its prefatory note, as the basis for one of his own,[23] one might have thought a brief acknowledgement, at least, appropriate. Her note on the *gentiana major* (a few paces from the everlasting ice) evidently struck him as a marvellous emblem of life juxtaposed with death which he transposed (with his 'Dejection' in mind perhaps) to an image of 'the boldness of human hope... venturing near, and as it were, leaning over the brink of the grave'. One or two other images of hers found a place in the poem itself.

More disturbing than the borrowings from the German original, however, is the tone of the poetry itself. It is perhaps significant that the section which moves most successfully is the one in which Coleridge brings to a new form the idea of stasis and movement (visible in the 'stationariness' of distant torrents):

> And you, ye five wild torrents fiercely glad!
> Who called you forth from night and utter death,

---

[20] Letter to Poole, 6 April 1799: *CL* I 479.

[21] *CBL* II 126 and chapter 22.

[22] He lifted notes from Darwin and Andrew Baxter for footnotes to his own poems: see *CPW* (Beer) 81–2n and *CPW* (EHC) II 1112.

[23] 'Hymn before Sun-rise in the Vale of Chamouny': *CPW* (CC) I ii 717–23.

> From dark and icy caverns called you forth,
> Down those precipitous, black, jaggéd rocks,
> For ever shattered and the same for ever?
> Who gave you your invulnerable life,
> Your strength, your speed, your fury, and your joy,
> Unceasing thunder and eternal foam?
> And who commanded (and the silence came),
> Here let the billows stiffen, and have rest?

Taken as a whole, the 'Hymn' is the first example of Coleridge's move to close the gap between the philosophy of the 'one Life' and his moral concerns; immediately after its composition we find the argument quoted above in favour of the superiority of Hebrew poetry over Greek, on the grounds that the Hebrew poets surpassed all others by possessing 'Imagination, or the modifying, and co-adunating Faculty':

In the Hebrew Poets each thing has a Life of it's own, & yet they are all one Life. In God they move & live, & have their Being—not had as the cold System of Newtonian Theology represents / but have.[24]

The process of co-adunation between a 'natural' poetry and the Hebrew insistence on morality and theology is now here visible; a similar process may well inform the long discussion of Milton's 'haemony', which follows, and which begins by contemptuously dismissing commentators who, simply concerned to find an English plant equivalent, have identified it as the 'English Spleenwort'. Coleridge insists instead on an allegorical interpretation:

Now what is Haemony? Αἷμα-οἶνος—Blood-wine.—And he took the wine & blessed it, & said—This is my Blood— / the great Symbol of Death on the Cross...[25]

This is an ingenious and by no means implausible explanation of Milton's use,[26] but if the reader is conscious of a certain disappointment as it proceeds, the reason may not unjustly be traced to Coleridge himself: for although he points to other meaningful phrases in Milton's description and deplores the ridicule commonly cast against allegorizers of poets, his explanation of 'haemony' is open to a charge not altogether dissimilar to that which he has just been preferring against Bowles. The

---

[24] *CL* II 866.   [25] Ibid., 867.
[26] For a full account, including other proposed interpretations, see *The Poems of John Milton*, eds. John Carey and Alastair Fowler (London: Longmans, 1968), pp. 207–8.

meaning which he is tracing has an arbitrariness—the cleverness of a good riddle perhaps, but not the wisdom of a profoundly illuminating analogy. And this is enough to make one ask whether Coleridge has revealed the whole of his meaning here. One is also led to reflect on the unexpected reference to the doctrine of atonement through sacrifice—a doctrine which Coleridge all his life found difficult to accept. May it not be that his mind, in playing over this analogy, had also been working at a lower level, connecting the 'blood-wine' concept with that of the 'one life', and so moving towards a conception of Christ's death which would make it not expiatory but revelatory of the link of life between all men, their unity of consciousness at the 'genial' level? Such an interpretation is not incompatible with an earlier expression of his, 'Lovely was the Death | Of Him, whose Life was Love!',[27] though it marks a development from it. (It may further be observed that the idea of the disregarded flower is one that links readily to the conclusion of Wordsworth's Immortality Ode.) Coleridge seems here to be guilty of falsification—at least in so far as he is neglecting the process underlying the point he earlier made about the necessity of 'passion' in a 'great poet'.

Coleridge's poetic and intellectual processes during this period repay close investigation. Underneath all can be detected the same need for 'the Permanent' that he looks for in the 'Letter'. How is he to deal with the phenomena of love, for example? It was one thing to accept the impossibility of his love for Sara Hutchinson, another to put that resolution into practice. The debate in himself which ensued may best be examined by looking at the long poem of that summer entitled 'The Picture, or the Lover's Resolution'.[28] This poem has been related to Gessner's 'Der feste Versetz', and no doubt took its departure from it. In itself, however, it marks an advance on Gessner's theme rather than simply repeating it. The original poem is about a lover's resolution to forsake his love, and his inability to keep it. It is in the best 'sentimental' tradition, by which the dictates of the heart can never be flouted. Coleridge's poem, written after he has decided that his moral responsibilities must take precedence over the dictates of the heart, cannot move to such a simple conclusion. Yet he is also in the process of realising that any sense of freedom which is generated by such a resolution can be temporary only, for reminiscence will soon come flooding in.

---

[27] 'Religious Musings', lines 34–5.   [28] *CPW* (CC) I ii 711–17.

Coleridge's lover, devoted to a young woman Isabel, sets off firmly into a landscape which cannot possibly speak of love and its languorous sensations: 'Through weeds and thorns, and matter underfoot | I force my way.' Passing over rocks, hearing scared snakes rustle over dry leaves, he becomes conscious of a sense of freedom, which is expressed through images, successively, of light, energy and spring:

> A new joy,
> Lovely as light, sudden as summer gust,
> And gladsome as the first-born of the spring,
> Beckons me on, or follows from behind,
> Playmate or guide! The master-passion quelled,
> I feel that I am free.

With these lines, Coleridge might seem to have restored himself to the landscape of North Somerset in 1797–8, when all around him seemed to speak of genial power. Not quite, however, for he goes on to speak of this landscape as one which might give rest to the love-lorn man, who, sick in soul,

> And of this busy human heart aweary,
> Worships the spirit of unconscious life
> In tree or wild-flower.—Gentle lunatic!
> If so he might not wholly cease to be,
> He would far rather not be that he is;
> But would be something that he knows not of,
> In winds or waters, or among the rocks!

The worshipper of nature as the link between the spirit of unconscious life and the emotion of love has become a 'gentle lunatic'—to be pitied as much as indulged; and the poem continues with an attack on the god of Love as one who would instantly be rejected by the wild landscape which would be too harsh for his daintiness. The stream 'that murmurs with a dead, yet tinkling sound', the wild bees making honey in a nearby tree, the breeze that blows through the trees, are all antitypes of the stream, the bee-murmur or the soft breeze that might be associated with love.

Yet the fact that his thoughts keep turning to the emotions of which this landscape does *not* speak is indicative of his abiding obsession; and it is not surprising therefore that soon we find ourselves in the looking-glass world of romance after all, as the lover looks in a pool, visualizes the experience of seeing the 'stately virgin' look at herself likewise, and finds himself able to contemplate her reflection as he would never be able to look at her actual face. But then, with equal arbitrariness, she plucks the heads of various flowers that grow around and scatters them on the pool:

> Then all the charm
> Is broke—all that phantom world as fair
> Vanishes, and a thousand circlets spread,
> And each mis-shape the other.

The lovelorn youth stays, but when the pool is calm again, the reflection of the girl is gone, leaving him to return to the pool day after day in the hope of seeing her again.

The other possible world of love thus envisaged is also rejected: this kind of wild pool is not the kind where such an event might happen: the lover is emancipated from such morbidity. Instead, he is free to roam through the dark landscape—though still haunted by images of true love, such as two streams parting to reunite again 'in deep embrace, and open to the sun' or two crescent hills folding in behind one another to make a circular vale. Eventually he emerges near some peaceful cottages, where he comes across a picture of the pastoral scene which he recognizes as having been painted by Isabel, and only recently left by her. At the same moment we learn that she is a 'child of genius':

> O Isabel!
> Daughter of genius! stateliest of our maids!
> More beautiful than whom Alcaeus wooed,
> The Lesbian woman of immortal song!
> O child of genius! stately, beautiful,
> And full of love to all, save only me,
> And not ungentle e'en to me! My heart,
> Why beats it thus?

He resolves to pursue her with the picture:

> She cannot blame me that I followed her:
> And I may be her guide the long wood through.

As mentioned above, the poem has been regarded as the description of a 'resolution that failed', though it is probably not the reading Coleridge himself had in mind. Rather, he was intent to present a 'resolution' through recognition that even if he no longer indulged soft thoughts of love towards Isabel, he might still honour her blend of genius and sensibility by acting as a guide to her through the forest.

In this inner argument of the poem it is difficult not to recognize a parallel to the argument which was proceeding simultaneously in his mind concerning his relationship to Sara Hutchinson. If he could no longer indulge soft thoughts of love towards her, he could at least honour her spirit and seek to communicate at the level of human 'genius'.

There is, however, an obvious limitation here. Coleridge had for some time found delight in speaking to Sara of his intellectual speculations. In September 1801 he wrote,

Endeavouring to make the infinitely beloved Darling understand all my knowledge I learn the art of making the abstrusest Truths intelligible; & interesting even to the unlearned.[29]

In 1804, similarly, he sent her a copy of Sir Thomas Browne's works with a long disquisition on the nature of that writer's genius.[30] Sara, of course, lacked artistic gifts of her own, and the relationship could not have been other than that of genial communication between the learned and unlearned. Perhaps it was some recognition of this difficulty that prompted Coleridge, at about the same time as his composition of 'The Picture' to send some lines to Matilda Betham,[31] whom he had never met, but in whom he could recognise a feminine genius like that of Isabel's. To describe the effect on him of her verses ('the fair, wild offspring of thy genius') he used an image of genial power from the *annus mirabilis*:

> (So have I heard a Nightingale's fine notes
> Blend with the murmur of a hidden stream!)

expressing the hope that she would prove

> Great, as th' impassion'd Lesbian, in sweet song
> And O! of holier Mind, and happier Fate.

Although both 'The Picture' and the 'Lines to Matilda Betham' gain in interest when one traces in them the presence of a continuing argument in Coleridge's own mind concerning the universality of genius, they lack, as poems in their own right, the life of the earlier conversational poems. The landscape described in 'The Picture' is very like that of

---

[29] NB 21 f 32^v (cf. *CN* I 984).   [30] *CL* II 1080–3; see also *CM* I 741–99.
[31] 'To Matilda Betham, from a Stranger': *CPW* (CC) I ii 726–8.

'This Lime-tree Bower', yet the poetry describing it lacks the delicate flow of the earlier poem. And this phenomenon may be legitimately related to the process of self-deception which Coleridge had initiated in himself at this time. To use the language of E. M. Forster's early novels, he was in the process of 'muddling himself': he was imagining that he could in some sense continue to give moral assent to his own marriage while continuing to love Sara at the level of the genial. But of course (as the imagery of the poetry itself makes clear) the genial was associated with the whole emotional aura of his early relationship with the Words-worths and so with the working of his own imagination. His problem, therefore, was to keep his imagination in line with the accepted actual-ities of his moral situation, which must involve an element of self-deception—even self-betrayal.

The process was necessarily taking place at a wider level than that of his love relationship, of course; the whole body of his thought was intimately involved. Somehow he must continue to align the grounds of the moral responsibility on which his marriage was based with the sense of the 'one Life'. One may see him facing the dilemma in actual life as he set off for his long walking-tour in the summer of 1802. Like the lover of 'The Picture', it would seem, he was endeavouring to escape from 'morbidly soft' thoughts by a programme of rigorous exercise on the fells—from which he sent Sara continuous accounts of his adven-tures. In one of these same letters he acknowledged that to pursue the wild and the genial in nature involved a kind of gambling 'not of the least criminal kind for a man who has children & a Concern': he was liable, for instance, when descending from a mountain, not to look for a suitable path but to climb down by the first descent that presented itself. On this occasion[32] he had moved away from the edge of the precipice, but had not looked round for a beaten track, so that when he finally saw a possible ledge he also realized that

if I dropt down upon it I must of necessity have fallen backwards & of course killed myself. My Limbs were all in a tremble—I lay upon my Back to rest myself, & was beginning according to my custom to laugh at myself for a madman, when the sight of the Crags above me on each side, & the impetuous Clouds just over them, posting so luridly & so rapidly northward overawed me / I lay in a state of almost prophetic Trance & Delight—& blessed God aloud, for the powers of Reason & the Will, which remaining no Danger can

---

[32] *CL* II 840.

overpower us! O God, I exclaimed aloud—how calm, how blessed am I now / I know not how to proceed, how to return / but I am calm & fearless & confident / if this Reality were a Dream, if I were asleep, what agonies had I suffered! what screams!—When the Reason & the Will are away, what remain to us but Darkness & Dimness & a bewildering Shame, and Pain that is utterly Lord over us, or fantastic Pleasure, that draws the Soul along swimming through the air in many shapes, even as a Flight of Starlings in a Wind.[33]

The terms in which he expressed his relief show with curious precision the point to which his thinking had brought him. Amused by his own calmness in the face of terrible danger, he recalls by contrast the feelings he would have if such a situation were to come on him in a dream. Daylight reality permits the operation of reason and the will, whereas in a state where they were impotent the whole mental experience would be of darkness, pain, and shame. As a vivid dreamer he found it a relief that in spite of his danger there was not the paralysing hold of nightmare states which, from other experiences, he knew all too well.

There is a not unfamiliar oddity at the end of his account, however. An argument which seems to be pointing firmly in one direction turns out to contain within itself a counter-current, suggesting somewhere an alternative motion of the mind. For while it was natural enough to welcome the distancing of himself from darkness, pain, and shame, the mention of 'fantastic Pleasure' and 'a Flight of Starlings' is a different matter—particularly when we remember the event which gave rise to that particular metaphor. Late in 1799, when he had just met Sara Hutchinson, Coleridge had been riding in a stagecoach into London in the early morning and had scribbled into his notebook a description of bird behaviour nearby:

Starlings in vast flights drove along like smoke, mist, or any thing misty [without] volition—now a circular area inclined [in an] arc—now a globe— [now from a complete orb into an] elipse & oblong—[now] a balloon with the [car suspended], now a concaved [semi] circle & [still] it expands & condenses, some [moments] glimmering and shivering, dim & shadowy, now thickening, deepening, blackening!—[34]

The experience, which had been of considerable delight, would still be recalled a year after the Scafell adventure:

[33] Ibid., 841–2.   [34] CNB 4 ff 1–1ᵛ (= 21f 56ᵛ) (cf. *CN* I 582 and I 589).

> My spirit with a fixed yet leisurely gaze
> Following its ever yet quietly changing Clusters of Thoughts,
> As the outward Eye of a happy Traveller a flock of Starlings...[35]

The full succession of this thought-process moves first against the stubborn resistance created by an awareness of things as they are, and then enters, as if by an instinctive reversion, the infinite, unlimiting world of the subliminal, whether of nightmare or pleasure.

Eventually, having seen the dangers of the ledge still more clearly, and the body of a sheep which had become cragfast at the same spot, he spotted a solution to his difficulty. As he looked down he could see stones on the ledge far beneath him which must have been piled there by a shepherd trying vainly to reach the cragfast sheep whose body he had just passed. But then he saw something a little less alarming:

> As I was looking at these I glanced my eye to my left, & observed that the Rock was rent from top to bottom—I measured the breadth of the Rent, and found that there was no danger of my being wedged in / so I put my Knap-sack round to my side, & slipped down as between two walls, without any danger or difficulty—the next Drop brought me down on the Ridge called the How / I hunted out my Besom Stick, which I had flung before me when I first came to the Rocks—and wisely gave over all thoughts of ascending Doe-Crag.[36]

That escapade of Coleridge's, descending heedlessly into an apparently impossible position and then finding a way out by discovering a space where he could fit and manipulate himself, was an apposite emblem for much of his later course through life, caught between the contradictory demands of two visions of the world, both of which he believed in profoundly, yet which he could not satisfactorily reconcile, allowing him only to argue his way through this position and that, sometimes offering aids to those in a similar predicament.

The whole experience on Scafell clearly remained important to him. Like Wordsworth, in 'Resolution and Independence' (a poem composed during the same year), he gained from his experience in this wild place a strong sense of his own ability to survive so long as Reason and Will were functioning. And this in turn, it would seem, gave, or restored to him, a sense of human identity intimately related to his old themes of form and energy. Despite the pleasures of energy it was the duty of the human being to be at heart an oak-tree, an organism whose branches act

---

[35] CNB 16 f 50ᵛ (cf. *CN* I 1779).   [36] *CL* II 842–3.

as a reminder of the central life binding all together, just as the excitement of his physical descent and danger initiated an unusual sense of calm repose. Writing to Sotheby a little later, he quoted some lines that he had written for the poem to Matilda Betham:

> Poetic Feelings, like the flexuous Boughs
> Of mighty Oaks, yield homage to the Gale,
> Toss in the strong winds, drive before the Gust,
> Themselves one giddy storm of fluttering Leaves;
> Yet all the while, self-limited, remain
> Equally near the fix'd and parent Trunk
> Of Truth & Nature, in the howling Blast
> As in the Calm that stills the Aspen Grove.—

He continued, 'That this is deep in our Nature, I felt when I was on Sca'fell.'[37]

To write from a deep conviction had evidently now become for him the best way to achieve the sublime. It was a view that would not serve him altogether well as a poet, threatening to drain away some of the imaginative lubrication that kept his meditative poetry sharply alive; yet it offered one means of holding in tension the play of that imagination with the need to accept the demands of the real world. Without awareness of such demands, and such compensatory play, his later writing cannot easily be understood.

---

[37] *CL* II 864, quoting (*variatim*) from the poem in *CPW* (CC) I ii 717–23.

8

Public Journalism, Private Affections

As Coleridge set out at the turn of the century on what seemed a promising journalistic career in London, his thoughts had naturally been dominated by English relations with France. After 1795, shame at what had been happening in Paris had been overtaken by a burgeoning patriotism that swiftly turned into thoroughgoing nationalism. His own thought then was primarily focused in dislike of the new mood in French politics that had made it possible for their army to suppress the Swiss cantons, in contravention of the earlier revolutionary ideals. His feeling echoed the disillusionment felt by others at such an ignominious end to what been regarded as a promising phase in European affairs. Yet there was also a positive element in his thinking. While political matters continued to absorb English thinkers, as they would for many years to come, the sense persisted that new and adventurous thinking was stirring. It has already been suggested that the *Lyrical Ballads* volume could be seen as an attempt to provide a third force in culture, based on cultivation of the imagination and the universal affections of the human heart; but how might humanity move on and develop such themes?

For Wordsworth the solution seemed to lie not only in writing further poems about isolated individuals and the universality of the human heart, as he showed in his contributions to the second volume of *Lyrical Ballads*, but in exploring his own earlier experiences and intuitions, as described in successive drafts for *The Prelude*. For Coleridge, on the other hand, the possibility of progress lay rather in developing the ideas that he had recently entertained in exploring the concept of genius; in this context he could not ignore a new avatar, in the shape of Napoleon Bonaparte—a figure of 'commanding genius' if ever there was one. For the time being, however, he had to be thought of as a powerful figure but, as it were, kept in reserve. As Coleridge had shown recently in 'Fears in Solitude', and other political statements, he was fully aware of the horrors of warfare. His own instincts, as voiced in leading articles contributed, with Stuart's connivance, to the *Morning Post*, were initially devoted to the desirability of averting full-scale war, and of adopting a more conciliatory attitude towards France. More than once he iterated the foolishness of lightly undertaking warfare which could bring about disastrous human suffering and waste of material resources.[1] At the same time he perceived that when Napoleon's overtures of peace at the end of 1799 were rejected by Pitt, England was left in a position where any outcome must be unsatisfactory:

Her factions suspended by national danger, and her pride insulted by rejected proffers, France will have placed herself like an army under the first military genius of the modern world! The fear of a threatened invasion will have restored to him all his popularity! And the man, who has atchieved by his exploits the splendour of a hero in romance, wields at his will the whole force of a romantic people, and unites in his single government the dispatch and unity of a despotism, with the enthusiasm and resources of a Republic![2]

While mistrusting Napoleon's overtures, Coleridge argued that they should be taken seriously and dealt with fairly; otherwise, the potentiality for favourable propaganda was forfeited to the other side. He also understood the unwillingness of the French to opt for a weak ruler, and thus the advantages of accepting Napoleon, despite what they must nevertheless acknowledge to be his usurpation:

We admit that an honourable Treaty concluded with Buonaparte would tend to confirm his power, and that by this and his subsequent moderation it may continue, till the revival of commerce and manufactures in France calls into active power the spirit of property, and consequently brings with it a Government modified accordingly.[3]

The alternative might face them with an even less welcome usurper; the quality of this one, at least, could not be in doubt:

In conniving at the usurpation of Buonaparte, they have seated on the throne of the Republic a man of various talent, of commanding genius, of splendid exploit, from whose policy the peaceful adherents of the old religion anticipate toleration; from whose real opinions and habits men of letters and philosophy

---

[1] See e.g. his articles of 6 January 1800 (addressed to ministers): 'under what pretext do you persist in wasting the blood and treasures of your country?' and 8 January: 'War ... can do no more for us than it has already done: and the longer it is prolonged, the heavier will be the burthens which it will leave behind it'; *CET* 1 78, 86.
[2] Ibid., 71. [3] Ibid., 78–9.

are assured of patronage; in whose professional attachment and individual associations the military, and the men of military talent, look confidently for the exertions of a comrade and a brother; and, finally, in whose uninterrupted felicity the multitude find an object of superstition and enthusiasm.[4]

Despite this tribute to Napoleon's 'commanding genius', however, Coleridge was cautious. The question of Napoleon's sincerity or otherwise was widely discussed. Despite his pacific attitude in 1800, moreover, the next few years were to witness a change of attitude on Coleridge's part as he became steadily more convinced of Napoleon's aspirations to dominance. Exactly when he fully formulated his twofold conception of 'commanding genius'—in peacetime enabling its owner to embark on great works of construction but in wartime emerging as 'the shaping spirit of Ruin'—is not clear, but it fitted his view of Napoleon to a T; so that it is no surprise to find that a classic formulations of its characteristics, in *The Statesman's Manual*, concludes with the statement

These are the Marks, that have characterized the Masters of Mischief, the Liberticides, and mighty Hunters of Mankind, from NIMROD to NAPOLEON.[5]

Illness, and a growing distaste for journalism, with its ambiguous prospects, led Coleridge to seek a period abroad. His immediate hope was that a stay in a warm and dry climate might assist him to overcome his health problems, but he could not enter the service of a colony in the Mediterranean at that time without being aware of the fraught political situation. One effect of the geographical location he chose was to make him more vividly aware of the manner in which European affairs were being changed by Napoleon's successes.

In going to Malta, it is true, he could still hope to exercise some influence over political events, but the surviving records show his active role to have been somewhat limited. Acting as public secretary following the illness of Alexander Macaulay (who died on the 18th of January) and filling the need for a stop-gap until Macaulay's successor, E. F. Chapman, could take up his duties, he was not formally appointed, and so had little public standing. The amount of thought and writing undertaken during his time as a journalist meant that in spite of this he was able to express an opinion of some weight on constitutional issues—even if he lacked the legal expertise required to draft the necessary legislation properly.

---

[4] Article of 11 March 1800: ibid., 208–9.   [5] *CLS* 66.

His other roles, so far as can be established, were those of humdrum administration: they included such things as countersigning passports and distributing bounty. His general sense that he could have been more profitably employed is indicated by a letter to Stuart late in 1806,

... tho' no emolument could ever force me again to the business, intrigue form and pomp of a public situation, yet beyond all doubt I have acquired a great variety of useful knowlege, quickness in discovering men's characters, and adroitness in dealing with them.[6]

The period spent overseas proved to be a time of self-examination. For the first time Coleridge found himself surrounded by men of affairs, and despite his experience as a journalist was made to feel how far he had failed in life through not having been forced to pit himself against men of action. In a later notebook he wrote ruefully of the recognition that came upon him in Malta that he could no longer hide behind the excuse of immaturity:

... the melancholy dreadful feeling of finding myself to be *Man*, by a distinct division from Boyhood, Youth, and 'Young Man'—Dreadful was the feeling— before that Life had flown on so that I had always been a *Boy*, as it were—and this sensation had blended in all my conduct, my willing acknowlegement of superiority, & *in truth*, my meeting every person, as a superior, at the first moment.[7]

He also found himself indulging in self-criticism for not suiting the level of his discourse to that of his interlocutors:

Coleridge! Coleridge! Will you never learn to appropriate your conversation to your company? Is it not desecration, indelicacy, a proof of great weakness & even vanity to talk to &c &c as if you talked with Wordsworth & Sir G Beaumont?[8]

From certain points of view the period marked a disjunction in his career. From domestic considerations and problems associated with Grasmere he was separated, temporarily at least, by physical distance. Indeed, he felt encouraged to cultivate other friendships. In Rome he established contact with a number of German scholars, including Wilhelm von Humboldt and Johann Ludwig Tieck, and heard about recent work by writers such as Goethe and Schelling. There was also, as Eduardo

---

[6] Letter to Stuart, 22 August 1806: *CL* II 1178.
[7] Entry of 18 May 1808: CNB 21 f 11 (cf. *CN* III 3322).
[8] Entry of 5 October 1804: CNB 21 f 2ᵛ (cf. *CN* II 2193).

Zuccato has considered in detail, a distinct move towards familiarizing himself with Italian culture. This was partly accidental, a result of southern sojourning for health reasons, but it is also not unlikely that the offer of work in an Italian-speaking community such as Malta, followed by a stay in Italy, was assisted by his recognition that Italian civilization might be of service to his own development. In certain respects he had found German culture stimulating; and at regular intervals throughout his career he would turn to one or another of their writers whose ideas he found chiming with his own—at which points the knowledge could be fortifying; yet there was a sense in which such discourses were insidiously undermining. The German tendency to approach matters systematically, to schematize, was subtly different from his own tendency to embrace less tangible modes of thought—as when he wrote of an extinction of light in his mind during his German visit or criticized Kant's elimination of feeling from moral judgment.

In these respects the Italian writers were more congenial. Perhaps they too were subtly different in content, cultivating an elegance in expression unlike his own delight in spontaneity of response—but if so they could be creatively misread. Among those whose writings Coleridge came to know during his Mediterranean sojourn the one closest to his own concerns was Petrarch. Kathleen Coburn remarked on the similarities between their careers[9]—and even commented on the ease with which Coleridge seemed able to overlook the adulterous implications of Petrarch's loves.

In Rome also the acquaintance of various painters, including the American Washington Allston, produced profitable cross-influence. Coleridge, who seems to have found Allston an easier artistic companion than Wordsworth, would renew the friendship happily when the American visited England, subsequently showing himself extremely active on his behalf.[10]

Gradually, however, the need to return to England was asserting itself. It was not altogether easy to secure a passage at a time when the French armies controlled much of continental Europe, and the continuing availability of intellectual relationships was no doubt a factor in delaying his return to England, where he knew that domestic

---

[9] She lists them in a note to her edition of the *Philosophical Lectures* (London: Routledge & Kegan Paul, 1949), p. 443.

[10] See also pp. 212–13 below.

complications awaited him. Eventually, however, he secured a passage on an American vessel.

Persistence of his bad health, not to mention continued resort to opium and spirits, had taken their toll, and on meeting Coleridge again after his return, Dorothy recorded her pained reaction:

> ... never never did I feel such a shock as at first sight of him. We all felt exactly in the same way—as if he were different from what we have expected to see; almost as much as a person of whom we have thought much and of whom we had formed an image in our own minds, without having any personal knowledge of him.[11]

It was, in general, difficult for Wordsworth and Coleridge to pick up the threads again. Both men had been forcibly changed by events of the two years: Wordsworth by the death of his brother John at sea, Coleridge partly by his immersion in the world of affairs, and partly by continuing ill-health and increasing dependency on opium.

If in one sense Coleridge seemed little altered, retaining his ability to pour out a profusion of thought and knowledge on any subject—to the degree that a single letter could be a miniature masterpiece—in other and slightly subtler respects he had undergone a deep and fundamental change. The notebooks and letters of the period before Malta convey an ebullient and burgeoning sense of ideas and thoughts developing, along with an enthusiasm to follow speculations wherever they may lead; after 1806 there is an increasing sense of restraint, even of underlying weakness. The difference might best be indicated as that between the sparkle of an ebullient spring and the eddies and currents of a moving stream.

When Wordsworth voiced his disquiet in his poem 'A Complaint', he adapted Coleridge's favourite imagery to further effect:

> There is a change, and I am poor;
> Your love hath been, nor long ago,
> A fountain at my fond heart's door.
> Now for that consecrated fount
> Of murmuring, sparkling, living love
> What have I? shall I dare to tell?
> A comfortless and hidden well.[12]

---

[11] Letter of 6 November 1806: *WL* (1806–1811) 86.   [12] *WPW* II 34.

The landscape continued to be important for both men. The familiarity
of the term 'Lake poets' for Wordsworth, Coleridge, and their friends
can actually mask the degree to which the physical fact of the lakes
mattered to them. Their desire for calm made the stillness of the lake a
perfect analogue for the happy state of the heart they looked for; the
most satisfying of their experiences could come at the moment when its
still water was ruffled by a light breeze. Yet Coleridge had to acknowledge that things were not the same. In his own public attitude, including
statements to friends and published works, he could express unreserved
admiration for his friend, but this was not necessarily endorsed by his
subconscious. It was impossible for him always to suppress a sense of
envy, particularly when he saw that Wordsworth had ready access to Sara
Hutchinson while he could see her, as it were, only on sufferance. While
he had had to recognize that his own sensitivity led to a lack of manliness
(he had written of this to his wife in 1804, together with an assurance that
'I shall grow firmer & Manlier'[13]) Wordsworth had no such problem.
The irony was that, following his fathering of a child while he was in
France, his failure to marry Annette Vallon now left him free to choose a
permanent wife. What little we know of his nature points to the probability that while he could recognize in Mary Hutchinson something of the
impulse that had guided him in writing the 'Lucy' poems, he could also
acknowledge the impossibility of relying on this in her as a constant
resource. He explored the paradox in a well-known poem:

> She was a Phantom of delight
> When first she gleamed upon my sight;
> A lovely Apparition, sent
> To be a moment's ornament;
> Her eyes as stars of Twilight fair;
> Like Twilight's, too, her dusky hair;
> But all things else about her drawn
> From May-time and the cheerful Dawn;
> A dancing Shape, an Image gay,
> To haunt, to startle, and waylay.

This tribute to her elusive charms was followed by appreciation of the
mature woman:

> A Being breathing thoughtful breath,
> A Traveller between life and death;

---

[13] *CL* II 1038.

The reason firm, the temperate will,
Endurance, foresight, strength, and skill;
A perfect Woman, nobly planned,
To warn, to comfort, and command;
And yet a Spirit still, and bright
With something of angelic light.

If Wordsworth could enjoy the nice balance between her spiritual and physical aspects in this manner, no such solution was available to Coleridge. He had already made his marriage choice some years before, sealing it with the birth of their children. However much he might love Sara Hutchinson, there was no chance that he could ever feel free to ask her to be his wife. But even when he recalled wistfully how he had urged William to pursue the happy consequence of being untrammelled by a previous marriage, he had to confess that he had not foreseen some of the inevitable consequences:

—O God! If it had been foretold me, when in my bed I—then ill—continued talking with Wordsworth the whole night till the Dawn of the Day, urging him to conclude on marrying Mary Hutchinson—[14]

What he had not foreseen, of course, was that marriage to the beloved woman must necessarily entail the forfeiting of the single lives that William and Dorothy had hitherto known and the establishing of a respectable domesticity—to be followed in due time by full family life. He could not deny that for the Wordsworths it had been a happy decision and had turned out well; yet this, by abating the memory of their previous deprivation, had also necessarily led to blinkered self-regard:

A blessed marriage for him & for her it has been! But O! Wedded Happiness is the intensest sort of Prosperity, & all Prosperity, I find, hardens the Heart—and happy people become so very prudent & far-sighted—but they look forward so constantly as never to have glanced at the retrospect, at their own feelings, & the principles consequent on them, when they were themselves disquieted, & their physical & moral Instincts not gratified!.[15]

If the conviction on which his love for Sara had been based had been lost, meanwhile, that was not altogether unexpected, since Wordsworth was not fully sympathetic to such an ideal: in the 'Lucy' poems he had shown himself aware of the possibility of an 'eternal moment' like that

---

[14] CNB 23 f 6ᵛ (cf. *CN* III 3304).   [15] Ibid., ff 6ᵛ–8.

described in the first stanza of the poem 'A slumber did my spirit seal...', yet, as Coleridge had come to realize, he was incapable of fulfilling the promise of falling in love. In a meditation of 1808 concerning the true love of fame Coleridge dwelt on the degree to which it involved the satisfying of one's moral yearnings. The implication was that Wordsworth was lucky in not having such yearnings, whereas his own case was of one whose nature forced him 'to seek for a completer of whose moral nature he shall be the completion':

... if this innermost & holiest Instinct have discovered its Object, as by a flash of Lightning, or the Strike of a Horse's Shoe, on a Flint, in utter darkness—if on after knowlege & tender affection one look of the eyes, one vision of the countenance, seen only by the Being, on whom it worked, & by him only to be seen,

> 'All Look or Likeness caught from Earth,
> All accident of Kin or Birth,
> Had pass'd away: there was no trace
> Of aught upon her brighten'd face,
> Uprais'd beneath that rifted Stone
> But of one image—all <u>her own!</u>
> She, She alone, and only She
> Shone thro' her body visibly.'[16]

Under the impact of that recalled momentary vision, swift as a flash of lightning, he had not only fallen in love with Sara, but done so with an absoluteness that (to cite another of his favourite formulations)[17] replaced the feeling of positiveness with the sense of certainty.

Yet if there was any retraction in his admiration for Wordsworth, he would not have acknowledged any connection with his own lack, rather a sadness that William and Dorothy Wordsworth did not acknowledge or even, perhaps, understand the full depth and purity of his passion for Sara. William, who, in his writing of the 'Lucy' poems, had seemed to appreciate, more than anyone else, the nature of love,[18] seemed not to perceive the corresponding intensity of his friend's emotion. As he put it that autumn,

It is not the W's knowledge of my frailties that prevents my *entire* Love of them / No! it is their Ignorance of the Deep place of my Being—and o! The cruel cruel

---

[16] CNB 23 ff 3–3ᵛ (cf. *CN* III 3291).
[17] See CNB 19 f 11 (cf. *CN* II 3095).
[18] For a fuller discussion, see the first chapter of my *Providence and Love* (Oxford: Clarendon Press, 1998).

misconception of that which is purest in me, which alone is indeed pure—My Love of ασρα could not be, did I did not know that she knew it as if she was it—herself & the Conscience of that self, beyond the bounds of that form which her eyes behold when she looks up on herself / O there is a form which seems irrelative to imprisonment of Space![19]

Since at no moment had he doubted that that knowledge existed on her part, any recognition of a mistake in so thinking was particularly agonizing:

O ΣΑΡΑ! ΣΑΡΑ!—what have you done in deceiving him who for 10 years did so love you as never woman was beloved! in body, in soul, in brain, in heart, in hope, in fear, in prospect, in retrospect—! Not he alone in the vulgar meaning of he, but every living atom that composed him was wedded & faithful to you / Every single thought, every image, every perception, was no sooner itself, than it became you by some wish that you saw it & felt it or had—or by some recollection that it suggested—some way or other it always became a symbol of you—I played with them as with your shadow—as Shakespere has so profoundly expressed it in his Sonnet—[20]

In Coleridge's case, meanwhile, it gradually becomes clear to the external observer that his decision to stake everything on the absoluteness of his vision of Sara was mistaken. The beauty she had revealed in that single moment was one that would emerge in her from time to time, but could provide no basis for lasting love. Blake's injunction would have been a better guide:

> He who binds to himself a joy
> Does the winged life destroy;
> But he who kisses the joy as it flies
> Lives in Eternity's sun rise[21]

Wordsworth had discovered an alternative by accepting the dialectic between Mary's moments of 'celestial light' and her everyday homeliness. Coleridge, debarred from taking his love relationship to its highest level by asking Sara to marry him, was nevertheless unwilling to accept the necessary elusiveness of her fleeting moments of beauty—kissing the joy as it flew, as it were—but must require it as a permanent resource. For him she must be eternal angel or nothing.

---

[19] CNB 12 ff 40ᵛ–41 (cf. *CN* II 3146).
[20] CNB 25 f 23 (cf. CN III 3303). In 1805, a version of Sonnet 98 appeared in CNB 17 f 9ᵛ (Cf. *CN* II 2428).
[21] *BK* 179, 184.

Coleridge could believe that his lonely position had a virtue of its own. It might be difficult to identify the nature of the 'original unific Consciousness' or the exact working of the 'primary Perception', but were not the energies, self-denials and 'sweat-drops on the Brow' of the 'philosopher who has really been sounding the depths of our being' comparable to with the 'greatest and most perseverant Labors of Travellers, Soldiers, and whomever else Men honor & admire'?[22] Such isolated mental labours and the distillation of such tenuously maintained love must inevitably prove precarious as a stronghold, threatening to end in disaster, but for a time their opportunity for mediating between the two extremes had offered itself as heroic.

While tensions had been disturbing the calm surroundings of Grasmere life, however, different and more violent forces were operating in the world at large. Coleridge's consequent conviction that in the dire circumstances of the time some remedial action was called for led him to think that he must again try the expedient of writing for the public, with the hope, no doubt, of reforming the current mood. Meanwhile Sara—feeling some guilt, perhaps, at her inability to have lived up to all he called on from her—agreed to assist him in his planned course by acting as his amanuensis.

[22] CNB 25 f 19ᵛ (cf. *CN* III 3295).

9

Politics, Principle, and *The Friend*

By 1808 international affairs were increasingly dominated by events in Spain: this is what young Sara Coleridge was referring to when she wrote of her memories of visiting Allan Bank in the autumn:

It was during this stay ... that I used to see my Father and Mr De-quincey pace up and down the room in conversation. I understood not, nor listened to a word they said, but used to note the handkerchief hanging out of the pocket behind, and long to clutch it. Mr Wordsworth too must have been one of the room-walkers. How gravely & earnestly used STC and WW, & my Uncle Southey also, to discuss the affairs of the nation, as if all came home to their business & bosoms—as if it were their private concern. Men do not canvass these matters now days, I think, quite in the same tone: domestic concerns absorb their deeper feelings—national ones are treated more as things aloof, the speculative rather than the practical.[1]

There can be little doubt what they were discussing in such serious fashion. In the previous December the Peninsular War had begun, exciting considerable national feeling—intensified when the English generals, having achieved considerable success against the French, granted them an armistice which seemed very much to their advantage. De Quincey described the extreme anxiety for news that caused Wordsworth from time to time to go up to Dunmail Raise in the hope of meeting the carrier who would be bringing the latest newspapers from Keswick;[2] the events leading to and following the convention of Cintra caused him extreme disquiet.

[1] See Appendix, 'The Autobiography of Sara Coleridge': Bradford Keyes Mudge, *Sara Coleridge: A Victorian Daughter* ... (New Haven, Conn.: Yale University Press, 1989), pp. 261–2.

[2] Thomas De Quincey, *Recollections of the Lakes and the Lake Poets*, ed. David Wright (Harmondsworth: Penguin Books, 1970), p. 160.

So great was Wordsworth's agitation by November that he resolved to write on the question, his first reactions being published in the *Courier* for 27 December and 13 January. Attacking the actions of the British, he castigated the sheer incompetence of the generals in letting slip a chance of defeating a thoroughly immoral enemy; his main thrust, however, was directed against the utter lack of principle that had been shown by the British in the whole affair. So his title concluded with the words 'The whole brought to the test of those Principles, by which alone the Independence and Freedom of Nations can be Preserved or Recovered'; his repeated aspiration was 'that we may have steady PRINCIPLES to controul and direct us'. He deprecated the idea of 'a paramount reliance on superior valour, instead of a principled reposal on superior constancy and immutable resolve'. Such qualities could exist in conjunction with a moral character that was greatly perverted, but

to *consummate* this species of courage, and to render it equal to all occasions... *Principle* is indispensibly requisite. I mean that fixed and habitual principle, which implies the absence of all selfish anticipations, whether of hope or fear, and the inward disavowal of any tribunal higher and more dreaded than the mind's own judgment upon its own act. The existence of such principle cannot but elevate the most consummate genius, add rapidity to the quickest glance, a wider range to the most ample comprehension; but, without this principle, the man of ordinary powers must, in the trying hour, be found utterly wanting.[3]

The panegyric of principle concludes with a glance at those who might best be thought to have embodied it: Phocion, Epaminondas, and Philopoemen in ancient times; Sir Philip Sidney during the Renaissance; more recently, George Washington; Lord Peterborough in Spain a hundred years before; and, in his own time, Lord Nelson.

To read such words as written in 1808–9 is to recall that at just this time Jane Austen was writing fiction more serious than her early comedies, where too the question of principle was paramount. The shifts and turns of British policy had caused a new heart-searching among those who had been moved by the intellectual developments of recent years, as a result of which this idea came to replace the crumbling of other foundations.

Early on the general reaction to news of the Convention is recalled:

Yet was the event by none received as an open and measurable affliction: it had indeed features bold and intelligible to every one; but there was an under-expression which was strange, dark, and mysterious... we were... fearful like

---

[3] *WPrW* I 256.

men who feel themselves to be helpless, and indignant and angry like men who are betrayed.[4]

Years before Wordsworth had said something like this in *The Borderers*:

> Action is transitory—a step, a blow,
> The motion of a muscle—this way or that—
> 'Tis done, and in the after-vacancy
> We wonder at ourselves like men betrayed.[5]

—lines which he evidently liked so much that he used them again later:[6] this sense of subliminal reactions existing separately from what was being experienced and expressed at a conscious level provided a dominant motif in *The Prelude*, where the prevalence of terms beginning with the prefix 'under-' bears witness to a preoccupation with the subliminal that reflects Coleridge's. Here the usage serves simply to reinforce what is being said about the nature of the popular response. Wordsworth felt, at the same time, that he could take for granted patriotic feeling behind the popular disquiet at what had been quietly surrendered.

'Principle', then, was the key word of the moment. Coleridge's similar decision to regard his marriage as indissoluble reflected his earlier, tragic affirmation to Southey as he returned to fulfil his promise of marriage to Sara Fricker: 'Mark you, Southey! *I will do my duty*.'[7] Wordsworth, who had composed his own 'Ode to Duty' in 1804, had found confirmation from the death of his brother—doing his duty—in the following year. Coleridge echoed the sentiment in a notebook shortly afterwards:

Let us do our Duty: all else is a Dream, Life and Death alike a Dream / this short sentence would comprize, I believe, the sum of all profound Philosophy, of ethics and metaphysics conjointly, from Plato to Fichte.[8]

He would hardly have been so ready to embrace such a destiny had there not been something in his own nature, a yearning for the permanent, corresponding to that sense.

Against this background of the need for principle Coleridge planned to launch his new periodical—even though in the first version what

---

[4] Ibid., I 224.   [5] Lines 1539–42, *WPW* I 188.
[6] He later adapted these and the lines following for an epigraph to *The White Doe of Rylstone*: ibid., III 283.
[7] Letter to Southey, 29 December 1794: *CL* I 145.
[8] CNB 17 f 62 (cf. *CN* II 2537). See also his distinction between fame ('the pursuit of which is an absolute Duty of the great') and reputation: *CL* III 83.

emerged appeared to be more of a miscellany than might have been expected. Certainly the explanatory sub-title 'A literary, moral, and Political paper, excluding personal and party politics, and the events of the day' might seem wilful to those who pondered it. How could a paper be 'political' while *excluding* personal and party politics?

One of the chief impulses towards creating such a journal came from Coleridge's annoyance at the anti-Jacobean propaganda that had questioned his patriotism. Early in *The Friend*, he bitterly recalled the article that had accused him of deserting his own surroundings in proceeding to Germany.

This was not the only element that was driving him, however. Paramount in his motivation towards the new journal was the feeling concerning the current anarchic lack of firm affirmation among his contemporaries that, having come upon him during discussions in Malta, had been reinforced by discussions with friends and acquaintances after his return. After spending time with C. W. Pasley, who had joined him in inspecting the fortifications remaining for the defence of the island, he recorded in his notebook his remark 'that *men* themselves in the present Age were not so much degraded, as their *sentiments*'—an assertion which, modified, found a place in *The Friend.*[9]

This was only part of the reassessment his time in Malta had forced on him. As Deirdre Colman makes clear, his larger enterprise involved responding to the challenge of the French Revolution by reaffirming doctrines such as those of Hooker and Burke. This was not altogether satisfactory, however, since both men ultimately assumed that wisdom consisted in what had been accumulated over the years—particularly in the development of Christianity. Their writings conveyed little sense that new truths could still be discovered. When it came to Rousseau, certainly, Coleridge could not allow him to be criticized in the manner that came naturally to Burke, since to do so would have been to negate much of what he had most valued in his youth.

From this point of view, it was refreshing to discover Immanuel Kant, who had been sufficiently influenced by Rousseau to be vilified by some for what William Taylor referred to as the 'notorious Gallicanism' of his

---

[9] See CNB 17 f 111 (cf. CN 3627) and *CF* (1809) 23 (cf. *CFriend* II 28): 'at present THE PRINCIPLES ARE WORSE THAN THE MEN'. See also Wordsworth's *Cintra: WPrW* I 317.

opinions.[10] Kant also, however, insisted on reinterpreting his ideas, maintaining that the 'General Will', to which Rousseau attached central importance, must be thought of in terms of the categorical imperative.

As *The Friend* continues, the sense of it as a miscellany remains an important feature; indeed, during the period following, one is struck (as were also Coleridge's friends) by an extraordinary interplay of ruination and resilience in the editor's attitude. On the one hand, devastation, particularly of his private life; on the other, a determination to achieve, which continually regroups its forces, still finds ways of proceeding. Important things remained to be said. Political life must be brought back to a sense of principle; human beings must be reminded of their proper stature in the scheme of things. So Coleridge returned to the field of independent judgement into which he had ventured years before, hoping that the goal of producing a completed issue each fortnight would enable him to 'play off his intellect ad libitum' in the manner projected in 1798.[11]

As often happens with Coleridge, the event proved less impressive than he had forecast, but less disastrous than some feared. The magazine eventually ran into the sands, and in the course of producing it Coleridge was often forced to lay his friends under charge for contributions. Yet it is hard to contemplate the figure of this man, in by no means the best of health, handling not only the writing of his magazine but also its production and distribution—often walking over the fells from Grasmere to Penrith to deliver copy to the printer—without a sense of strange heroism. Even Southey was impressed, writing in December,

Coleridge has so pleasantly confuted my expectations concerning The Friend that I begin to look confidently forward to a continuance of his exertions.[12]

So far from folding after one or two issues, the periodical ran in fact to no fewer than 27. Its production, nevertheless, was fraught with problems. Above all, any attempt to find consistency in the writing itself brings us against the same problem encountered in interpreting *The Rime of the Ancient Mariner.* Trying to make sense of the earlier poem involved appreciating the various patterns of understanding that played

[10] See Deirdre Coleman, *Coleridge and* The Friend *(1809–10)* (Oxford: Clarendon Press, 1988), p. 133, citing the *Monthly Review*, 1799, XXVIII 65.
[11] Letter to Josiah Wedgwood of 5 January 1798: *CL* I 366.
[12] *Memorials of Coleorton*, ed. William Knight (2 vols., Edinburgh: D. Douglas, 1887), II 86–7.

in Coleridge's mind as he tried to maintain his Christian faith while also contributing all that he had learned from contemporary scientific lore and his reading of romances. By dramatizing the conflicts at work he was able to enhance his poetic achievement. By the time that he set to work on *The Friend,* by contrast, the contending strands were further apart; instead of enjoying an arresting story, which they were free to interpret in any fashion they chose, readers were faced with the need to make sense of Coleridge's own intellectual tensions of the time and his efforts to resolve them into an intelligible and acceptable pattern.

Deirdre Coleman draws attention to some of the factors at work in *The Friend.* In particular she suggests that some of the uncertainty in what he is doing may be traced to ambiguities in the terminology of two writers whom he saw as major predecessors in the field. Because the term 'liberty' was so crucial to the age, a thinker such as Rousseau, who not only made it central to his ideas but dealt subtly with its political implications, must command respect. Yet Coleridge was also aware of the centrality of those ideas to the French Revolution, and the need for considerable reserve in considering their implications. In these circumstances it was auspicious that Rousseau's ideas had already been accepted—even if guardedly—by Kant.

The main question that was likely to arise for those who made sweeping claims for liberty concerned the social sanctions that could be invoked for judging actions by the individual. In Rousseau's view those sanctions were furnished by the General Will as developed by the community to which the individual belonged; but awareness of the enormities to which the General Will might devote itself made his admirers conscious that as a guide to individual actions such a basis was vulnerable. The existence of such reservations made Kant emphasize the universality of the moral imperative.

The two thinkers were thus using terms in slightly varying senses. Both Rousseau and Kant extolled the paramountcy of Reason, but while for Rousseau there was little sense of problematic factors Kant was less assured of its moral powers. Coleridge, in turn, who had seen the failings of the General Will during the Revolution, was more firmly guided by the reservations of Hooker and Burke, with their awareness of an original defect in human nature that must undermine the Reason, if that were invested with an automatic moral authority of its own. He was increasingly persuaded of the existence of such a defect, both by the social ills revealed in France and by his own human failings.

The thinkers concerned all took for granted the existence of a single, consistent basis for truth. Coleridge was not only firmly convinced of this but gave the proposition even greater prominence than did Kant, assuming that the Reason to which he accorded supremacy was in itself an enlightening power, to be given precedence in all intellectual activity. This set up a further tension within his handling of *The Friend*, since it was hard to distinguish this power from the Inner Light acknowledged by the Quakers. To consider this, however, leads to a curious misunderstanding that involved the periodical's title. As Deirdre Coleman has suggested in her discussion of the reception of the 1809 *Friend*, it proved equivocal in terms of its audience. Through the efforts of Thomas Clarkson, it was partly sustained by Quakers who found Coleridge's stress on the importance of Reason as an inner light well suited to their own beliefs. As members of the Society of Friends, which had already had a journal of the same title, they were understandably likely to assume this as another: many signed up as subscribers, and Coleridge did little or nothing to disabuse them. They would only gradually have grasped that there was little in the new journal to appeal specifically to them—particularly as it became clear that the editor, who had once deplored resort to warfare, was now, in the shadow of the Napoleonic conquests, urging the need for physical resistance in the defence of freedom. However much he might approve of the Quaker stand for non-violence, it evidently seemed to him by now impossibly idealistic in practice, so that he had developed an ambiguous attitude towards them. He was to recall humorously how his enthusiastic fondness for Quakerism when at Cambridge had led to his attending one of their meetings—which cured him.[13] His contemporary remarks were increasingly lacking in sympathy: he believed them to be 'altogether degenerated from their ancestors of the seventeenth century', and deplored their strong streak of commercialism:

The Quakers educate upon a principle of suppressing all appearance of passion, where the exhibition of it can be injurious to their worldly interests; but they neither teach nor practise any inward subduing of the appetites; and accordingly they are the most sensual of any race of men I ever knew, within the sanction of certain public ordinances. A Quaker is made up of Ice and Flame—he has no composition, no kindly mean temperature, no Christian gentleness and cheerful charity. Hence he is never interested about any public measure, but he

---

[13] See his Table Talk of 21 April 1811: *CTT* I 12.

becomes a downright fanatic, and oversteps in his furious irrespective zeal every decency and every right opposed to his course. Of course there are some exceptions, especially amongst the women, but I believe what I say is true of Quakers in general—and I have seen a good deal of them.[14]

Coleridge's vehemence may well have been exacerbated by an uneasy consciousness that their belief in the 'inner light' corresponded so closely with aspects of his own doctrine. At all events, he was careful to exclude 'religion' from the topics to be dealt with specifically in his journal.[15] Yet he was still anxious to keep up a counterpoint between practical needs and his sense that in the end problems might be resolvable only by invoking human genius. This led him to pursue a zigzag course between, say, topics concerned with 'visionary' topics and those concerned with right conduct—which takes a new turn, for instance, when the fifth essay begins with an equivocation typical of his attitude at that time:

The Intelligence, which produces or controls human actions and occurrences, is often represented by the Mystics under the name and notion of the supreme Harmonist. I do not myself approve of these metaphors: they seem to imply a restlessness to understand that which is not among the appointed objects of our comprehension or discursive faculty.[16]

Coleridge's tendency first to give rein to a visionary speculation then to draw back is familiar enough; but he now allows himself a limited use of the idea to justify comparisons and contrasts between Erasmus and Voltaire, Luther and Rousseau and Robespierre and Munster (referring probably to Thomas Münzer rather than Sebastian Münzer, with the last pairing not in fact developed). It is a curious feature of these comparisons that in each case they are presented as demonstrating the superiority of the first figure named, yet that the contrast is not always compelling—which may, perhaps, be related to the fact that Coleridge is thinking partly in terms of a comparison between genius and talent, partly of one between rootedness in principle and unrestrained reason. On these terms, Erasmus can be made out as superior to Voltaire on both counts, for

the Wit of one is always bottomed on sound sense, peoples and enriches the mind of the Reader with an endless variety of distinct images and living interest; and that his broadest laughter is every where translatable into grave and weighty

---

[14] See ibid., I 415–16, 457–9.   [15] *Memorials of Coleorton* II 87–8.
[16] *CF* (1809) 114 (cf. *CFriend* II 111).

truth: while the wit of the Frenchman, without imagery, without character, and without that pathos which gives the magic charm to genuine humour, consists, when it is most perfect in happy turns of phrase, but far too often in fantastic incidents, outrages of the pure imagination, and the poor low trick of combining the ridiculous with the venerable, where he, who does not laugh, abhors.[17]

When Coleridge turns to Luther and Rousseau, on the other hand, he is on more difficult ground, for both are men of powerful imagination—and he is forced to confess that it may be only the accident of being born at a particular time that caused Luther to be what he was, 'a Giant awaking in his strength!' and not to have been 'the crazy ROUSSEAU, the dreamer of love-sick Tales, and the Spinner of speculative Cobwebs; shy of light as the Mole, but as quick-eared too for every whisper of the public opinion'.[18] He can return to his public themes by moving on to a detailed discussion of Rousseau's ideas, but the original plan of comparing him with Luther seems to have dropped out of account; it is now Burke who appears in the text as his proper counterweight, a point possibly due to the dilemma just indicated. Luther could have been cited as a true opponent to Rousseau only if established as a man of true genius, rooted in principle; the lack of a proper biography of him made this impossible.

Coleridge could not regard the matter as done with quite so easily, however, for the flaw in the argument of the Luther essay also undermined his discussion of Rousseau. While on the one hand he supports the conception of a transcendent Reason, available to all men, he draws back from any development which might suggest (in Rousseau's terms) that this universal reason was immanent in all men as a universal political wisdom. On the contrary, he founded the political bases of the country in the existence of property, arguing that universal suffrage would be a mistake. Any idea that the quest for true principle might lead to a theory of universal Democracy vanished as his essay proceeded, to end indeed with an attack on the theory of universal suffrage, since such principles

necessarily suppose uniform and perfect Subjects, which are to be found in the Ideas of pure Geometry and (I trust) in the Realities of Heaven, but never, never, in Creatures of Flesh and Blood.[19]

[17] *CF* (1809) 116 (cf. *CFriend* II 112).
[18] *CF* (1809) 117 (cf. *CFriend* II 113).
[19] *CF* (1809) 144 (cf. *CFriend* II 133).

This down-to-earth attitude is aligned with a basically practical streak. Coleridge later protested that he had always believed that

in every country where Property prevailed, Property must be the grand basis of the Government; and that that Government was the best, in which the Power or political Influence of the individual was in proportion to his property, provided that the free circulation of Property was not impeded by any positive Laws or Customs, nor the tendency of Wealth to accumulate in abiding Masses unduly encouraged.[20]

He specifically excluded from this statement the period of his allegiance to Pantisocracy; and indeed that scheme did not conflict logically with the principle, since it had been founded on the idea of a society where property did not prevail. Since human nature had shown itself resistant to the creation of such a society, however, Coleridge could not expect any realization in the near future. Indeed, he hoped for some reward from warning those who might think in such terms, if only he might

arm a single man of Genius against the fascinations of his own ideal World, a single Philanthropist against the enthusiasm of his own heart![21]

Yet he could not disprize the value of such aspirations; indeed in his very next sentences he warned practically-minded statesmen against rejecting such ideals and enthusiasms in favour of pure empiricism, for

every speculative Error, which boasts a multitude of Advocates, has its golden as well as its dark side... there is always some Truth connected with it, the exclusive attention to which has misled the understanding, some moral beauty which has given it charms for the heart.[22]

This may be a guide to political wisdom, but it clearly does not entail a specific political programme. A practising politician might agree with it yet not change his existing policies by an iota. And indeed, so far as a practical programme emerges from *The Friend*, it is of a different order. The underlying sense of the work is directed not to political thinkers, but to intelligent individuals, encouraging them to develop both heads and hearts and so leaven society. We are witnessing the germination of the idea of the clerisy which would become an important element in Coleridge's social theory.

---

[20] *CF* (1809) 161 (cf. *CFriend* II 146).
[21] *CF* (1809) 114 (cf. *CFriend* II 148).
[22] *CF* (1809) 164 (cf. *CFriend* II 149).

Insofar as *The Friend* includes a defence of property as the basis of political representation, we may perhaps trace the effects of Wordsworth's stress on the value of a society in which possession of a small plot of land acts as a focus for each individual's ties and affections. But we may also notice a favourite imagery in Coleridge's argument. When he urges that the free circulation of property should not be impeded by any positive laws or customs, nor the tendency of wealth to 'accumulate in abiding masses' be unduly encouraged, we are reminded of his preoccupation with the life of the human heart—the need, both at the physical and moral level, that its warm flow should not be chilled or arrested. The notion that Coleridge is using the heart and circulation as a controlling metaphor for his conception of property is reinforced when we turn to a later essay, on taxes and taxation, where he uses it explicitly in defence of taxation and the national debt:

A great statesman, recently deceased, in one of his anti-ministerial harangues against some proposed impost, said: the Nation has been already bled in every vein, and is faint with loss of blood. This Blood, however, was circulating in the mean time, through the whole Body of the State, and what was received into one chamber of the Heart, was instantly sent out again at the other Portal. Had he wanted a metaphor to convey the possible injuries of Taxation, he might have found one less opposite to the fact, in the known disease of aneurism, or relaxation of the coats of particular Vessels, by a disproportionate accumulation of Blood in them, which sometimes occurs, when the circulation has been suddenly and violently changed, and causes Helplessness, or even mortal stagnation, though the total quantity of Blood remains the same in the System at large.[23]

The early enthusiasms of the heart might have promoted radicalism in his attitudes, but a more literal attention to the workings of the heart in the body has led to a more conservative attitude which sees the organism of the state as one that is as likely to lose the warm flow of its inward subtle life through violent interference with the free flow of its processes as it is through the stoppages of custom or unnecessary accumulation of resource.

Though open to criticism the metaphor is not without virtue as a guiding image for the idea of government by freedom and consensus, since, like Burke's image of the vegetable organism, it allows for the fact that life has its own laws, differing from those which govern a machine,

---

[23]   *CF* (1809) 177–8 (cf. *CFriend* II 159).

and that they ought to be taken into account in framing political theory; unlike Burke's image it allows for a process of constant reform if the warm flow of life is being impeded at any point.

When the intellectual virtues of *The Friend* have been acknowledged, nevertheless, one may still register a disquieted sense that writing of such a kind lacks the specific note of brilliance to be traced in much of his poetry, notebooks, and letters. This is rather the Coleridge of the 1795 lectures, his public stance involving reasonable enquiry, unexception-able logic, a tendency (nevertheless) to digression, unexceptionable sentiments, and a rather heavy-footed humour directed against oppo-nents, real or hypothetical. It does not, like the best of Coleridge, give the sense of ideas sprouting and burgeoning; while marking an impor-tant stage in Coleridge's own intellectual and spiritual odyssey its proper place is in the history of social thought.

The importance of *The Friend*, however, lies not in its outward shape and development, but in a duality of structure which allows ideas of a different kind to be glimpsed stalking through its pages from time to time.

As the writing proceeds, therefore, one is aware of an increasing zigzag between public and private discourses, between enunciation of the need for principles and a tendency to draw upon old theories. A reader who had not followed the course of his development could be pardoned for imagining that the work was becoming totally digressive, but certain of the ideas voiced turn out to have a logical progression of their own. The early enthusiasms of the heart might have promoted a radicalism in his attitudes, but a more literal attention to the workings of the heart in the body has, as we have noticed, encouraged a more conservative attitude.

Although the 1809 *Friend* might seem to have broken off abruptly, it kept surprisingly closely to the Cintra pamphlet by ending with praise of individual public figures who had been just and honest in their dealings. Where Wordsworth had concluded by praising Peterborough and Nelson in modern times, Coleridge ended with Ball and Nelson, using the occasion of Ball's death to praise the man he had admired in Malta.

This conclusion had a fitting logic, therefore. Although it coincided with the ending of the close relationship with Sara Hutchinson it also marked a point where she had achieved what could really be of use to him; from now on he could consolidate his larger position. He had learned increasingly to value not only the challenges of intellectual and political argument, but the virtues of a practical and good man such as

Alexander Ball. Uneasy, perhaps, about the warlike stance into which the logic of philosophical and political argument had propelled him he could continue to explore deeper if more esoteric issues, while attacking the shallowness of thought betrayed by writers such as William Cobbett. The position from which he launched the periodical in 1809 represents, therefore, an amalgam of revised attitudes with those of Wordsworth. As Wordsworth had seen in his brother's death an exemplification of the virtue of duty and an implicit comment on the privacy he had allowed himself to adopt, Coleridge, studying the nation both as journalist and public servant, had come to accept the necessity of strong principle; at the same time, communality and the 'one Life' were still attractive powers, as in a forceful observation of 1799. The genial activity of insects and the effect upon it of a sudden flash of sunshine (we may compare the moon and nightingales or the moon and owls in poems written just before) had become a striking illustration for him of that master-Idea, celebrated in *Kubla Khan*, of the sun-like power of absolute genius to enthral and focus the human passions. In the context of *The Friend*, it could illustrate a less visionary (and less presumptuous) ideal, emphasizing less the inspired and transfigured Moses than the nature of the Law he promulgated, but it was not altogether lost.

The concluding of the journal in its original form coincided with the end of his relationship with Sara Hutchinson; increasingly, his position involved private retreat. In a letter to Thomas Smith he wrote, with sharp self-knowledge,

I was affected by your Present, and receive it with feelings correspondent to those, with which it was sent: and still more by your approbation of the Principle, on which I have grounded 'The Friend'. Believe me, nothing but a deep and habitual conviction of it's Truth absolutely, and of it's particular Importance in the present generation could have roused me from that dream of great internal activity, and outward inefficience, into which ill-health and a wounded spirit had gradually lulled me. Intensely studious by Habit, and languidly affected by motives of Interest or Reputation, I found in my Books and my own meditations a sort of high-walled Garden, which excluded the very sound of the World without. But the Voice within could not be thrust out—the sense of Duty unperformed, and the pain of Self-dissatisfaction, aided and enforced by the sad and anxious looks of Southey, and Wordsworth, and some few others most beloved by me and most worthy of my regard and affection.[24]

[24] *CL* III 216.

The kind of sensibility thus induced was indicated by his metaphor of the high-walled garden. Its presence is detectable even in the one or two poetic productions of this period, including his republication of 'Frost at Midnight'. In its first version the line 'Quietly shining to the quiet moon' had been followed by others describing his child's foreseen delight next day when he would stretch out his arms to the shining icicles 'as he would fly for very happiness'. Now these lines were cancelled, since, as he put it in a note in Sir George Beaumont's copy, they 'destroyed the rondo, and return upon itself of the Poem'.[25] To put it another way, however, the expansive element in his work was being taken over by enclosure within self-reflecting harmonies.

At the same time, such cultivation could indicate the existence of a mode in its own right still traceable within his more prosaic writing. In the early part of the 1809 *Friend* certain images appear in isolation, illustrating some point in the argument, yet resonating beyond themselves and back into a more excited past. It is worth registering further their existence and consistency: a continuing presence and resource.

---

[25] See *CPW* (CC) I i 456 and n.

10

Fascinations of the Esoteric

Although much of Coleridge's main work in the first decade of the new century was related to political and philosophical questions, a hidden spring in his mind was always bringing him back to matters related to his 'darling studies'. The text would then become at once riddling and attractive.

Some of his delights in the esoteric had been undermined by the visit to Germany. In the universities there he discovered little enthusiasm for the kind of lore that had entranced him during the fruitful years devoted to poetry.[1] Yet the possibility remained that if he were to continue exploring matters that had previously come to fascinate him he might produce an intellectual approach to supersede anything the German intellectuals could do. De Quincey's assertion that he intended to 'astonish the world with a Metaphysical work...on which he intends to found his fame', already mentioned,[2] suggests that he had gained some inkling of what was afoot.

Despite the scepticism of some associates, the belief that he could bring about such a revolution survived strongly in succeeding years. But many conflicting ideas were also claiming his attention: the conception of a single great study became elusive. He thought therefore of producing a serial work such as those that achieved success in the previous century: the *Spectator* or the *Tatler*. Arriving in Malta, he wrote in a notebook, 'I should *like* to dare look forward to the Time, when Wordsworth & I with contributions from Lamb & Southey—& from a few others—should publish *a Spectator*—.'[3]

---

[1] See above, pp. 23–6.
[2] *A Diary of Thomas De Quincey, 1803*, ed. H. A. Eaton, London, 1926, p. 191 (cf. above, p. 73).
[3] CNB 15 f 32ᵛ (cf. *CN* II 2074).

The political needs of the time had led to this conception being transposed into the political and philosophical disquisitions examined in the previous chapter, since they could be thought of as suited to the needs of the time. But he also wanted to produce something closer to the psychological explorations he had been carrying out in his note-books, devoted to what (using once more the metaphor of his mind as a version of the sea) he described as 'all the Flux and Reflux of my Mind within itself'.[4] Beyond such investigations lay the Grail of establishing a valid correspondence between the human psyche and the divine source of the Nature in which it participated. Visiting Sicily, he gratefully noted from John Smith's *Select Discourses* the thought that

the eye cannot behold the Sun ... unless it be Sunlike, and hath the form and resemblance of the Sun drawn in it; so neither can the Soul of man, behold God ... unless it be *Godlike*, hath God formed in it, and be made partaker of the Divine Nature.[5]

Years before, Lamb had rebuked him for trying to console him with the aspiration of becoming 'an eternal partaker of the Divine Nature'.[6] Now, fortifying himself perhaps with the thought that such language was authorized by the New Testament,[7] he could delight in Smith's use of the same term to support an asserted correspondence between the light of the sun as the central phenomenon of the natural world, and that of the divine illuminating human beings.

Although this symbolism was constant throughout Coleridge's career an even more intimate one, that of the moon, suited his nature even more closely. A few months later, in the small hours during a night of February 1805, the idea seized him almost involuntarily:

Unconsciously I stretched forth my arms as to embrace the Sky, and in a trance I had worshipped God in the Moon / the Spirit not the Form / I felt in how innocent a feeling Sabeism might have begun / O not only the Moon, but the depth of Sky!—the Moon was the *Idea* but deep Sky is of all visual impressions the nearest akin to a Feeling / it is more a Feeling than a Sight / or rather it is the melting away and entire union of Feeling & Sight / And did I not groan at my unworthiness, & be miserable at my state of Health, its effects, and

effect-trebling Causes? O yes!—Have Mercy on me, O something *out* of me!
For there is no *power*, (and if that *can* be, less *strength*) in aught *within* me!
Mercy! Mercy![8]

The concluding sentences, turning immediately from psychological speculation to confession of guilt, are characteristic of Coleridge's oscillations
between the two modes. And since he here confirms the importance to
him of the image of the moon, it is not surprising to find him a few
months later, in April 1805, employing that central symbol again, asserting even more closely its correspondence with the divine nature:

In looking at objects of Nature while I am thinking, as at yonder moon dim-
glimmering thro' the dewy window-pane, I seem rather to be seeking, as it were
asking, a symbolical language for something within me that already and for ever
exists, than observing any thing new. Even when that latter is the case, yet still I
have always an obscure feeling, as if that new phaenomenon were the dim
Awaking of a forgotten or hidden Truth of my inner Nature / It is still
interesting as a Word, a Symbol! It is Λογος, the Creator! and the Evolver![9]

Speculations of this kind continued to play their part in the development of his next enterprise, *The Friend*, helping to explain some of the
problems surrounding it. In his study of Coleridge's borrowings, Norman Fruman has pointed out that two sections of the 1809 version were
taken, with minimal acknowledgement, from articles that Jonas Ludwig
von Hess had published in Germany, and which he had presumably
come across during his stay there.

The lack of acknowledgement is certainly reprehensible, but another
question, and in some ways a more interesting one, is why he should
have been sufficiently interested in their content to have kept them and
brought them back to England. Was he already planning a periodical,
and conserving useful copy in readiness? This is unlikely. A more
probable explanation is that he retained them as interesting pieces of
evidence for studies concerning the nature of mental activity that were
already occupying him. His attitude to Luther was a case in point:
instead of developing a full critique of his theology, he analysed a
particular incident, the one involving Luther's vision of the Devil, in
which, working late at night in his study, he saw, or thought he saw, the
Devil so vividly as to hurl an inkpot at it. The incident plays a major
part in Hess's account. Coleridge may have been particularly interested

---

[8] CNB 17 ff 25ᵛ–26 f (cf. *CN* II 2453).   [9] CNB 17 f 69 (cf. *CN* II 2546).

in it at this time, as paralleling the experience that he claimed to have
had in writing *Kubla Khan*, when (according to his 1816 account) 'all
the images rose up before him as things, with a parallel production of the
correspondent expressions, without any sensation or consciousness of
effort'.[10] The tone of the account he offers of Luther's vision is strikingly
similar:

> Disappointed, despondent, enraged, ceasing to think, yet continuing his brain
> on the stretch, in solicitation of a thought; and gradually giving himself up to
> angry Fancies, to recollections of past persecutions, to uneasy Fears, and inward
> Defiances, and floating Images of the evil Being, their supposed personal Author;
> he sinks, without perceiving it, into a Trance of Slumber: during which his brain
> retains its waking energies, except that what would have been mere Thoughts
> before, now (the action and counterweight of his outward senses and their
> impressions being withdrawn) shape and condense themselves into Things,
> into Realities! Repeatedly half-wakening, and his eyelids as often re-closing, the
> objects which really surround him form the place and scenery of his Dream.[11]

The surrounding discussion brings with it favourite speculations and
investigations of Coleridge's, including his interest in the 'half waking
state' and the tendency in that state for the speculations of the mind to
assume a strong sense of reality. (In the case of *Kubla Khan* this had
happened when his mind was affected, he hinted, by the prescription of
'an anodyne'.)

In 1799, one imagines, he would have been more ready to believe
that the vision of the Devil was in some sense a genuine vision, in the
sense of realizing true evil; whereas his later speculations might produce
a more sceptical position, reducing the significance of Luther's vision to
that of a 'psychological curiosity'. The supposition that such a process of
interpretation has taken place is supported when we look further into
the origins of a particular illustration in the account. Coleridge tries to
explain his meaning by reference to an optical illusion sometimes visible
to him on winter evenings, when, looking out of his study to the scene
beyond, he would see the reflection of the fire apparently burning
among the bushes there, the illusion increasing in intensity as darkness
came on. In the context, it is a straightforward illusion, simply reducing
the reality of Luther's apparition still further; but when Coleridge
discussed it, in a notebook of 1803, the moral point was a more serious
possibility—even if, on further reflection, it seemed ultimately futile:

[10] *CPW* (EHC) I 215.   [11] *CF* (1809) 1267 (cf. *CFriend* II 120).

The Soul within the Body, can I any way compare this to the Reflection of the Fire seen thro' my window on the solid Wall, seeming of course within the solid wall, as deep within as the distance of the Fire from the Wall?—I fear, I can make nothing out of it . . .[12]

Coleridge's image, and his difficulty in rendering the point he wished for, is near the heart of his dilemma. Ideally he would like to make the illusion of the fire seen in the wall an image for the reality of the soul, despite its immateriality in the body, but his awareness of the normal conditions under which it occurs stands in the way of such an inference. The whole Luther anecdote, indeed, provides a solemn dance around ideas that fascinated him but could not adequately be harnessed to his philosophy. It is not surprising, then, that he continued by postponing to a later date his explanation of the mode in which

our Thoughts, in states of morbid Slumber, become at times perfectly *dramatic* (for in certain sorts of dreams the dullest Wight becomes a Shakespeare) and by what Law the form of the Vision appears to talk to us its own thoughts in a voice as audible as the shape is visible; and this too oftentimes in connected trains, and sometimes even with a concentration of Power which may easily impose on the soundest judgments, uninstructed in the *Optics* and *Acoustics* of the inner sense, for Revelations and gifts of Prescience.[13]

The number of *The Friend* containing the Luther episode, meanwhile, which enjoyed a considerable success with his friends, was followed six weeks later by a further translation (again from Hess, and again with insufficient acknowledgement).[14] The melodramatic story of Maria Eleonora Schöning (which he says he first read during his visit to Germany) described the ruin of a young girl who had spent her childhood and youth looking after her aged father and was treated after his death with inhumanity by the revenue officers, who looked over his effects and seized the whole. In her destitution she was raped in a churchyard and picked up by the police as a street-walker; befriended then by another woman with two small children she lived happily with them until their poverty grew so great that she forced herself back on the streets. Apprehended by the police again, she fabricated a false confession of infanticide which the other woman was eventually persuaded to corroborate in the expectation that, if she was executed, her children would be committed to

[12] CNB 16 f 39 (cf. *CN* I 1737).
[13] *CF* (1809) 124 (cf. *CFriend* II 117–18).
[14] *CF* (1809) 194–208 (cf. *CFriend* II 173–82).

an orphanage. Despite last-minute and passionate attempts to stay the execution, Maria's friend was beheaded, while, when the executioner came to Maria, it was found that she was already dead.

As one reads this long dramatic narrative, one might be forgiven for thinking that Coleridge had decided to prop up the fortunes of his periodical by including a sensational story. There is more to the affair than that, however. Coleridge begins his introductions to the narrative by a reference to the favourable reception of 'The Three Graves' and his intention of showing in that poem 'the effect, which one painful Idea vividly impressed on the mind, under unusual circumstances, might have in producing an alienation of the Understanding'. Acknowledging that many of the details in his poem had been fictitious, however, he turns to the German narrative as presenting an instance of

the same causes acting upon the mind, to the production of conduct as wild as that of madness, but without any positive or permanent loss of the Reason or the Understanding.

What has interested Coleridge, in other words, is the story of a human being, utterly innocent, being torn 'live-asunder' from nature and suffering a temporary alienation of her life-consciousness—which, subsequently unleashed in the processes and evolved to a point where her life itself was severed, had prompted her in her despair to seek death itself in the hope of saving the lives of the children. In the storms of passion which her action and its consequences brought about, the inner activity of life itself was destroyed—to such a degree that when she died she was found 'as cold as if she had been dead for some hours'. To quote Coleridge's concluding statement, 'The Flower had been snapt in the storm, before the scythe of violence could come near it.'

Coleridge did not himself pursue such significances fully, probably for reasons already indicated. As with the Luther anecdote, he offers his story as no more than a psychological curiosity, and uses the terms 'Reason' and 'Understanding' rather than 'life-consciousness', or any such phrase. The suggestion that some such speculation was working in his mind is furthered, nevertheless, by the additions he made to Hess's account. In characterizing Maria Schöning's original states, he inserted a long passage concerning her voice which had had no place in the original:

The peace, which passeth all understanding, disclosed itself in all her Looks and Movements. It lay on her Countenance, like a steady unshadowed Moonlight: and her Voice, which was naturally at once sweet and subtle, came from her, like the fine flute-tones of a masterly performer, which still floating at some uncertain distance, seem to be created by the player, rather than to proceed from the instrument. If you had listened to it in one of those brief Sabbaths of the soul, when the activity and discursiveness of the Thoughts are suspended, and the mind quietly *eddies* round, instead of flowing onward (as at late evening in the Spring I have seen a Bat wheel in silent circles round and round a fruit-tree in full blossom, in the midst of which, as within a close Tent of the purest White, an unseen Nightingale was piping its' sweetest notes) in such a mood you might have half-fancied, half-felt, that her Voice had a separate Being of its' own—that it was a living Something, whose mode of existence was for the Ear only: so deep was her Resignation, so entirely had it become the unconscious Habit of her Nature, and in all, she did or said, so perfectly were both her movements and her utterance without effort and without the appearance of effort![15]

Southey (perhaps detecting—acutely—the difference in tone from that of the German original) singled this passage out for especial comment:

The description of Maria's voice and countenance is too beautiful for its place; it is too much like poetry. We should beware of mingling fancy with the narration of what we believe to be the truth...[16]

Coleridge wrote to him defending the passage:

Your remark on the Voice is most just—but that was my purpose—not only so, but the whole passage was inserted, and intertruded, after the rest was written... in order to unrealize it even at the risk of disnaturalizing it—Lady B[eaumont] therefore pleased me by saying—never was the golden tint of the Poet more judiciously employed &c—For this reason too I introduced the simile of the Leaf &c—I not only thought the Voice part & Philomel out of place, but in bad taste per se.[17]

As a defence for a piece of writing this is extraordinary. Coleridge not only admits it to be in bad taste but argues that it was put in to 'unrealize' a passage the veracity of which he had just been defending. Yet he not only refused to admit a fundamental badness, but kept it in both subsequent editions. A clue to the reason for his truculence may perhaps be discovered by way of another passage where the word 'unrealize' appears:

...for from my very childhood I have been accustomed to abstract and as it were unrealize whatever of more than common interest my eyes dwelt on; and then by a sort of transfusion and transmission of my consciousness to identify myself with the Object.[18]

---

[15] *CF* (1809) 195 (cf. *CFriend* II 173–4.   [16] *Memorials of Coleorton*, II 87–8.
[17] *CL* III 266.   [18] *CL* IV 974–5.

What Coleridge seems to be indicating in his defence is that the process of 'unrealization' was intended to conduct readers towards a different level of perception, at which the nature of Maria might be apprehended by their primary consciousness and perceived as embodying the harmony to be discovered in some of the moods of nature. And indeed it will be observed that the images which he uses to describe her can be directly related to some elsewhere in his writings, helping to locate the significance of the passage in the visionary quality of the writing. The image of the bat, wheeling in silent circles around the fruit tree in which the nightingale is singing, immediately suggests cognate parallels: the 'rapid bat' wheeling 'silent by', while 'the solitary humble-bee sings in the bean-flower' in 'This Lime-Tree Bower my Prison'; the Lampads 'wheeling round the throne' in the 'Ode to the Departing Year'; the spectators circling the entranced bard of *Kubla Khan*. What seems to be suggested is that Maria Schöning was a true child of nature in that original state where her own indwelling vision could still cast her energies into charmed compliance.

Coleridge did not make it clear (apart from a brief and inadequate reference at the beginning of the Luther piece) that he was reproducing much of his accounts word for word,[19] and the monstrous insufficiency of his acknowledgement in some ways marks an important moment in his career. But when we have recognized an element of deception we are still entitled to ask whether there was not a particular reason why he should have taken over these stories, rather than many others that were available in German sources. His account of the deep impression made on his memory by the story of Maria Schöning assists his suggestion that the relating of the story on his part has a claim to originality, but it needs not be discounted therefore; for the poet who had left England with the first part of *Christabel* achieved but the rest still to be worked out, this tale would indeed have been significant, as the apparently authenticated story of a girl who had been painfully diverted from her original state of innocence and driven to more and more desperate acts in her efforts to atone for a steadily increasing sense of degradation after her father's death, until she succeeded in having herself executed for a murder, even though her claim to have committed it was false. To someone as deeply concerned with the nature of innocence and its corruption as was Coleridge, such a story would have had a striking appeal, seeming to

---

[19] See M. Eisler, 'Die Geschichte der Maria Eleonora Schöning und die Characteristik Luthers in Coleridge's Friend', *Englische Studien*, XLVII (Leipzig, 1913–14) 219–25.

provide in a very pure form a documented account of alienated under-standing. That primal estrangement, Coleridge seems to suggest, affect-ed Maria so sharply as to cast her into the opposite role as a creature seeking her own death—even if she hoped she would be acting for the good of others. And it may well be not without significance that another of the touches added by Coleridge to Hess's narrative again— if distantly—recalls the imagery of *Christabel*. When Maria, after a manic excursion to drown herself, is rescued by a soldier's wife and taken to her home, he describes the relief which came to her:

As when a withered Leaf, that has been long whirled about by the gusts of Autumn, is blown into a Cave or hollow Tree, it stops suddenly, and all at once looks the very image of quiet. Such might this poor Orphan appear to the eye of a meditative imagination.[20]

Whereas Christabel had been still alive, like the 'one red leaf, the last of its clan', Maria Schöning's wild activities were a counterfeit of living activity from one who, in one sense at least, had long been dead. Small wonder, then, that when her execution finally came, the hangman discovered that he was not needed. Coleridge then goes on quickly to affirm that the tale 'overflows with a human interest, and needs no philosophical deduction to make it impressive.' The preceding avowal is worth lingering over, however, since the reference to 'The Three Graves' again suggests that he had read the story in the light of immediate excitement produced by psychological speculations. Maria Schöning's derangement might well suggest an extraordinary reversal of the poles at the deepest level, transforming all that had previously enhanced life into a principle working irresistibly towards death.

These are by no means the only cases where Coleridge's more esoteric ideas intervene in a more staid narrative. A moral illustration may prove unexpectedly resonant:

Truth considered in itself and in the effects natural to it, may be conceived as a gentle Spring or Water-source, warm from the genial earth, and breathing up into the Snow-drift that is piled over and around its' outlet.[21]

What might at first sight appear no more than a decorative flourish reveals itself on examination to be a closely-wrought image of corre-spondence, the 'genial warmth' of the earth being related to that of the

---

[20] *CF* (1809) 201 (cf. *CFriend* II 178).
[21] *CF* (1809) 53 (cf. *CFriend* II 54).

body, while the spring is that of the 'heart of hearts', making its pulsing presence felt against the weight of freezing custom. These implications are not pursued, however; in the same way, there is nothing further to indicate the depth of the correspondence that is being proposed when Coleridge turns to Bell, the educationalist, and visualizes extravagantly how glorified spirits in Heaven might praise him, and

> give thanks for his earthly Virtues, as the chosen Instruments of Divine Mercy to them, and not seldom, perhaps, turn their eyes toward *him*, as from the Sun to its image in the Fountain, with secondary gratitude and the permitted utterance of a human love![22]

One of the most striking examples of this tendency for attractive trains of thought to obtrude on a discussion has already been mentioned as an example from *The Friend* (where he writes of the necessity for making 'every fair appeal to the Feelings, the Imagination, and even the Fancy'):[23]

> On some wide Common or open Heath, peopled with Ant-hills, during some one of the grey cloudy days of late Autumn, many of my Readers may have noticed the effect of a sudden and momentary flash of Sunshine on all the countless little animals within his view, aware too that the self-same influence was darted co-instantaneously over all their swarming cities as far as his eye could reach; may have observed, with what a kindly force the Gleam stirs and quickens them all! and will have experienced no unpleasurable shock of Feeling in seeing myriads of myriads of living and sentient Beings united at the same moment in one gay sensation, one joyous activity! But aweful indeed is the same appearance in a multitude of rational Beings, our fellow-men, in whom too the effect is produced not so much by the external occasion as from the active quality of their own thoughts.[24]

A whole range of such observation and imagery is now geared (if sometimes uneasily) to his main assertions, so identifying principles with the central fountainous power:

> The widest maxims of Prudence are like Arms without Hearts, disjoined from those Feelings which flow forth from Principle as from a Fountain . . . [25]

In writing so, Coleridge may be aligning his own apparently good faith with the needs of society, but if so he seems to be simultaneously guilty of bad faith with himself. What he might originally have described were

[22] *CF* (1809) 71 (cf. *CFriend* II 69).   [23] *CF* (1809) 26 (cf. *CFriend* II, 31).
[24] Ibid.   [25] *CF* (1809) 86 (cf. *CFriend* II 85).

those feelings which flow forth from the workings of genius as from a fountain; but his glimpse of the nature of some of those feelings has been succeeded by a misleading identification of genius with ordained law. If in so doing he has forged a link back with society and kept alive his association with Wordsworth's mind, it has been at the expense of cutting himself off from the source of some of his most valuable psychological insights.

One can see the process of self-adjustment in process on one of the very first pages of *The Friend*:

In health and youth we may indeed connect the glow and buoyance of our bodily sensations with the words of a theory, and imagine that we hold it with a firm belief. The pleasurable heat which the Blood or the Breathing generates, the sense of external reality which comes with the strong Grasp of the hand or the vigorous Tread of the foot, may indifferently become associated with the rich eloquence of a Shaftesbury, imposing on us man's possible perfections for his existing nature; or with the cheerless and hardier impieties of a Hobbes, while cutting the gordian knot he denies the reality of either vice or virtue, and explains away the mind's self-reproach into a distempered ignorance, and epidemic affection of the human nerves and their habits of motion . . . I shall hereafter endeavour to prove, how distinct and different the sensation of positiveness is from the sense of certainty, the turbulent heat of temporary fermentation from the mild warmth of essential life.[26]

So far, Coleridge's statements are well in line with researches noted earlier. He is exploring the sense of heightened reality which may accompany the intensification of warmth, and relating this to the flow of animal spirits in youth. The development of the idea shows the old reluctance to pursue the sense of reality thus given, however; there is an insistence rather that the more temperate flow, the mild warmth of ongoing life, provides a more permanent vehicle of truth.

A further development follows. As a later editor points out, this distinction between positiveness and certainty had already been used in other places. In a notebook entry defining the nature of true love he wrote:

Even as the youth who carried away by eloquent books had felt all the fermenting & busy heat of utmost positiveness, the first time he has been made to demonstrate a problem of geometry, feels the sense of *certainty*, &

---

[26] *CF* (1809) 4 (cf. *CFriend* II 7). A distinction between 'the feeling of positiveness' and 'the sense of Certainty' is implicit in a notebook entry of June 1803: CNB 8 f 54ᵛ (cf. *CN* I 1410).

finds no difficulty save in words to distinguish it infallibly from the sensation of positiveness.[27]

In a letter of 1808 to De Quincey, likewise, he claimed 'a *sense* of *certainty* intuitively distinguished from a mere delusive *feeling* of *positiveness*', asserting that he had little partiality to his own productions or thoughts.[28]

A similar mutation is evident in the *Friend* passage. As great a degree of 'certainty' is now being assigned to the great laws of morality as to those of geometry:

Suffice it for the present to affirm, to declare it, at least, as my own creed, that whatever humbles the heart and forces the mind inward, whether it be sickness, or grief, or remorse, or the deep yearnings of love (and there have been children of affliction, for whom all these have met and made up one complex suffering) in proportion as it acquaints us with 'the thing, we are,' renders us docile to the concurrent testimony of our fellow-men in all ages and in all nations. From PASCAL in his closet, resting his arm, which supports his thoughtful brow, on a pile of demonstrations, to the poor pensive Indian, that seeks the missionary in the American wilderness, the humiliated self-examinant feels that there is Evil in our nature as well as Good, an EVIL and a GOOD for a just analogy to which he questions all other nations in vain...[29]

He is moving into more difficult terrain; for however unexceptionable the quotation from Horace, he is still faced with the task of justifying his own conception of good—which involves the circular paradox that those who most easily accept it will be those who least need to:

Would to Heaven that the Verdict to be passed on my Labours depended on those who least needed them! The Water Lilly in the midst of Waters lifts up its' broad Leaves, and expands its Petals at the first pattering of the Shower, and rejoices in the Rain with a quicker Sympathy, than the parched Shrub in the sandy Desart.[30]

There follows a crucial passage, in which Coleridge tries to establish his point by a long series of analogies between the 'higher faculty' in man and that in animals. But he is again on dangerous ground, veering towards some form of pantheism; and so it is not surprising to find

---

[27] CNB 19 f 11 (cf. *CN* II 3095).   [28] *CL* III 48.
[29] *CF* (1809) 4 (cf. *CFriend* II 7–8). The quotation is from Shakespeare's *Rape of Lucrece*, line 149.
[30] *CF* (1809) 78 (cf. *CFriend* II 75).

him three years later relegating the passage to a footnote, four years later severely questioning it in a marginal note, and finally, in 1818, dropping it altogether. The process exemplifies in unusually sharp form the dilemma presented by animal life and its potential significance.

Even in this early version, however, Coleridge tries to get the best of both worlds by arguing both that nature is revelatory in man, and that man, as created in the image of God ('the image of his own Eternity and Infinity') is given a Reason which creates for itself the Ideas of Soul, the Free Will, Immortality, and God—'without which the Conscience would be baseless and contradictory'. Though not Kantian, this could hardly have been phrased so if Kant had not written. It displays the degree to which he took hold of his predecessor's philosophy, reinterpreting it in his own terms to build a bridge between his own psychology (despite its ever-present danger of pantheism) and eternal and immutable morality. Thus equipped, he can treat nature in both guises, allowing for the possibility of revelation in nature yet also acknowledging that at other times the same nature is morally neutral:

With this Faith all Nature

> ... all the mighty World
> Of Eye and Ear...

presents itself to us, now as the Aggregate Materials of Duty, and now as a Vision of the Most High revealing to us the mode, and time, and particular instance of applying and realizing that universal Rule, pre-established in the Heart of our Reason: as

> The lovely shapes and sounds intelligible,
> Of that Eternal Language, which our God
> Utters: Who from Eternity doth teach
> Himself in all, and all things in Himself![31]

At this point, also, Coleridge brings in, as a kind of sublime groundswell to his text, the passage from Giordano Bruno in which philosophical contemplation of the divine is praised as initiating man into knowledge of 'the Omnipotent, in the illimitable etherial space, in the infinite power, that creates all things, and is the abiding Being of all things', and Trismegistus quoted on man as 'the great Miracle',

---

[31] *CF* (1809) 81–2 (cf. *CFriend* II 79–81).

Inasmuch as he has been made capable of entering into Union with God, as if he were himself a divine nature; tries to become all things, even as all things are; and in limitless progression of limited States of Being, urges onward to the ultimate Aim, even as God is simultaneously infinite, and every where All![32]

In the very course of his quoting, Coleridge interjects comments to guard Bruno against possible charges of pantheism; and after his own visionary passage in the text feels bound to defend himself immediately against the possible charge of 'Enthusiasm'.

From the point of view of Coleridge's visionary speculations, this is the high point of *The Friend*; he moves immediately into less controversial ground, a long disquisition on the extraordinary degree of power which can be exerted by an individual who throws off the restraints of conscience—which soon leads him, via an echo of Satan's 'Evil, be thou my good!', to reflect on the need for men of virtue to stand together during the current violence, and so to affirm that contemporary fashions in taste, morals, and religion are false, while the materials and opportunities for acquiring correct principles by reflection are available to all.

The filament of logical development is still just visible, however, for in this essay Coleridge is intent to present the portrait of a man who exists at the opposite extreme from the fearful hero of *Kubla Khan*, yet to draw upon the same powers: to offer a figure of Genius, but in its positive rather than its destructive form.

At this moment the inherent tensions of *The Friend* are most evident, for the figure upon whom Coleridge chose in 1808 to draw for his depiction was, as already noticed, no inspired bard or entranced prophet but the more mundane and sober figure of Sir Alexander Ball, the main anecdote recording Ball's success in quelling a state of near mutiny on a ship in which he succeeded by the simple expedient of enforcing the processes of law: making sure that the rules were known and that they were always fairly applied. The previous attempt to rule by terror had had an effect which Coleridge describes by a metaphor drawing on his favourite imagery of ice and warmth: as

like that of a Polar Winter on a Flask of Brandy; the furious Spirit concentered itself with ten-fold strength at the heart. . . .[33]

---

[32] *CF* (1809) 82fn (cf. *CFriend* II 81fn and I 117n).
[33] *CF* (1809) 100 (cf. *CFriend* II 99).

If Ball's rule, on the other hand, also penetrated to the heart, it did so more subtly:

An *invisible* Power it was, that quelled them, a Power, which was therefore irresistible, because it took away the very Will of resisting! It was the aweful power of LAW acting on natures pre-configured to its influences....[34]

This same spirit of rule is presented in the role of a daemonic presence, to which the spirit may answer but which it cannot body forth in physical form:

Strength may be met with strength; the Power of inflicting pain may be baffled by the Pride of endurance; the eye of Rage may be answered by the stare of Defiance, or the downcast look of dark and revengeful Resolve; and with all this there is an outward and determined object to which the mind can attach its passions and purposes, and bury its own disquietudes in the full occupation of the Senses. But who dares struggle with an *invisible* Combatant? with an Enemy which exists and makes us know its existence—but *where* it is, we ask in vain?—No Space contains it—Time promises no control over it—it has no ear for my threats—it has no substance, that my hands can grasp, or my weapons find vulnerable—it commands and cannot be commanded—it acts and is insusceptible of my re-action—the more I strive to subdue it, the more am I compelled to think of it—and the more I think of it the more do I find it to possess a reality out of myself, and not to be a phantom of my own imagination; that all, but the most abandoned men, acknowledge its authority, and that the whole strength and majesty of my Country are pledged to support it; and yet that *for me* its power is the same with that of my own permanent Self, and that all the Choice, which is permitted to me, consists in having it for my guardian Angel or my avenging Fiend![35]

In this paragraph, Coleridge's enquiries into the nature of the daemonic are brought into the service of something resembling Kant's categorical imperative. That very Law which is normally thought of as deposited in dry statute-books, the residue of bygone dead decisions, is converted into an effect more like that produced by Moses on Mount Sinai. The true law-giver is not a judicious and blindfolded figure, measuring and punishing, but an inspired prophet: the comparison is enforced by the author's rapturous conclusion:

This is the Spirit of LAW! the Lute of Amphion, the Harp of Orpheus! This is the true necessity, which compels man into the social State, now and always, by a still-beginning, never-ceasing force of moral Cohesion.[36]

---

[34] *CF* (1809) 102 (cf. *CFriend* II 100).
[35] *CF* (1809) 102–3 (cf. *CFriend* II 101 (I 171)).
[36] *CF* (1809) 103 (cf. *CFriend* II 101).

Despite the power of this *tour de force* on Coleridge's part, one senses the strain of the divergent impulses that he is trying to reconcile. The reader need only reflect that the subject of this rhapsody is an English commander who put a set of rules in his ship and insisted that all his men obey them, in order to see how far we have moved in reality from the visionary protagonist of *Kubla Khan*'s final stanza, Apollo and other such figures of intoxicated prophecy. Although the power that can bring together these images may still be maintaining its self-consistency, it is by now doing so in a process of contortion that the straightforward reader is hardly likely to follow.

Reversion to the central relationship between Will and Intelligence raises a crucial issue in Coleridge's moral psychology, where he argues against the positions of necessitarianism that might be thought of as predestinarian. In an important statement of his own faith he contends,

... I maintained, that a Will conceived separate from Intelligence is a Non-entity, and a mere Phantasm of Abstraction; and that a Will not *free* is an absolute contradiction. It might be an Instinct, an Impulse, a plastic Power, and if accompanied with Consciousness, a desire; but a Will it *could* not be; and this *every* Human Being *knows* with equal *clearness*, though different minds may *reflect* on it with different degrees of *distinctness*; for who would not smile at the notion of a Rose *willing* to put forth it's Buds and expand them into Flowers?[37]

The illustration is worth lingering over, including the possible significance of the fact that Coleridge turns to the vegetable world rather than the animal—and to the expansive power of the rose at that. Had he spoken of an animal willing its actions, the illustration might not have appeared so evidently absurd; instead, he turns to the rose for an exemplar of 'an Instinct, an Impulse, a plastic Power'.

He concluded, finally, (in words no doubt intended to realign him with traditional religious attitudes) that the human will,

though diseased, is yet free, and being at the same time an intelligence, must be capable of being acted upon by different forms of intelligence; that the opposite assertion contradicts the whole Tenor of the Gospel, which informs us not simply, that Christ brought Immortality into the World, but LIGHT and Immortality; and by a mystery awfully significant, attributes in the divine Economy the *origination* and *peculiar* office of Redemption to the WORD, or *intelligential* Wisdom, which from all Eternity is with God and is God. I utterly disclaimed the idea, that any *human* Intelligence, with whatever power it

---

[37] *CF* (1809) 333 (cf. *CFriend* II 280).

might manifest itself, was *alone* adequate to the office of restoring health to the Will; but at the same time I held it impious and absurd to hold, that the Creator would have *given* us the faculty of Reason, or that the Redeemer would in so many varied forms of Argument and Persuasion have *appealed* to it, if it had been either totally useless or wholly impotent.[38]

In this way Coleridge tried to reconcile the power of human Reason with that of the will, invoking arguments that could find a sympathetic audience among the Christian faithful. One of the most thoughtful and penetrating critiques of the 1809 *Friend*, indeed, was written by John Foster, a Baptist minister and litterateur who lived near Bristol at the time and must have known Coleridge by reputation even if he never managed to meet him.[39] In a long review of the volume in the *Eclectic Review* for September 1811 he dwelt on Coleridge's relationship to nature:

... we will confess that this author, beyond any other (Mr Wordsworth is next), gives us the impression, or call it the fancy, of a mind constructed to bear a certain indescribable analogy to nature—that is to the physical world, with its wide extent, its elements, its mysterious laws, its animated forms, and its variety and vicissitude of appearances. His mind lives almost habitually in a state of profound sympathy with nature, maintained through the medium of a refined illusion of genius, which informs all nature with a kind of soul and sentiment, that brings all its forms and entities, animate and inanimate, visible and invisible, into a mystical communion with his feelings. This sympathy is, or involves, an exceedingly different feeling from that with which a strictly philosophical mind perceives and admires in nature the more definable attributes of variety, order, beauty and grandeur. These are acknowledged with a vivid perception; but, in our author's powerful imagination, they become a kind of moral attributes of a half-intelligential principle, which dimly, but with mysterious attraction, discloses itself from within all matter and form. This sympathy has retained him much more effectually in what may be called the school of nature, than is usual to men of genius who enter so much into artificial society, and so extensively study the works of men. And the influences of this school have given that form to his habits of thinking which bear so many marks of analogy to the state of surrounding physical nature. To illustrate this we may observe, that he perpetually falls on analogies between moral truth and facts of nature.[40]

---

[38] *CF* (1809) 334 (cf. *CFriend* II 280–1).

[39] See *The Life and Correspondence of John Foster*, ed. J. E. Ryland, *With notices of Mr. Foster as a preacher and a companion*, by John Sheppard (2 vols., London: Jackson & Walford, 1848).

[40] John Foster, review in *Eclectic Review* (1811) VII 912–31: *CH* I 99–100.

To have read *The Friend* in 1810 in this way was to have grasped how it fulfilled the kernel of Coleridge's aspirations hitherto; but it was also to glimpse the fault-line that would be more evident in his later thinking—reflecting a suspicion that 'facts of nature' might after all obstinately refuse to cohere with what was required from them by the demands of 'moral truth'.

The esotericism in Coleridge's thinking as it had now developed was in fact crystallizing into an assurance that human beings must learn to rely on the kind of certainty that could derive only from a sublime intuition. The process had involved increasing exacerbation of the tension between his stern devotion to 'principle' and the free play of mind that could explore new ideas by sporting with the esoteric. The tension thus created could be relieved only by cultivating his critical powers still further.

11

The Poet as Critic, Critic as Poet

The judgement that Coleridge was the most important English critic of his age is, in the end, hard to resist; yet the one major critical book published in his lifetime, *Biographia Literaria*, is digressive and unpredictable in arrangement. Beyond that we have sets of lectures and essays published after his death, together with critical judgments scattered in short essays, notebooks, marginal comments, recorded conversations, and letters. Leading ideas and central passages can be located, seminal thoughts traced; yet it remains the case that a reader coming to Coleridge for the first time may be bewildered.

Faced with this situation it may be better to approach *Biographia Literaria* more obliquely, reading it less as a kind of autobiography than as a document calling for genetic criticism. Through the progress of Coleridge's critical statements during his early years it is possible to detect certain contradictory strains, exhibiting more clearly the nature of that brilliant but strangely riven document.

The characteristics of Coleridge's mind early disclosed themselves as ill attuned to those of the immediately preceding period, with its taste for large schematizations. By comparison with the underlying single-mindedness encouraged by such a search, his psyche was shifting and versatile, developing different kinds of discourse in correspondence with strains in his own psyche.

He had both predecessors and heirs, of course. One can already trace something of the kind in Johnson's habit of blending discourses of nature with those of morality. Later, Matthew Arnold would develop this mode further, mingling Hellenistic and Hebraistic values. There is no great problem here, since the nature of such discourses is easy to discern. With Coleridge, however, the tendency to move between their various kinds means that those who are looking for some uniting singleness may soon find themselves in difficulties. It is not simply a matter of two or three clearly defined and clearly understood lines of thought that can be traced throughout a writing that has its own homogeneity. In Coleridge the inter-running of discourses formed a mode of writing so deep as not always to be fully under his own control. His main aim was to bring everything he had to say into a single harmonized pattern, and while he was remarkably good at this in local instances, an element of *legerdemain*, or of uneasiness, can sometimes be detected—as if he were already aware of fissures opening in what he was trying to bring together. A suggestion that had been shadowed in the passage about the Hebrew poets also emerges more clearly into the light of day when Imagination, viewed as the modifying power, is contemplated and something of the process in the Divine creation itself is glimpsed.

Meanwhile, a rift opened out in the relationship with Wordsworth, corresponding to a suspicion that his idol might after all have feet of clay. As Coleridge's devotion to nature became less prominent, the impulse to poetry gave way to a concern with literary criticism; and for several years after this his chief critical—indeed literary—activity would be the giving of lectures—some the fruit of a growing delight in Shakespeare. Important and illuminating comments developed Johnson's view of the latter as a poet of nature, the sphere of Coleridge's activity being now extended to the element of nature found in the human consciousness. An important factor, also, was the emergence of further criticism relating to the role of imagination and the workings of the 'one Life'. Throughout the period, as Coleridge had been working on literary criticism, A. W. Schlegel had been developing his own positions in different European universities, giving the Romantic Movement in Germany an intellectual basis. An important element in his contribution had been to give centrality to the concept of organic life. Coleridge took a deep interest in what he had to say—modified, however, by the fact that the concept of 'the one Life', by which his own criticism had already been deeply affected, was in many ways subtler. Whereas the German critics thought of the organic basically in terms of growing organic form, their basic conception being that of a vegetable, unfolding itself according to the inward image already existing in its seed, Coleridge's view went further. Organic life was also characterized by the play of energies; if one were thinking of art in those terms, therefore, one should think in terms of energies as well as of forms. Nor were they to be treated in a simple fashion, since they had passive as well as active modes—a fact which applied also to the responding mind. Finally, following the intuition already mentioned, he believed that if the mind was allowed to submit itself in passivity not to the external world but to its own powers it would discover in its depths a secret creativity which would reveal something of the divine. One of his main keys for unlocking Shakespeare, was therefore at once his masterstroke and his point of vulnerability, for orthodox theological tradition was always likely to reject, as overweening arrogance, too ready an identification between the creativity of human beings and that of God.

The comprehensiveness and subtlety of Coleridge's thinking, and its vulnerability, are thus equally apparent. On the one hand he had produced a form of organic thinking which was intricate in its approach, allowing for energies both passive and active. In the process of doing so he had given it a beguilingly human reference by binding it back to basic activities such as the indrawing and expelling of air—the act of breathing, or the systole and diastole inherent in every heartbeat, or the necessary interchange between waking and sleep. At the same time, moreover, by being drawn into unity, this whole could be made revelatory of the larger divine process.

In more sober moments it might appear a grand fantasy rather than a system by which human beings could hope to live; and this was particularly likely to be the case when he went on to bring everything back into the Christian tradition. In his own states of guilt, indeed, identification of the artistic process with the workings of God could appear blasphemous. Yet the concatenation of ideas remained engaging, strangely compelling in its hint of answering to many basic human needs.

Coleridge's quarrel with Wordsworth in 1810 had been patched up; but it was followed by other wounding blows when Wordsworth produced the 1815 edition of his poems, where he saw fit to add a preface in which, describing the Imagination as the power which 'draws all things to one', he ascribed the view to one of his 'more esteemed friends'—the 'friend' being not, as one might have expected, Coleridge himself but Charles Lamb.[1] In his supplementary essay, similarly, he paid tribute to the Germans for having awakened his own countrymen to the understanding of Shakespeare,[2] making no reference to the fact that Coleridge had spent the past seven years trying to do just that. It was this slighting of his achievements which no doubt persuaded

---

[1] *WPrW* III 34.   [2] Ibid., III 69.

Coleridge that he must express his own view—and in the process try to probe differences between himself and his old friend which he had already sensed some years before. So it was that a projected preliminary essay to the new edition of his own poems turned first into an 'Auto-biographia literaria' and then into *Biographia Literaria*.[3]

The existence of varying powers in the consciousness throws light on various of the phenomenon which Coleridge describes in the *Biographia*, such as his postulation of 'that willing suspension of disbelief for the moment, which constitutes poetic faith'.[4] If such a process is to be supposed, there must be a level at which it can take place; the existence of two levels of consciousness allows for a condition in which the powers associated with primary consciousness can have a greater sway, while the checking and inhibiting functions of the secondary when engaged with the objective world are held in abeyance.

The supposition that he held such a theory also helps elucidate Coleridge's theory of 'commanding' and 'absolute' genius. Men of absolute genius, resting content 'between thought and reality, as it were in an intermundium of which their own living spirit supplies the substance, and their imagination the ever-varying form', can be seen to draw on the full power of their primary imagination, the interaction between that and the secondary 'living spirit' being totally self-satisfy-ing; men of commanding genius, on the other hand, 'must impress their preconceptions on the world without, in order to present them back to their own view with the satisfying degree of clearness, distinctness and individuality'.[5] Their energies, having no rootedness in primary vision, will be rather like bees seeking a place to swarm;[6] the effects of their labours, accordingly, will be determined by the spirit of the times, either finding expression in the construction of great works or, in times of tumult, coming forward as the shaping spirit of ruin.

The levels of consciousness described here can also link very naturally with the processes of the organic and the vital as they operate in the natural world. When the primary Imagination is held to be 'the living Power and prime Agent of all human Perception',[7] it resembles the mysterious power in the organism which unfolds it according to its

---

[3] See the Editor's Introduction to *CBL*. A more concise account may be found in *CL* IV 578–9 and nn.

[4] *CBL* II 6 (chapter 14).   [5] Ibid., I 31–3.

[6] Note the mention of bees on the previous page (ibid., p. 30).

[7] *CBL* I 304 (chapter 13).

preordained form. The secondary imagination, by contrast, is essentially a mode of energy: 'It dissolves, diffuses, dissipates, in order to recreate; or where this process is rendered impossible, yet still at all events it struggles to idealize and unify.' As Coleridge also put it, 'It is essentially vital, even as all objects (as objects) are essentially fixed and dead.'[8]

Such statements can apply to the processes of artistic creation in more than one way. They also throw light on the question how far Coleridge's early literary theories could properly be described as 'organic' and how much truth (if any) there is in his assertion that his views of Shakespeare had been thought out long before he could have read Schlegel—indeed, before he went to Germany. He remained stubborn in this asseveration and was particularly hurt when Wordsworth, in his 'Essay Supplementary' of 1815, praised the Germans for their originality in appreciating Shakespeare's genius. Norman Fruman believes that Wordsworth's comment must have been intended as a deliberate slight to Coleridge and that when he and Hazlitt made such statements they were quite specifically denying his priority.[9] But in the *Biographia* he also points out in some puzzlement that Coleridge had already, two years before, conceded a priority to the Germans:

It was Lessing who first introduced the name and the works of Shakespeare to the admiration of the Germans, and I should not perhaps go too far, if I add, that it was Lessing who first proved to all thinking men, even to Shakespeare's own countrymen, the true nature of his apparent irregularities. He proved that in all the essentials of art, no less than in the truth of nature, the plays of Shakespeare were incomparably more coincident with the principles of Aristotle, than the productions of Corneille and Racine, notwithstanding the boasted regularity of the latter.

This Fruman describes as 'a passage which for all time must baffle any student of Coleridge' since if true 'it would render almost meaningless the very questions of priority between himself and Schlegel'.[10]

Although the statement is indeed surprising, it is 'baffling' only if we assume that the question of organic form was, for Coleridge himself, central in the manner familiar in Germany. It is, however, possible to pursue a different possibility. One of the points made by those who urge total plagiarism on Coleridge's part is that when the term 'organic' was

---

[8] Ibid.
[9] Norman Fruman, *Coleridge: The Damaged Archangel* (Scranton, Penn.: George Braziller, 1971), pp. 149–51.
[10] Ibid., 149.

used before 1808 it was in a context of physiology, not art.[11] This, however, is a blinkered view, since the organic concept is after all an analogy relating art directly to questions concerning natural phenomena. Since it asserts that the laws of art are consistent with those of nature, physiology can hardly be irrelevant—least of all for a writer such as Coleridge, whose mind characteristically made such connections.

Many of the dogmatic statements that are made about the question of 'plagiarism' are in fact assisted by the modern tendency to consider intellectual statements so far as possible in separate compartments. When the question of organic form is raised in terms of art, it is natural to turn to Coleridge's critical writings, where there is indeed little to suggest that he was thinking in exactly the same terms as Schlegel before 1810. Meanwhile, however, other critics, in other places, may be working on Coleridge's vitalistic theory, including his formula that 'Each thing has a Life of it's own, & that we are all one Life', but treating them as statements restricted to nature—even though in one instance the sentence is used about 'the Hebrew poets'.[12] Because the two spheres of discourse are not brought together, the fullness of Coleridge's position is missed: sources for his statements about organic form are looked for in his German contemporaries, but the fact that he was thinking hard about the nature of life, and that this might have had its own part to play in developing his ideas about art, is ignored. Instead of poring again over the statements of his that were either clearly or possibly influenced by Schlegel, it is better to examine the question from a different point of view, asking whether Coleridge did not develop a view of art that was founded in his thinking about the nature of life itself.

Before grappling with the matters implicit in Wordsworth's corresponding essay, Coleridge tried to tease out his own views on the question of the Imagination. He was well aware of the danger that he might seem to be supporting a pantheistic view. In consequence, he found himself driven to the desperate expedient of appropriating, with a little rewriting, large chunks of Schelling on the subject, and then cutting across the whole problem by reporting the receipt of a letter (written, he later acknowledged, entirely by himself[13]), dissuading him from continuing the enterprise and advising him to save the subject for another work. He then moved into the gnomic vein, setting down his

---

[11] Norman Fruman, *Coleridge: The Damaged Archangel* (Scranton, Penn.: George Braziller, 1971), 206.
[12] Letter to Sotheby, 10 September 1802: *CL* II 866.
[13] See *CBL* II vii, citing a letter to Curtis, *CL* IV 728.

own version of the Imagination, in which he characterized the two versions as primary or secondary, distinguishing both from 'Fancy'.

These paragraphs have probably engendered more subsequent discussion among critics than any others that Coleridge wrote. They have been defended and praised as a kind of bedrock upon which a defence of the role of the imagination can be mounted; they have also—more often, perhaps—been attacked as offering distinction without difference. Many have been baffled by the attempt to separate two powers, imagination and fancy, which strike them as more or less synonymous; they have found themselves still more bewildered when the imagination itself is divided into two further areas, of which the 'secondary' seems to correspond most recognizably with what many artists would normally think of themselves as primary.

The very terms in which these distinctions are presented—'like those of a royal proclamation', Hugh Sykes Davies once said—assist the sense that Coleridge's categories are presented as if they heralded a final judgment on literature. Discussion of the passage has not been helped, either, by the fact that many critics have followed I. A. Richards in taking Primary Imagination (described as 'the living Power and prime Agent of all human Perception') to be something very homely, to be equated with normal perception: 'the world of motor-buses, beef-steaks, and acquaintances, the framework of things and events within which we maintain our everyday existence'.[14] If we regard it simply in these terms we shall indeed have some difficulty in distinguishing it from the Fancy. And Coleridge cannot altogether be exempted from responsibility for such readings. He does indeed make the secondary Imagination the active and vital power, but it was crucial to his view of the matter that the energies of the mind were in their operation both active and passive. If the imagination allowed itself to become simply passive to the external world it would indeed enter the realm of Fancy, where it would have nothing to play with but the dead counters of objects; if, on the other hand, it attended to its own subconscious powers it would, he trusted, find itself in correspondence with the true sources of creativity. When Coleridge speaks of the primary imagination as the 'prime Agent of all human Perception' his reference is to the level of creative activity at which the artist allows the shaping power of imagination to take over. At that point, he believes, the artist is, however minimally, in

---

[14] *Coleridge on Imagination* (2nd edn., London: Routledge & Kegan Paul, 1950), p. 58.

touch with the creative powers of the divine—repeating in the finite mind 'the eternal act of creation in the infinite I AM'.[15]

Once he had set forward this gnomic formulation he could feel free to judge Wordsworth's achievement, suggesting where he fulfilled it and where he fell short. Shrewdly, he located the core of their difference in certain particular words of the Preface:

A selection of the REAL language of men.

objecting to an equivocation in the use of the word 'real' and arguing that for 'real' one ought to substitute the word 'ordinary'—referring to the concept of lingua communis that must have been in Wordsworth's mind. He then went on to query the wisdom of his friend in adding to 'real' the words 'in a state of excitement'—which he felt simply darkened counsel. If for Coleridge's purposes the word 'real' meant 'ordinary' this justified his then drawing attention to the fact that 'ordinary speech' could be of many kinds, so that praise of it should not be confined to the speech of those who by rural employment were constantly in touch with objects of the natural world. But for Wordsworth himself, in any case, it had meant something different. He had not written 'in a state of excitement', but 'in a state of vivid sensation'.[16] Other writings of his make it clear that he was not simply praising ordinary usage at the expense of artificial diction (as many of his followers, accepting Coleridge's discussion, would feel encouraged to think) but was praising language that sprang from deep and real feeling, so that a starving woman saying (apparently nonsensically), 'That waggon does not care for us' or another, who had lost her baby, repeating continually the words 'O misery' were actually speaking a truer language than that of ordinary acceptable civilized discourse, being truly 'in a state of vivid sensation'. When Coleridge said, in 1803, 'Wordsworth's words always mean the whole of their possible Meaning',[17] he was, perhaps, speaking better than he knew; in any case, however, it is in this sense of 'the real language of men' that Wordsworth's own contributions should be read. Coleridge meanwhile continued to explore the question of the subconscious powers themselves, as in the chapter on metre; ending the book with its 'act of inward Adoration to the great I AM and to the filial WORD...whose choral Echo is the Universe'.[18] It was suggested

---

[15] *CBL* I 304 (chapter 13).   [16] *WPrW* I 119.
[17] Letter to Southey, 14 August 1803: *CL* II 976.
[18] *CBL* II 247–8 (chapter 24).

earlier that as Coleridge's most compressed statements of the years up to 1808 are examined, many can be seen to contain a germinal point, to find fuller expression in the next. But there is also a counter process at work, foreshadowed as early as 'The Eolian Harp', by which the poet feels the whole creative process to be under divine judgement and invokes divine mercy. Despite the creative burst that enabled him to complete *Biographia Literaria* rapidly this is true also of his later work, so that some years later, according to Sara Coleridge, he even went so far as to strike out from one copy the passage about the 'infinite I AM'.[19] For the same reason his critical powers turned increasingly to religious questions and the Bible. The development is by no means to be disprized. The idea that Coleridge may also have felt himself to be under judgement does not, in the end, indicate weakness. It may have inhibited him from developing some of his critical insights to the extent that some readers would like, but it also showed another aspect of his awareness— that of his existence as a human being in a universe that was, in the end, riddling and mysterious.

The levels of consciousness described here can also link very naturally with the processes of the organic and the vital as they operate in the natural world. When the primary Imagination is held to be 'the living Power and prime Agent of all human Perception',[20] it is pre-eminently the mysterious power in the organism that unfolds it according to its preordained form. The secondary imagination, by contrast, is especially a mode of energy: 'It dissolves, diffuses, dissipates, in order to recreate; or where this process is rendered impossible, yet still at all events it struggles to idealize and unify.'[21] As Coleridge himself puts it, 'It is essentially vital, even as all objects (as objects) are essentially fixed and dead.'[22]

This can be applied to the processes of artistic creation in more than one way. The work of art may be seen as gaining in power when the unified object which the artist sets before his or her audience is redolent also of vital energies. Coleridge presents an example of his own when he draws attention to the difference between the effect produced by the lines

> Behold yon row of pines, that shorn and bow'd
> Bend from the sea-blast, seen at twilight eve.

and the same lines when revised to read

---

[19] See her edition of *Biographia Literaria* [1817]: *CBL* (1847) I 297n.
[20] *CBL* I 304 (chapter 13).   [21] Ibid.   [22] Ibid.

> Yon row of bleak and visionary pines,
> By twilight-glimpse discerned, mark! how they flee
> From the fierce sea-blast, all their tresses wild
> Streaming before them.[23]

There are various means by which such effects may be achieved, ranging from the presentation of a plot (as for example that of *The Rime of the Ancient Mariner*) in which the interplay is constantly present, to the employment of certain rhythmic techniques (the likening of the work of metre in poetry to that of wine in animated conversation,[24] for example). It can further be urged that the mind of the artist should itself exhibit such a working together of the two principles. Coleridge's use of the water-insect, 'winning' its way upstream, to illustrate the alternation between passive and active powers in creativity, points the way: in such a case the artist's mind works alternately through direct action and passive submission to a higher, subconscious power.[25] Coleridge's conception of the artist as needing certain kinds of beneficent stimulation if creation is to be successful ('I could write as good verses now as ever I did, if I were perfectly free from vexations and were in the ad libitum hearing of fine music . . .'[26]) follows a similar pattern: it reaches an early culmination in *Kubla Khan*, with the man of absolute genius building his dome in air to the sound of 'symphony and song'.

Coleridge's sense of the work of artistic energies links above all with his interest in manifestations of 'genial' powers. The interplay of the organic and the vital is seen to be essential in the production of beautiful forms, whether in nature or in works of art. Coleridge's interest in the co-operation between musical energies and the elaboration of artistic form coloured his aim to 'elevate the imagination & set the affections in right tune by the beauty of the inanimate impregnated, as with a living soul, by the presence of life'—a formula which included direct quotation from Milton;[27] it added also, presumably, to his delight in Milton's sardonic creation of Pandaemonium, that 'Fabrick huge', which rose out of the earth 'like an Exhalation, with the sound | Of Dulcet

---

[23] *CBL* II 23 (chapter 15).   [24] Ibid., II 66 (chapter 18).
[25] Ibid., I 124, II 66 (chapters 7 and 18).
[26] Table Talk, 1 July 1833: *CTT* I 409.
[27] Letter to George Coleridge, 10 March 1798: *CL* I 397. 'Set the affections in right tune' is from *The Reason of Church Government*, ii, preface (identified by J. S. Hill).

Symphonies and voices sweet.'[28] The role of Satan's energies in making him attractive to the reader could be seen as an allegorization of the secondary powers when detached from the primary: Satan and his like must forever be involved in fruitless acts of creation, reflecting their subconscious desire for reunion with the unifying and vivifying primary power that had been forfeited by their revolt against the heavenly order.[29]

The production of *Biographia Literaria* was part of the process of self-rehabilitation that Coleridge set in motion following the period of crisis at Bath and Bristol in 1813–14, which also included his decision to put together a new edition of his poems, to be called *Sibylline Leaves*. The very title indicates something of the defensive manner in which he now addressed the public. He had evidently been disturbed and distressed by slighting references to his work that continued to appear in the public presses. He tended to exaggerate the extent of these, ignoring the favourable references, but his reaction reflects the degree of his exposure. For many years he had resisted the prospect of settling down into a professional career that might have offered financial security. At the back of his mind there was always the sense of being called to a destiny that demanded his independence. Yet his personality called for some stability in which to anchor itself. For ten years his belief in Wordsworth's genius had given him something of what he was looking for. It was not simply that he could feel his efforts to create a philosophy for the age strengthened by the awareness of Wordsworth labouring in his vicinity; the two enterprises could be felt to be complementary. Wordsworth's *Prelude* and his own 'Logosophia' could be regarded as mutually supportive enterprises.

Biographia Literaria and *The Prelude* were not, however, works of the same kind. *The Prelude* was in many respects a self-justifying work: validating its account of Wordsworth's growth as a poet it was itself a fine poem. The *Biographia* could not hope to emulate it, though Coleridge may well have hoped for it a propaedeutic function, preparing readers for the fuller presentation of his thought that might eventually be found in the 'Opus Maximum', once that was ready.

---

[28] *Paradise Lost*, i, 688–730. Another part of this description is quoted in CNB 26 f 74ᵛ (cf. *CN* IV 5395). See also my *Coleridge the Visionary* (London: Chatto and Windus, 1959), pp. 223–4.

[29] Cf. the traditional fate of the descendants of Cain: ibid., pp. 118–23.

As he worked on it, however, the *Biographia* came to express less the march towards such a conclusion than a laying out of his fuller personality, with all its tensions and contradictions. As was mentioned earlier, his mind although logical, could be brought into the service of contrary impulses—even if he was sometimes unable to recognize that in other circumstances he might have behaved differently. He laughed at this tendency in himself in the *Biographia* itself, recalling how, at an evening gathering in the course of a tour to publicize his journal *The Watchman*, he had replied to the question 'Have you seen a paper to day, Mr Coleridge?' with the words 'I am far from convinced, that a Christian is permitted to read either newspapers or any other works of merely political and temporary interest.'[30]

This element of comic play had its own part to play in the work. It has been noticed by more than one critic that the title-page, with its secondary title, Biographical Sketches of my Literary Life and Opinions, carries a distinct echo of Sterne's *Life and Opinions of Tristram Shandy, Gent.* The general lack of organization, with its chronological framework playing host to numerous disquisitions, bears more than a passing resemblance to Sterne's negligent treatment of chronology. The most striking similarity, however, comes in the author's attitude to central events. The actual birth of Tristram somehow eludes attention; in the same way, the most crucial aspects of Coleridge's career, the growth and subsequent decline in his personal relationship to Wordsworth from 1798 onwards, and the fate of his love for Sara Hutchinson, are neglected in the narrative as a whole, which instead circles round and round the *annus mirabilis*, leaving space only for the German trip immediately afterwards and for passing references to his stay in Rome. The other events mentioned were crucial to his life in the first decade of the century, and the fact that they are not touched upon at all suggests their traumatic status. Although an understanding of them is crucial to that of his total life during those years, it seems as if he cannot bear to think about them directly.

This bears on another facet of the book. As is well known, I. A. Richards derived his influential concept of 'practical criticism' from Coleridge's use of the phrase at the start of chapter 15 in the *Biographia*; and his subsequent examination of Wordsworth's verses is often thought to exemplify the ideal of that practice. Yet if one were to read

[30]   *CBL* I 183: chapter 10.

those chapters innocent of the biographical facts behind them one might well come to believe that the main poems described had been written away from Coleridge and after the time of their collaboration. The fact that he was just as active then as before throws an interesting light on his critical comments. Either voluntarily or involuntarily he clears his mind of his accumulated knowledge concerning these poems and thus achieves an effect as if he were reading and criticizing them for the first time. This, we are told, is a model of the effect at which all practical criticism should aim, but some account ought also to be taken of the fact that Coleridge's treatment here is, as a result, highly artificial.

At other times, however, particularly when he was less constricted by memories of the immediate past, he would show his mastery of the critical mode. His sense of the positive gain to be derived from 'hovering between images', for example, marked a distinct advance on the view of Burke, who had stressed the advantage of words over visual images, in offering the chance to enhance passionate effects through skilful use of combinations, but still found some difficulty in differentiating between the effects available to 'strong' and 'weak' language.

Coleridge's own poetry, meanwhile, took a different turn, with the exploration of sensibility no longer his primary theme. In his new, critical frame of mind, John Donne came to the fore. As long ago as 1796 he had planned, among various projects, to write satires in his manner.[31] Now, his mind sapped by disillusion, Donne's wit seemed more attractive than before. He scribbled in a copy of Chalmers's *Poets* lines dwelling on what he now found most attractive:

> With Donne, whose muse on dromedary trots,
> Wreathe iron pokers into true-love knots;
> Rhyme's sturdy cripple, fancy's maze and clue,
> Wit's forge and fire-blast, meaning's press and screw.[32]

The compelling poetic power of Donne by no means meant that Wordsworth's poetry must be abandoned, however; indeed, he might have found a notable link between his friend's 'She was a phantom of delight...' and the first stanza of 'Air and Angels'. From his seventeenth century hero, however, he could borrow imagery for a vision of negativity unknown to the contented Wordsworth, in which, for example, souls might be annihilated through the administration of pulverized fleas:

---

[31] CNB G f 23ᵛ (cf. *CN* I 171).   [32] *CM* II 16.

Even now it shrinks them! they shrink in, as Moles
(Nature's mute Monks, live Mandrakes of the ground)
Creep back from Light, then listen for its Sound—
See but to dread, and dread they know not why
The natural Alien of their negative Eye.[33]

Coleridge could also write, as has already been mentioned, eloquent expressions of despair, coupled with verses querying the validity of visionary experiences in the service of love. If he could not easily resume love poetry as such he could experiment with the poetry of negativity, inspired not only by a poem like 'The Flea', but by Donne's successful explorations of loss, as in 'A Nocturnal upon St. Lucy's Day'. If such poems seemed to begin unrelentingly in the negative mode, the very wittiness of their wordplay set up a tribute to positivity—or even, if only by contrast, succeeded in suggesting the positiveness that was being denied. Despite his devotion to poets such as Butler, Pope, Congreve and Sheridan, Donne remained for him the embodiment of true wit:

Wonder-exciting vigour, intensity and peculiarity of thought, using at will the almost boundless stores of a capacious memory, and exercised on subjects, where we have no right to expect it—this is the wit of Donne![34]

It must also have nursed, on occasion, a nostalgia necessarily to have haunted someone who in his youth had shown such intellectual power that his friend Charles Lamb, thinking about his promise in retrospect, could find no other words to describe it than those which, according to Izaak Walton, had been reported of the young John Donne himself: 'That this age had brought forth another Picus Mirandula'.[35]

---

[33] CNB 18 f 146 (cf. *CN* III 4073).   [34] *CM* II 17.
[35] See Izaak Walton's account of the young Donne in his *Life* (London: John Major, 1825, p. 4) and Lamb's account of Coleridge as 'the young Mirandula' in his essay for *Elia*, 'Christ's Hospital Five and Thirty Years Ago'.

12

Shakespeare's Plays of Passion

As Coleridge's uncertainties about his own intellectual position made him less and less able to contemplate the creation of great poetry, he was increasingly drawn to critical engagement with the achievements of others, especially Shakespeare, who—without providing a good template for a view of the world that he might accept—seemed frequently to provide nourishment for his psychological speculations by way of telling illustrations from human nature.

His valuation had risen with the years. In 1797, for example, he had been set a little lower than Wordsworth, whom he praised for 'profound touches of the human heart, which I find three or four times in "The Robbers" of Schiller, & often in Shakespeare—but in Wordsworth there are no inequalities'. In the following year came his somewhat baffling remark to Hazlitt that Shakespeare was a 'stripling in the art' who if he had come to man's estate would have been a monster.[1] If correctly reported, this may have indicated a suggestion that Shakespeare's gifts were those of an immature genius, compared with the fully responsible vision of a Milton or a Wordsworth.

The remark, however, ought to be read in conjunction with some comments by Hazlitt a few years later during a discussion at Charles Lamb's house, on 27 November 1811, during which John Payne Collier took some notes. Hazlitt reportedly claimed on this occasion that Coleridge was not competent to lecture on Shakespeare, since he was not well read in his work:

He knew little more than was in the Elegant Extracts & Hazlitt himself had told him of many beautiful passages that Coleridge had never before heard of. It was owing to this ignorance that Coleridge had not yet exemplified any of his positions by quoting passages—and he doubted if he ever would.[2]

---

[1] 'My First Acquaintance with Poets', *HW* XVII.   [2] *CLects (1808–1818)* I 233.

The editor at this point simply notes this as an 'insulting remark', the unspoken implication being, given the elementary nature of Vicesimus Knox's *Elegant Extracts*, that this was simply a typically bad-tempered assertion. Hazlitt was not denying, however, that Coleridge held certain positions in relation to Shakespeare. On the same occasion he actually spoke warmly of his knowledge of Milton, while according to Coleridge he had on another (and in spite of his known *animus*) defended him against the charge of plagiarism from Schlegel, saying 'That must be a Lie: for I myself heard Coleridge give the very same theory before he went to Germany and when he did not even understand a word of German.'[3]

It is worth considering, therefore, whether his reported comment on Coleridge's lack of familiarity with Shakespeare's plays might not have contained a limited truth. Hazlitt had not, after all, had much recent contact with Coleridge, following his disastrous departure from the Lakes in 1803, while there is no evidence of Coleridge's having read deeply in Shakespeare earlier, though he evidently read *King Lear* attentively during his Bristol years.[4] If one takes Hazlitt's comments at their face value it becomes possible to think that Coleridge (having been stung at the time, possibly, by Hazlitt's demonstration of superior knowledge) had from that time onwards devoted more time to detailed reading in Shakespeare. Once resident in London, Hazlitt would not have known about this.

In the early years of the decade, certainly, it was more the *idea* of Shakespeare than particular texts of his that preoccupied him. By 1802 he could value Shakespeare at his best for his pure energy, able to pass out of his own living form and inhabit others, a view developed in a letter of July: 'It is easy to cloathe Imaginary Beings with our own Thoughts & feelings; but to send ourselves out of ourselves, to think ourselves into the Thoughts and Feelings of Beings in circumstances wholly & strangely different from our own / hoc labor, hoc opus / and who has atchieved it? Perhaps only Shakespere.'[5] In April 1804 he wrote: 'A Shakespeare, a Milton, a Bruno, exist in the mind as *pure* Action, defecated of all that is material & passive'; seven months later he referred to 'the imitation instead of copy which is illustrated in very nature shakespeareanized/—that Proteus Essence that could assume the

[3] *CL* IV 831.   [4] See CNBG ff 15–16 (cf. *CN* I 121–7).
[5] Letter to Sotheby, 13 July 1802: *CL* II 810.

very form, but yet known and felt not to be the Thing by that difference of the Substance which made every atom of the Form another thing'.[6]

Proteus, too, was a monster; but when his image was used again in *Biographia Literaria* it was to praise Shakespeare—who 'darts himself forth, and passes into all the forms of human character and passion, the one proteus of the fire and flood'.[7] This passage comes shortly after one in which (adapting a line from the 1798 'France: An Ode') he characterized original genius as a power to transfer life to images from the poet's own spirit, 'which shoots its being through earth, sea and air'.

His feeling for his predecessor was enhanced by his love for Sara Hutchinson, which was no doubt responsible for his copying into a notebook during his first months in Malta several of the sonnets, including the one that begins 'From you have I been absent in the spring...'. With Shakespeare he could readily identify—particularly in his potential for 'myriad-mindedness'.[8] If it was not a capability that he could altogether trust in himself he could enjoy it all the more in Shakespeare, where he was equally at liberty to exercise moral censure when he felt it to be called for.

Shakespeare, after all, could be thought of as supremely a man of play—in all the connotations of the word—and there are signs that he thought of the word more particularly in connection with the less rational aspects of the psyche. 'All deep Passions a sort of Atheists, that believe no Future—' he wrote, annotating a speech of Romeo's,[9] with an implicit suggestion that intense passion takes human beings beyond rational consciousness—a point further stressed by his analysis of Lear's condition in old age, where the clash between fidelity and ingratitude among those around him has left him 'the open and ample Play-room of Nature's Passions'.[10]

As it happens, events conspired to assist his exploration in more than one direction. When he arrived back in England from Malta, urgently concerned with finding means to support himself, he received an offer from the Royal Institution (probably through the good offices of Humphry Davy, who in 1805 had urged him to lecture there) to give

[6] CNB 15 f 7 and 21 f 59 (cf. *CN* II 2026, 2274).

[7] *CBL* II 27 and n. The image of Shakespeare as a Proteus did not originate with Coleridge: it had been used, for example, by William Richardson: 'He is the Proteus of the drama' (1774) in *Shakespeare: The Critical Heritage*, ed. B. Vickers, VI (1981), 118–19.

[8] Cf. his entries of December 1801 and spring 1808: CNB 21 f 38[v] and 15 f 123[v] (cf. *CN* I 1070, III 3285); also *CBL* II 19.

[9] *CM* IV 834.   [10] Ibid., 820.

lectures on the Principles common to the Fine Arts; after some thought and discussion he accepted. It is indicative of a growing obsession with Shakespeare's works that he spent a good deal of time in the following years reading and annotating them.

Study of Shakespeare enabled him to explore further some of his psychological insights in recent years without having to grapple intensely with oppressive theological matters: he could respond critically without having to make up his mind on moral and religious issues.

The fruits of the intellectual liberation thus experienced can be found in the lecture on *Romeo and Juliet* that he gave a few years later, in which he described how poets working, by shifting words and images, to create newness, 'hover between images'. The purpose may be, as he said, 'to reconcile opposites and qualify contradictions'. This could have the remarkable result of creating unprecedented states of mind—even, perhaps, 'the substitution of a sublime feeling of the unimaginable for a mere image'.[11] This remarkable insight exemplifies Coleridge's skills at mediation, and the positive manner in which he could profit from his own criticism. By such means the mind of the reader might find itself energized into activity of its own.

The lectures were taking place from 1808, but less is known of the first ones and their content than of the later series; this is all the more unfortunate since in the very same year Schlegel delivered his lectures in Vienna. Knowledge of what Coleridge was saying in those years would have made it more possible to compare the views of the two men when expressed independently. The remarks of 1811 just quoted, however, suggest something of what they may have contained, even in their earliest form.

Certainly, the mind that Coleridge brought to Shakespeare was not simply blank and receptive. Apart from the various passages he had found to quote from in his early notebooks, the sonnets had been a particular source of consolation during the early years in Malta. Not only that, but he found the plays a constant source of wisdom—often amazingly condensed and encapsulated. In 1808, for instance, when his love for Sara was under stress, he copied into a notebook lines from *Hamlet,*

> There lives within the very flame of Love
> A kind of wick or Snuff, that will abate it,

commenting:

---

[11]   *CLects (1808–1819)* II 496 (cf. I 311).

Merciful Wonder-making Heaven! What a man was this Shakespear! I know no better epithet than . . . myriad-minded.

The element in his work that seems to have impressed him most was his acute insight into the nature of human passions, always for him an ambiguous subject. His own principles encouraged him to take a moral standpoint, urging that they be subordinated to a rational view, yet he remained fascinated by the matter, particularly when passions—such as the 'involuntary jealousy' mentioned earlier—rose from his own subconscious.

As one puts together the evidences of his thinking about the passions, the 'genial' powers, and the roles of the organic and the vital at the time of his early conversations with Wordsworth, the probability grows that, at the time when Schlegel was beginning to present his idea of 'organic form' in Germany, Coleridge was developing a body of thought concerning the relationship between the organic and the vital—whether in nature, the mind, or art—which was bound to affect his own reading of works from the past. For if the true artist was the one in whom the relationship between organic and vital powers could be seen most successfully at work, whether in the presentation of subject, the organization of the work itself, or the powers of mind exhibited, it would be natural to look for evidences of such interactions in existing great works. The most obvious area for deployment of such theories in criticism lay in the work of Shakespeare, offering opportunities at all levels. Defending himself later against the charge of plagiarism he called in evidence his lectures of 1808, when he could not have known Schlegel's lectures, appealing to 'the most adequate judges'[12]—though it is not clear how many of these attended the lectures of 1808. In particular, he turned to three individuals: firstly to Sir George Beaumont, especially in connection with *Hamlet*: '*Hamlet* was the Play, or rather Hamlet himself was the Character, in the intuition and exposition of which I first made my turn for philosophical criticism, and especially for insight into the genius of Shakespear, noticed, first among my Acquaintances, as Sir G. Beaumont will bear witness . . .'.[13] He also invoked Wordsworth at this point, though without further details, and then Hazlitt, whose indignant rebuttal of the charge that he plagiarized from Schlegel has already been quoted.

---

[12] Letter to William Mudford, 18 February 1818, *CL* IV 839.
[13] *CM* IV 836, note of 7 January 1819. Cf. *CLects (1808–1819)* II 293.

Coleridge protested that he had applied his own philosophical ideas to the study of Shakespeare, at least so far as the character of Hamlet was concerned, as early as 1798, in the hearing of Hazlitt, and that he continued to develop his analyses with Wordsworth, being heard this time by Sir George Beaumont. There is evidence to support the latter claim in a letter to Beaumont about his plans for work on Shakespeare and his contemporaries in February 1804: 'Thus I shall both exhibit the characteristics of the Plays—& of the mind—of Shakespere—and of almost every character at greater or less Length a philosophical Analysis & Justification, in the spirit of that analysis of the character of Hamlet, with which you were much pleased, and by being so, I solemnly assure, gave me Heart & Hope....'.[14]

Hamlet, Lear, Othello, and *Romeo and Juliet* were named by Coleridge in 1797 as the most popular tragedies of Shakespeare, but it is likely that his early conversations with Wordsworth included also discussion of *Macbeth,* a play which both poets had already quoted in their writings.[15] For men who had turned aside from direct political writings to the contemplation of human motives and the composition of dramas, *Macbeth* was an obvious topic, since the issues of violence that had bedevilled the French Revolution were adumbrated with admirable clarity in a plot where one act of violence engendered another in succession, each being necessary to reinforce the previous one. In terms of the theory outlined above, Macbeth could be seen as a man of unusual energies who had deliberately cut himself off from the resources of his primary imagination (resources which were effortlessly expressed in every gesture of Duncan's). Given that condition it was a logical consequence that the violence of his energies should dominate his actions more and more, leading him into a vortex of destruction, while privately he might mourn his separation from the world of primary natural innocence, discovering that his natural feelings had themselves atrophied. That Wordsworth and Coleridge discussed the significance of the play in such terms is suggested by the fact that both took the unusual locution 'The time has been' (used twice by Macbeth, the second time to suggest the decay of his feelings) to produce their own version, 'There was a time', used first by Coleridge in his poem

---

[14] *CL* II 1054.
[15] *CLects (1795)* 226; Wordsworth, letter to W. Mathews, 7 November 1794, *Letters: The Early Years, 1785–1805,* ed. E. de Selincourt, revd. C. Shaver (Oxford, 1987), p. 135.

'The Mad Monk', along with the line 'If I must live to know that such a time has been', to describe a state of consciousness in which a violent act has engendered an obsession with blood that colours everything around him. It was then taken up by Wordsworth as the opening phrase for a poem describing the decline of his own imaginative powers in a manner which suggests a process deeper than the one through which Macbeth had forfeited his resources of feeling.[16]

The most central comment in this context, however, is Coleridge's: on the lines beginning 'It will have blood', he writes, 'Who by guilt tears himself live-asunder from Nature is himself in a praeternatural state; no wonder, therefore, if inclined to all Superstition & Faith in the praeternatural.'[17] The phrase 'live-asunder' can hardly have been coined casually; the rest of this present sentence gives clues to the possible contents of the Essay on the uses of the Supernatural which Coleridge promised to write as a preface to *The Ancient Mariner*.[18] It implies that by existing as a living being in separation from the powers of nature Macbeth has laid himself at the mercy of the more fearful powers of his own primary consciousness—an implication which may be linked to the account of the Weird Sisters ascribed elsewhere to him by his son-in-law: 'Their character consists in the imaginative disconnected from the good; they are the shadowy obscure and fearfully anomalous of physical nature,—elemental avengers without sex or kin . . .'.[19]

A similar interpretation can be applied to *King Lear*, Lear's condition being that of a great organism which has been uprooted in old age and exposed to the destructive energies of the elements. As elsewhere in Shakespeare, a creature fundamentally innocent (in this case Cordelia) is victim of the violence thus unleashed. One of Coleridge's comments on the play suggests the nature of these energies: 'Lear combines length with rapidity,—like the hurricane and the whirlpool, absorbing while it advances.'[20] (Elsewhere in his work the whirling vortex is an image of energies released freely into destruction.) When he comes to the relationship between Lear and Edmund, Coleridge proposes an opposition between passive and active similar to that already noticed in connection with his primary and secondary imagination: 'From Lear, the persona PATIENS of his Drama, Shakespeare passes without delay to the second in importance, to the Main Agent, and prime Mover—introduces

---

[16] 'Ode: Intimations of Immortality...', *WPW* IV, 279–85.   [17] *CM* IV 729.
[18] *CBL* I 306.   [19] *CShC* I 67n.   [20] Ibid., I 54.

Edmund to our acquaintance.'[21] As in *Paradise Lost*, the order of things has been reversed. Lear, who as king should be exercising over his kingdom a function akin to the agency of the primary imagination in the human mind, has become purely passive and a natural prey for the active Edmund, whose energies, cut off from any roots in ordained society and owing allegiance to nothing except his long-nurtured pride, work in pure destructiveness.

One of Coleridge's late comments on the play shows this body of ideas still at work in his mind, with Lear's madness the product of mental energies that can no longer flow in an onward current: 'In Edgar's ravings Shakespeare all the while lets you see a fixed purpose, a practical end in view;—in Lear's, there is only the brooding of the one anguish, an eddy without progression.'[22] It is particularly interesting, in view of the organic image proposed above for his view of Lear, that the image of great trees should have brought Lear, along with Wordsworth, readily to his mind when he came across it in Drayton:

> . . . our trees so hack'd above the ground,
> That where their lofty tops the neighbouring countries crown'd,
> Their trunks (like aged folks) now bare and naked stand,
> As for revenge to Heaven each held a wither'd hand.[23]

In the case of Othello, Coleridge always insisted on his lack of true jealousy, the real exemplar of that passion being Leontes in *The Winter's Tale*. The Moor was to be seen as truly noble, vulnerable only to the wickedness of Iago. Coleridge's insistence possibly owed something to puzzlement how a love as noble as his own for Sara could have proved susceptible to intervention from his subconscious. Othello could be interpreted another way, however, exemplifying Coleridge's man of 'commanding' genius, who needs to see his power reflected and echoed from without. Othello's nature and status set him quite naturally in that category. Yet his powers are still those of genius, with all its compelling quality: hence his attractiveness to Desdemona as he relates his exploits. His determination to live by the dictates of honour is both his pride and his fate, nevertheless, since it exposes him to the intellectual wiles of Iago. Othello's commanding genius is, at its best, beautifully matched to the sensibility of Desdemona—of whom Coleridge once remarked,

[21] *CM* IV 815 (cf. *CLects (1808–1819)* II 326).
[22] *CShC* I 65 (from *CLR*).
[23] Table Talk, 11 September 1831: *CTT* II 147.

'Every one wishes a Desdemona or Ophelia for a wife—creatures who, though they may not always *understand* you, do always *feel* you, and *feel* with you.'[24] At the point when Othello's toils of jealousy are being exacerbated by Iago's wiles Desdemona enters and immediately his attitude is transformed:

> If she be false, O, then heaven mocks itself!
> I'll not believe it.

Coleridge comments, 'Divine! the effect of innocence & the better genius'.[25]

But this appeal by Desdemona's sensibility to the heart of Othello's genius is to be thwarted by his growing belief that she has betrayed his honour. The agent of this destruction is a being whose energies are almost totally disembodied—hence Coleridge's famous term 'motiveless Malignity'.[26]

In his later writings, Coleridge returned to Iago to consider again the question of the self from which he operated. Interestingly, the old theory of single and double touch was revived. Attacking the idea that the self can be regarded as an object created by our own perceptions, he remarked,

Even the combination of the sense of Touch and more strictly of Double-touch with the visual image of such parts of our body as we are able or accustomed to behold is so far from being the only possible representative of Self that it is not even the first; in the earlier periods of infancy, the mother or the nurse is the Self of the child.[27]

Coleridge's initial reservation invokes the condition of single touch, which in the human being, brings into play primary consciousness, below even the conscious self. In Iago there is no self, only a congeries of energies, lacking relationship to an organic centre. One of Coleridge's comments on him is particularly interesting in this connection: Iago, he writes, could not have uttered the 'To be or not to be...' soliloquy, for it would have suggested 'too habitual a communion with the heart'. He is also at pains to point out, nevertheless, that Iago's fiendishness is never absolute ('In itself fiendish—while yet he was allowed to bear the divine

---

[24] *Table Talk*, 26 September 1830: *CTT* I 208 (cf. II 124).
[25] *CM* IV 868.   [26] *CM* IV 862.
[27] *Op. Max* Fragment I f. 49, cited by E. S. Shaffer, 'Iago's Malignity Motivated: Coleridge's Unpublished "Opus Magnum"', *Shakespeare Quarterly* 19 (1968), 195–203, my main source for these citations (cf. *COM* 30).

image, too fiendish for his own steady View.—A being next to Devil—only not quite Devil'; 'not absolute fiend—at least, he wishes to think himself so'). Only the truly Satanic could be so absolute; Iago, as a human being, exists rather in a state of false choice keeping him from any proper ground of motive, a prey to his own distorted energies:

> now assigning one & now another & again a third motive for his conduct, each a different motive and all alike the mere fictions of his own restless nature, distempered by a keen sense of his own intellectual superiority & a vicious habit of assigning the precedence or primacy to the intellectual instead of the moral; and haunted by the love of exerting power on those especially who are his superiors in moral and practical estimation.[28]

Particularly in his later thinking, then, Coleridge associates the primary and organic with the moral. This can set in motion a contradiction between the workings of the moral and the natural which may be disabling—a point relevant to some of Coleridge's comments on *Hamlet*.

Of all Shakespeare's plays the latter one offers the most fascinating field for the present discussions, since the figure at its centre is close to Coleridge's conception of absolute genius. The description of Hamlet's qualities suggests that in him the highest possibilities of artistic and mental energy combine; yet he also exhibits the corresponding human defects of such a character when called upon for specific action. The relationship between Ophelia and Hamlet is as tragic as that between Desdemona and Othello: in both cases, fine sensibility is destroyed by the powers of genius. Hamlet's intellectual energies, unlike Iago's, are not harnessed to an ignoble aim; he has a 'habitual communion with the heart'. The chief characteristic of his character, nevertheless, is an intellectual energy running to excess.

The various lectures on *Hamlet* give evidence at every point of the further enquiries that could be stimulated by Coleridge's ideas. In the depths of the subconscious extremes meet: emotion generates its opposite by natural recoil and reaction, reflecting the workings of the human heart itself in constant alternation of systole and diastole:

> These complex causes will naturally have produced in Hamlet the disposition to escape from his own feelings of the overwhelming and supernatural by a wild transition to the ludicrous: a sort of cunning bravado, bordering on the flights of delirium.[29]

---

[28] *CM* IV 850, 862, 867; Shaffer, p. 196: I f 57 (cf. *COM* 34).
[29] *CLects (1808–1819)* I 544–5.

The most striking example of the way in which his sense of two modes of consciousness in the human mind might work together, producing a marvellously dramatic and complex effect, is in his analysis of the early scene in *Hamlet* where the ghost is addressed as it appears. The plausibility of this he attributes to the psychological dynamism of the scene following the prince's vivid response to the noise of the feasting:

The knowlege, the *unthought-of* consciousness, the *Sensation*, of human Auditors, of Flesh and Blood Sympathists, act as a support, a stimulation *a tergo*, while the *front* of the Mind, the whole Consciousness of the Speaker, is filled by the solemn Apparition.[30]

A similar use of such preoccupations to throw light on incidental elements in Shakespeare's writing can be found in *Romeo and Juliet*, where the speeches of Mercutio have all the vivacity, the felicity in making unusual connections, that characterize the secondary imagination in the service of Fancy, while the Nurse shows similar powers in decline: the goodness of her heart cannot prevent her associations of ideas from falling into delirium.[31]

One of Coleridge's most cogent and original applications to Shakespeare of his critical principles comes in a passage concerning *Venus and Adonis*. The poetic genius reveals itself there first as a musical power: 'the sense of musical delight with the power of producing it, and the Gift of true Imagination'. As soon as this has been established Coleridge passes to the poetic mind, which, in its apparently impersonal activity, exhibits the energy and vitality of the secondary imagination at its extreme:

as if a superior spirit more intuitive than the Parties themselves not only of every Motion, Look & Act but of every subtle Thought & feeling, the whole flux and reflux of the Mind, were placing the whole before our view.[32]

Coleridge argues further that the very nature of the energetic imagination renders the resulting work immune from the moral censure which might otherwise be incurred:

The reader's Mind & Fancy are forced into too much action to sympathize with the merely *Passive* of our Nature—As little can the mind thus roused & awakened doze and be brooded on by indistinct Passions, as the low lazy Mist can creep upon the surface while a strong Gale is driving the lake on in waves and billows before it—/[33]

---

[30] Ibid., II 299.   [31] Ibid., I 306–7.

[32] CNB M f 27ᵛ(cf. *CN* III 4115). *CLects (1808–1819)* I 241.

[33] CNB M ff 26–7.

Here, as elsewhere, Coleridge's thought reveals its true originality. Schlegel, drawing on his reading of Kant while at the same time relating the work of the artist to that of nature, had based his memorable theory on the simple concept of organic form; Coleridge, meanwhile, bringing to bear a larger body of speculation relating the organic to the vital powers, has introduced greater complexity. Schlegel's treatment of *Romeo and Juliet*, for instance, centred in the sensuous qualities of the nightingale and the rose which furnished Shakespeare's drama with two major images, seeks to epitomize the spirit of spring, locating the energy of the play largely in the action, the unfolding of its single central idea. Coleridge, by contrast, associates the working of energy in the plot itself with particular characters, tracing in it a dialectic between the unfolding of form and the play of energy. Coleridge's spring is not only intoxicating in its odours but sharp with precipitancies, recalling the reader to a version of the organic in which forms and energies are both equally involved.

A passage such as this suggests the extent to which Coleridge was justified in asserting that he too could claim to have been a pioneer in explaining the virtues of Shakespeare in terms of the 'organic'; it also helps to explain why he felt particularly bitter at Wordsworth's omission of his contribution, since Wordsworth above all had been in touch with him at the time when he was elaborating his conceptions of the organic and the vital. Any sense of grievance mingled, nevertheless, with an awareness of having been betrayed by opium, that literally organic means of mental illumination which had at times promised a sense of revelation into the heart of things. He expressed his disillusionment in a mention of the 'dire poison' which, 'for a delusive time', had made 'the body, (i.e. the *organization*, not the articulation (or instruments of motion)) the unknown somewhat, a fitter Instrument for the all-powerful Soul';[34] in another elaboration of the organic image he looked back in disenchantment to a time when he had been 'intoxicated with the vernal fragrance & effluvia from the flowers and first-fruits of Pantheism, unaware of its bitter root'.[35] In such a state Coleridge could no longer delight wholeheartedly in the play of energies and the unfolding of organisms, whether in nature or in Shakespeare's text. He never lost his admiration for Shakespeare, but the focus of his admiration shifted to a more purely 'spiritual' level; writing about the role of the idea in great works of literature many years later he put it as

[34] CNB $21^{1/2}$ f 8^v (cf. *CN* III 3320).
[35] Marginal note to Jacob Boehme, *Works* (London, 1764–81): *CM* I 602.

follows: 'in every *Epos*, that is the Work of Genius, there is an IDEA, that is at once the final cause of the whole, and the spiritual Life and Light pervading and shining thro' the literal sense and proximate purposes of the component parts'.[36] The coarctation of energy and vitality into the word 'life' in the formula 'spiritual Life and Light' allows little play for forces that had formerly made his criticism particularly fertile.

Coleridge came to distrust the free play of energy, which in his own experience he had found misleading. In consequence, his criticism of Shakespeare became more conventionally moralizing, flashing less frequently with the twin insights that led him to striking perceptions—to a modern eye often the most memorable. A further, paradoxical effect, through his increasing moralizing emphasis, could be to increase the inhibition of spontaneous activity that he had remarked as an element in Hamlet's behaviour, thus fulfilling the account of his character in new and even subtler ways. If Hamlet was the victim of his own powerful intellectual energies, in Coleridge's case the inhibitions abounding from plenitude were further cut across and reinforced as they were checked by moralizing and passive reflections upon his own experience.

Coleridge's twelfth lecture on Shakespeare during the 1811–12 series was devoted to *Hamlet*, and was generally acknowledged to be one of his most brilliant. In the course of it he developed the point just alluded to by the self-reflexive device of identifying himself not with the playwright but with the central character of the play under discussion. Crabb Robinson, who described it enthusiastically, was particularly struck by one passage at the end:

Last night he concluded his fine development of the Prince of Denmark by an eloquent statement of the moral of the play: 'Action,' he said, 'is the great end of all—No intellect however grand is valuable if it draw us from action & lead us to think & think till the time of action is passed by and we can do nothing.' Somebody said to me, this is a Satire on himself; No, said I it is an Elegy.[37]

If it was indeed, it was an elegy on a career that his wealth of moral, as well as intellectual, reflections had gradually rendered more intricate, more cross-cut with contradictions, than Hamlet's, even.

---

[36] CNB 42 f 9 (cf. *CN* V 6116).
[37] Letter from Henry Crabb Robinson to Mrs Clarkson, 3 January 1812: *CLects (1808–1819)* I 391.

13

Mental Energies, Ancient
and Modern

During the Napoleonic Wars, Coleridge had wondered how to address his fellow countrymen about the problems facing the nation. His ultimate solution was to recommend superseding the supposed dominance of the philosophical attitudes inspired by Locke, Newton, and Hartley in favour of a position based on alternative doctrines. These involved a reaffirmed belief in the Bible, while grafting on to traditional scholarship the need to support the living values that he had been exploring in his recent work. It was in many ways a further development from the view of life and the appreciation of Hebrew poetry that he had evolved earlier. The divine creator of the universe was not a supreme watch-maker who had wound it up as a machine and set it to work its way according to an inbuilt programme, but the 'living God', constantly revealing himself with all the attributes of life. This God was equivalent to Reason—not the goddess whom the Revolutionaries had in mind when they dressed her as a courtesan, but the enlightening power of true wisdom. To this God could be applied what had been said in 1802 about the animated creation: 'Each thing has a life of its own and we are all one Life':

In the Bible every agent appears and acts as a self-subsisting individual: each has a life of its own, and yet all are one life.[1]

In this view of the world, the Imagination which had been so exalted in *Biographia Literaria* reappears as

that reconciling and mediatory power, which incorporating the Reason in Images of the Sense, and organizing (as it were) the flux of the senses by the permanence and self-circling energies of reason, gives birth to a system of

---

[1] *CSM* 31.

symbols, harmonious in themselves, and consubstantial with the truths, of which they are the conductors.[2]

Coleridge conveyed little sign that he had been affected by the biblical advances of his time in Germany, which challenged its status as a source of revelation. He had not felt obliged to address such issues in earlier years; and now he was content to take for granted the conventional view that the Bible consisted of inspired scripture and accept that there was no getting behind its basis, or point in seeking further foundation for what was in itself the ground. One could not reason about Reason: it must be treated as self-affirming, just as God alone could say, simply, 'I am that I am'. Such an insight was not to be reached through processes of logical thought, but by what should be described as an 'intuitive beholding'.

In one sense, this affirmation of the need less for thought than for something more like an act of vision had a long history. From the beginning of his career Coleridge had been fascinated by the problems of philosophy. The details of his interest are fragmentary, but the hints surviving from various memoirs suggest an omnivorous love of books and the search for a key to knowledge which in adolescence focused particularly on Jacob Boehme's *Aurora* and the writings of the Neoplatonists. James Vigus suggests convincingly that the course of study Coleridge recommended for young clergymen in a notebook entry of 1810[3] corresponds to a record of his own development. In that case the inspired schoolboy recalled by Lamb as unfolding 'in thy deep and sweet intonations, the mysteries of Jamblichus, or Plotinus' had not in those days pitted himself against the difficulties posed by the philosopher himself. That Coleridge himself in time did so can be judged from the minuteness of the reading which his notebook entry sets in the way of the clerical student.

The existence of this interest is particularly relevant to his life following the rupture with Wordsworth, when he attempted to come to terms with recent developments in German philosophy. As Ross Wilson and others have pointed out, discussion of this has been largely skewed by the discovery of his plagiarisms, notably the paragraphs from Schelling lifted for *Biographia Literaria*. The shock of this discovery has led writers to concentrate on psychological speculation about possible reasons for what seem like criminal acts. The idea that he was also

---

[2] Ibid., 29.   [3] CNB 18 ff 67ᵛ–69 (cf. *CN* III 3934).

actively engaged with the questions approached by thinkers who were not necessarily of his own country has thus been set to one side.[4] As a result, Walter Pater's supposition that Coleridge was indebted to Kant for an absolutist philosophy and consequent anti-relativist attitude that was untrue to the needs of the age is unfair to both men, since their demand for a 'critical' philosophy excluded both absolute and relative positions.

More important than this is Coleridge's actual relationship to Kant, understanding of which calls for an equal recognition of his allegiance to Plato. The imagery of 'dazzling', associated with Plato in early references, can be set beside his reminiscence in the *Biographia* that Kant 'took possession' of him 'as with a giant's hand'.[5] Yet later critics claimed that he had basically misinterpreted Kant, René Wellek, for instance, maintaining that instead he had set up a crazy and unsatisfactory edifice pieced together from Kant, the post-Kantians, and Anglican theology.[6]

Vigus argues that Coleridge's ambiguous attitude to Kant was heavily coloured by his earlier Neo-Platonic enthusiasm, coupled with the growing need to complement the current fashion for Locke and Hartley by pursuing a Berkeleyan insistence on the active power of the mind. He was thus led to believe that in his published writings Kant must have wanted to convey more than he was able to state openly.

Meanwhile, he was himself advancing a mode of thought which did not fall into simple categories. His thinking about symbolism provides a good case in point:

It always partakes of the Reality which it renders intelligible; and while it enunciates the whole, abides itself as a living part in that Unity, of which it is the representative.

To say that a symbol actually forms part of the reality it reveals is to demonstrate its complexity as a concept. To think properly in response requires something more than the binary process which assumes that an object must be either one thing or another. In making such demands Coleridge was displaying a characteristic subtlety of mental process— and requiring it from his readers.

---

[4] Ross Wilson, 'Coleridge's German "Absolutism"', in *Coleridge's Afterlives*, ed. J. Vigus and J. Wright, (London: Palgrave Macmillan, 2008), pp. 171–87.

[5] *CBL* I 153.

[6] James Vigus, *Platonic Coleridge* (Leeds: Modern Humanities Research Association (Legenda) and Maney Publishing, 2009), p. 49, citing Wellek, pp. 67–8.

The first Lay Sermon, *The Statesman's Manual*, had all the marks of a paean to the forces, material and moral, that had secured victory in the Napoleonic conflict. At that time he had found it most profitable to read recent events in the light of biblical prophecies, his quotations being taken from major prophets such as Isaiah and Jeremiah. There was also a further issue. *The Statesman's Manual* was addressed on its title-page to the 'Higher Classes of Society'; in reviewing it, Hazlitt noted an apparent discrepancy between this and the author's insistence that he was addressing not 'a promiscuous audience' but 'men of clerkly acquirements, of whatever profession'.[7] Coleridge, protesting that his instructions for the title-page had not been properly carried out, added the words 'and to the Learned' in one copy, at least—presumably as a counter to charges that he was adopting a snobbish approach: his aim was to exclude not a particular class of people but the thoughtless in all classes.

Despite the falseness of this charge, however, there are some grounds for Hazlitt's complaint, in that the pamphlet could be charged with advocating élitism. The audience assumed (implicitly or explicitly) is strictly limited. Coleridge could protest that his thinking had not been confined to the higher classes; he was able to complain in turn that Hazlitt had not noted the further issues addressed by the second of his Lay Sermons, including his awareness that despite the successful con-clusion to the Napoleonic Wars temptations to triumphalism must be more than undermined by the current murmurings of discontent. He claimed, indeed, that the new enterprise had been started off by his chancing to light on the words of Isaiah: 'We looked for peace, but no good came; for a time of health and behold trouble.' He was particularly disturbed by the increasing tendency for trouble-makers and rabble-rousers to make their voices heard. Hazlitt would no doubt have failed to agree, but Coleridge's admonitory tone chimed with the support for the status quo voiced by people such as Hannah More. His mind was by no means closed, nevertheless, to social ills, particularizing some, such as the fluctuation in the wages of labour in the towns, and in the country-side 'a peasantry sinking into pauperism, step for step with the rise of the farmer's profits and indulgencies'.[8] He was also aware of the periodic 'gradual expansions of credit ending in sudden contractions (in mercantile language, a Crash)' with which society was threatened,

---

[7] *CSM* 36.   [8] *CLS* 212.

and the common usage by which such phenomena were rationalized and regarded as examples of things 'finding their own level': an expression perhaps fitting a mechanism but not, he maintained, human beings properly treated—in Kantian terms—as 'persons', rather than as 'things'.

He also argued that in this discourse his present concern was more with 'the requisite correctives of the commercial spirit', than with religion conceived as a 'counter charm to the sorcery of wealth'; in this respect the instances he gives of encounters with people who impressed him by their insight into the social ills about them were diverse. Some were from his Scottish tour of 1803, while the children who were stunted by their lack of sunshine were seen in Dorset, and therefore presumably at the time when he was staying in Wiltshire in 1813–16. His present concern continued with several publications on the plight of the factory children.

At the same time, other issues were coming forward. After the end of the Napoleonic wars, and with the reopening of contact with continental Europe, much that had been happening abroad came to be known, either through the importing of previously unavailable books or through the advent of scholars from those countries. So far as Coleridge was concerned, the most important visitor of this kind was Ludwig Tieck, whom he met at the house of J. H. Green and who came, at his invitation, to Highgate in June 1817. Tieck he had known in Rome, and had long admired him from a literary point of view. One of the gifts he brought with him now, however, was news of the respectability with which animal magnetism was now viewed by many important figures—including Blumenbach himself, whose change of attitude was for Coleridge a significant development. When he visited Germany at the beginning of the century Blumenbach's scepticism on the subject had apparently been a powerful deterrent to further speculation. Reference to hypnotic power, a notable feature of the 1798 version of *The Rime of the Ancient Mariner*, disappeared from the 1800 version; and no more was heard on the subject from Coleridge for many years. In September 1809 he was able in *The Friend* to number 'Animal Magnetizers', along with Richard Brothers and Joanna Southcott, among the irrational thinkers of the time, so lumping them with the French thinkers on whom he was turning his back. But when he found this passage repeated in his 1818 rewriting he added annotations recanting his sentiments, stating that Blumenbach and a number of other former disbelievers now accepted the factual existence of hypnotic phenomena, even if they could not account for them. He was still somewhat nonplussed by the situation—particularly since he could hardly forget how fruitful his speculations had proved during the time of his poetic flowering. His rejection of French thought and all that it represented had been easily maintained in the years after his return from Germany: it was of a piece with the general revulsion against the violence that followed the Revolution; but to devise an attitude that could maintain that rejection while acknowledging the factual accuracy of the magnetizers' claims required unexpected and more complex intellectual contortions. It intrigued him, for instance, to think that the phenomenon might throw new light on 'the oracles and mysteries of Greek, Roman, and Egyptian Paganism', yet he was anxious to rescue it from those whose main object would be 'to undermine the divine character of the Gospel history, and the superhuman powers of its great founder'.[9]

As mentioned already, Tieck is the most likely source of the new information; certainly by July Coleridge had not only been able to question him about his own experience of magnetism but complained to him that Gillman could not yet rid himself of his 'professional Anti-belief in Animal Magnetism'—though he believed that the aversion among medical men might have been less had it been called the 'Galvanism of organic bodies'.[10]

His sense of religious significance to the phenomenon probably reflected a theory that the magnetic effects had to do not with the magnetist's ability to awaken sexual appetite through the effects of touch but with something more subtle: the ability 'to transmute the infra-abdominal Appetite into pectoral Sentimental Fruition or Sensation'. This was an effect that he had noted as produced similarly by opium in 'men of feminine Constitution'—including, no doubt, himself.[11] Presumably he regarded the ability to transmute physical desire into sentimental fruition as an important key to religious meliorism, opening possibilities of spreading widely religious beliefs that were constructed on such sentiments.

For the time being the effect of his reconciliation with the newly authenticated phenomena was to urge an attitude of simple toleration; an abandonment of disfavour. In the longer term, however, he thought that the effect of such forbearance would be valuable in promoting a

---

[9] See his letter of 1 December 1818 to Thomas Curtis, proposing to publish an account of his own: *CL* IV 887.

[10] *CL* IV 745, 751.   [11] CNB 29 ff 4–4ᵛ (cf. *CN* IV 4512).

better attitude towards the miracles of the first-century church, since it would assist the formulation of a distinction between the miracles of Christ and those performed by his followers.

Intellectual concerns remained uppermost. One of the immediate fruits of the more orderly life that he was pursuing under the watchful eyes of Mr and Mrs Gillman from 1816 onwards was his decision to undertake what he referred to as a 'rifacciamento' of *The Friend*. Much of the work that had related to his larger enterprises would now be given a subordinate position, relegated to the 'Landing-Places' which provided entertainment for the reader, as opposed to the main sections. These, under the revised formulation, were intended to provide a long exercise in self-training by which the mental powers could be encouraged to pursue lasting truths.

Certain things remained constant. The opening still made some play with the fable of the maddening rain, and in the conclusion the figure of Alexander Ball remained prominent as an example of the condition to which the good ruler might aspire. His most anxious concern, however, was with communication. Instead of expressing his thought in long, considered periods amounting to extended argumentation, he felt obliged to protest continually concerning the difficulty of making his audience respond to points which, he felt, ought to be all too obvious. In marginal comments on several copies, as on one presented to J. G. Lockhart in 1819, he wrote again of the recently rehabilitated animal magnetism,

Since Cuvier has asserted the truth of the poets, and that they are not adequately solved by imagination, in any received sense of the word; and since *Hufeland,* Stieglitz, above all, *Blumenbach,* the for so many years zealous Opponents & almost Persecutors of Animal Magnetism, have openly retracted their verdict, surely, I need not be ashamed to join in the recantation. The Problem was this: whether the nervous system of one body can, under certain circumstances, act physically on the nervous system of another living body?—and this seems to have been solved in the affirmative, & placed beyond the reach of any rational scepticism...[12]

Previously, his main assurance had been based on the Royal Commission under the auspices of Benjamin Franklin in 1784 which concluded that its effects were the result of 'imagination'. Awareness of the new

---

[12]   *CF* (1818) (cf. *CFriend* I 59n).

development encouraged Coleridge to undertake urgent enquiries into the new research and thinking that was becoming increasingly available, particularly in Germany.[13] Yet at the end of his long investigation he had to confess himself baffled:

Were I asked, what I think—my answer would be—that the Evidence enforces Scepticism and a Non liquet. Too strong & consentaneous for a candid mind to be satisfied of its falsehood, its solvibility in the supposition of Imposture or casual Co-incidence;—too fugacious and infixible to support any Theory that supposes the always potential & under certain conditions & circumstances occasionally actual existence of a correspondent faculty in the human Soul. And nothing less than such an hypothesis would be adequate to the satisfactory explanation of the Facts—tho' that of a metastasis of specific functions of the nervous energy taken in conjunction with extreme nervous excitement, + some delusion, + some illusion, + some imposition, + some chance & accidental coincidence, might determine the direction, in which the Scepticism vibrated. Nine years has the subject of Zoo-magnetism been before me—I have traced it historically—collected a Mass of documents in French, German, Italian, & the Latinists of the 16th century—have never neglected an opportunity of questioning Eye witnesses, (ex. Gr. Tieck, Treviranus, De Prati, Meyer, and others of literary or medical celebrity) and I remain where I was, & where the first perusal of Klug's Work had left me, without having advanced an Inch backward or forward. Treviranus the famous Botanist's reply to me, when he was in London, is worth recording. . . . I have seen what I am certain I would not have believed on your telling; and in all reason therefore I can neither expect nor wish that you should believe on mine.[14]

Much of 1818 was taken up with the *rifacimento* of *The Friend,* Coleridge evidently feeling that the first edition had petered out without a firm conclusion—a fate which his longer, three-volume version would, he hoped, avoid. Still there lurked the dream of a Great Work; and it was presumably in the hope of moving further towards that that he arranged at the end of the year to begin lecturing on the history of philosophy.

---

[13] Coleridge's change of opinion apparently dates from the spring of 1817. A long note of 8 July pleaded for disinterested examination of the facts (Cornell UL & BL Add MS 36532 ff 5, 7–12: cf. *CSWF* I 588–95). Another long note on zoomagnetism followed in 1821 (BL add ms 34225 ff 146–7; cf. *CSWF* II 911–14). See also CNB 29 ff 67–69 (cf. *CN* IV 4908) for a further discussion in July 1822.
[14] Marginal annotation on Southey's *Life of Wesley* (2 vols., London 1820) I 301–5, in the BL (corrected from *CM* V 141–2).

Careful re-editing of his philosophical lectures has enabled readers to see more clearly than before the details of the materials he had at his disposal. He was able to draw both on works published in recent years and on unpublished entries in his notebooks; he was also conscious, however, that the enterprise was a longstanding one, and that he had carried out much of his thinking towards it in the early years of the century. Increasingly he had come to see the history as one of distinctive thinkers, needed under a providential dispensation to correct the short-comings of their predecessors, the supreme example being the inade-quacies of the Stoics and the Epicureans, balanced against one another at the height of the Roman Empire, yet unable to confront the inade-quacies of the civilization about them until the coming of Christ, the supreme thinker who reconciled the contraries of their philosophy.

The centrality of this perception helps to explain why Coleridge chose to concentrate on ancient philosophy when he might have ad-dressed the more contemporary work of Kant and the neo-Kantians. He used the work of W. G. Tennemann heavily in preparing his lectures, though, as Vigus maintains, any charge of plagiarism from them is invalidated by the amount of his marginal commentary. He was not (as Vigus also points out) antagonistic to the fact that Tenneman opposed the neo-Kantians' supposed misunderstanding of Plato, but was probably swayed by his larger achievement to feel justified in focusing on the ancients.

Re-editing for the *Collected Works* has also emphasized the extent to which Coleridge relied on his own previous writing and thinking for the first lectures, while from the seventh onwards he turned gratefully to Tennemann's recently published history in German, which he bor-rowed from J. H. Green. He could do this with a better conscience since his use of the volume was largely for the facts collected in it. So far as Tennemann's philosophy was concerned his thoroughgoing Kantian-ism could be regarded as acceptable but preliminary: Coleridge, who believed that he was moving beyond Kant and towards a greater synthesis reinstating the position of Christianity, could feel that taking issue with him was fully justified—even if he was also drawing on him for his factual provision.

Even while he embarked on this larger struggle, however, he was also driven back to take account of theories that had fascinated him at an earlier stage. One of the most important was the theory of human evolution, which he had tried to dismiss when writing to Wordsworth in 1815 of his failed hopes for *The Excursion*, saying,

I understood that you would...have exploded the absurd notion of Pope's Essay on Man, Darwin, and all the countless Believers—even (strange to say) among Xtians of Man's having progressed from an Ourang Outang state—so contrary to all History, to all Religion, nay, to all Possibility...[15]

The outline which Coleridge provided here was not strictly accurate. In his *Essay on Man* Pope had not described an evolutionary process, simply a version of the Great Chain of Being:

> Far as creation's ample range extends,
> The scale of sensual, mental powers ascends:
> Mark how it mounts, to man's imperial race,
> From the green myriads in the peopled grass.[16]

An 'evolutionary' belief could more properly have been ascribed to Erasmus Darwin—though even he was inclined to believe in an ascending order:

> Hence without parent by spontaneous birth
> Rise the first specks of animated earth;
> From Nature's womb the plant or insect swims,
> And buds or breathes, with microscopic limbs.
>
> ORGANIC LIFE beneath the shoreless waves
> Was born and nurs'd in Ocean's pearly caves
> First forms minute, unseen by spheric glass,
> Move on the mud, or pierce the watery mass;
> These, as successive generations bloom,
> New powers acquire, and larger limbs assume;
> Whence countless groups of vegetation spring,
> And breathing realms of fin, and feet, and wing.[17]

Coleridge could recognize the force of Darwin's rhetoric, even if he did not acknowledge that the true author of the cult was Lord Monboddo. For his own part he recalled Voltaire's anecdote of a lady who responded to the assertion that a saint had walked two leagues with his severed head in his hand with the comment that the first step was the most difficult. The basic question, in other words, concerned the initial premise. The original human being must have been endowed, like any animal, with instinct, though in the human instance that instinct must have involved both a physical and an intellectual nature.

---

[15] *CL* IV 574–5.   [16] Pope, *Essay on Man*, I 207–10.
[17] Erasmus Darwin, *The temple of nature; or, The origin of society: a poem, with philosophical notes* (London: J. Johnson, 1803).

Some of the ideas that had intrigued him in the 1790s were still worrying him, evidently, if only by their attractiveness. So as in his lectures he surveyed the state of philosophy in the decades immediately preceding the rise of Christianity he paid tribute to the achievement of the Stoics, but then wrote more admonishingly of the rise of the Eclectics:

But the more dangerous sect was arising, the rival of Christianity, namely the sect which is said to have begun in Alexandria about the beginning of the third century, but which in truth had begun somewhat earlier. It is very difficult to speak accurately of the opinions of a sect whose great pride was to combine and to reconcile all the truths of the other philosophers who had appeared in the world, in that very instant presenting itself as the mimic of Christianity and pretending to do what had been really done by Christianity.

Continuing to indicate how this school of thought might have arisen, Coleridge supposed that it answered the need to find a single religion 'common to all men as men'—one which reconciled all the varying cults then in existence and in addition took account of all the superstitions answering to human need for 'a support from a higher cause':

This was so strong that the old augurers . . . were grown into utter neglect . . . From Persia, Egypt, and other places, a perfect stream of astrologers and nativity-casters and magicians or whatever they might have been, inundated Italy. This was too strong to be resisted, and this Eclectic system adopted it, and we have to contemplate the strange and unnatural union of the abstrusest philosophy with the basest superstitions.[18]

At this point, however, the argument takes an unexpected turn, as Coleridge suggests that recent thinkers may have been mistaken in discounting the tradition of the decline of the oracles:

Many are the difficulties that press on this subject, more so in consequence of the determination with which the literati of the last century and a half have had to consider all the ancient oracles, all the facts related concerning extraordinary circumstances among the ancients, as mere delusions, as poor conscious tricks of the priesthood, little considering whether it was possible that, century after century and century after century, an acknowledged imposture could have prevailed and could have produced such belief in the sacredness of an oath, and such a constant superintendence in conscience, in an imperfect morality indeed, but yet still in a morality, as appeared in the Roman Empire for so

[18] *CPL* (1949) 238 (cf. *CLects (1818–1819)* I 315–16).

many centuries, when their generals after conquering kings came back and humbly laid their fasces at the foot of the Jupiter Capitolinus.

That some unspecified event occurred was suggested by the decay of oracles mentioned by Plutarch and the sense of loss felt by the Romans. The point induced further thoughts about animal magnetism:

I say this because in the writings of [Philo Judaeus] not to mention some striking passages in Plato himself I find references to secret arts in their mysteries which correspond so strangely and minutely to the facts which have been lately brought forward on the continent (and permit me to say I am not passing any judgment on those facts because what I state will be true, whether we take the report of Dr. Franklin and the philosophers who made their report before the American war, or the reports made by other governments which bear a different complexion, still it remains fact that means exist by which a mutual action of the imagination upon the nervous system and the nervous system upon the imagination will produce most extraordinary phenomena). For these phenomena have never been denied; the facts themselves cannot be disputed. The only question has been whether it is necessary to assume a new principle of physiology, or whether what we know of the human frame the power of imagination is sufficient to explain the fact, the facts being the same. Now from this (which I find to have been the constant practice in their higher mysteries so that Philo Judaeus declares that he has no confidence in their writings but such as were composed when he was in one of those extasies) conclude that those arts which may be practised among the meanest of men were among the main secrets of the Eclectics, and constituted those pretences to revise his view of the last-named and to magic and to a divine communion which appears everywhere in their writings.[19]

During the spring, while these lectures were being given, Keats encountered him, with Green, in a lane near Highgate and found himself exposed to the full play of his mind for two miles.[20] Apart from comments on nightingales and poetic sensation, Coleridge was evidently still preoccupied by the implications of recent work on animal magnetism and what it suggested about differing levels of consciousness in human beings. He spoke of single and double touch and of how there were 'so many metaphysicians from a want of smoking the second consciousness'—the existence of which threw light on many superstitions.

---

[19] *CPL* (1949) 239–40 (cf. *CLects (1818–1819)* I 318–19).
[20] For Keats's account, see *Letters of John Keats, 1814–1821*, ed. H. E. Rollins (2 vols., Harvard University Press and Cambridge University Press, 1958) II 88–9. I have considered the possible reordering of Keats's ideas as a result of this event in chapter 4 of my *Romantic Consciousness: Blake to Mary Shelley* (London: Palgrave Macmillan, 2003).

His revived fascination with hypnotic phenomena lasted for several years, with the result that he could be described by Carlyle in 1825 as 'a kind good soul, full of religion and affection, and poetry and animal magnetism'.[21] Although his final position was one of scepticism there evidently survived the sense that it might still be a key to religious truth. He indicated what he had in mind in a marginal comment on F. A. Mesmer's *Mesmerismus*:

It is . . . no sound Objection to the facts of Animal Magnetism, that it's most successful Professors have been men of weak Judgement. For the prevention of distraction of mind, and earnestness of Volition are ex hypothesi the conditions of concentering and emitting the influence, even as Anger, and the energy of self-defence are the conditions of the Gymnotus accumulating its galvanism.— but this devotion of thought, freedom from disturbing Doubts, and even from the activity of philosophic Inference, in short, Faith (as a unifying energy) are most likely to exist in weak & credulous but sincere, sensitive and warm-hearted Men.—Just such a man is Dr. Wolfart . . . I think it probable that An. Magnetism will be found connected with a Warmth-Sense: & will confirm my long long ago theory of Volition as a mode of double Touch.[22] . . .

Taken with the ability 'to transmute the infra-abdominal Appetite into pectoral Sentimental Fruition or Sensation', an effect he believed to be produced by opium in 'men of feminine Constitution', the nature of Coleridge's continuing esoteric speculation emerges. The phenomenon of animal magnetism could be related to that of single and double touch, by which passive human beings, the most open to magnetic force, would live in possession of truth, their hearts responsive to their own deepest will, while predominantly active natures, responding to the compulsions of double touch and so at the mercy of passing volitions and contemporary fashions, would be anxious always that their actions should be reflected back to them.

The position he had reached by 1824 precluded the possibility of further advance. He had established to his own satisfaction that zoo-magnetism was a fact, and that the hostility of English thinkers should be modified at least to the extent of taking it more seriously; on the other hand, his esoteric doctrine of single and double touch was open to question. It might be supported to the degree of exploring further the relationship between active and passive states of the consciousness, yet it

---

[21] See the letter to his brother, John Carlyle, quoted below at p. 230 and n. 23.
[22] F. A. Mesmer, *Mesmerismus* (Berlin 1814, 1815), transcribed *CM* III 867–8.

risked giving too much weight to sensibility. In his own life he was by now too much of a chronic invalid to be able to allow the virtues of the passive consciousness to be given too much positive value, though he was still impressed by the power of opium to produce the therapeutic effects of magnetization on 'men of feminine Constitution'.[23]

For the time being the effect of his reconciliation with the newly authenticated phenomena was to urge an attitude of simple toleration; an abandonment of disfavour. It was too late, however, to revisit some of the possibilities that had presented themselves in earlier years; the main force of his thinking as it had now developed was to stress above all the non-sensuous nature of the Reason that must be thought of as the main guide for humanity.

As the years passed, the hope of establishing a firm conjunction between nature and morality faded, yet the conviction that magnetism enshrined an important truth refused to go away. The source of that conviction lay in his abiding faith in the power of the human heart. When *The Friend* had been reassembled as a three-part volume, the ending remained, as before, Coleridge's panegyric on the qualities embodied in Alexander Ball which could be regarded as a final public statement. The core of the work, on the other hand, lay in the concluding climax of the preceding section, in which he insisted that the ultimate truth for which he was contesting, stressing above all the super-sensuous, could not in the end be 'a sort of knowledge':

This elevation of the spirit above the semblances of custom and the senses to a world of spirit, this life in the idea, even in the supreme and god-like, which alone merits the name of life, and without which our organic life is but a state of somnambulism; this it is which affords the sole sure anchorage in the storm, and at the same time the substantiating principle of all true wisdom, the satisfactory solution of all the contradictions of human nature, of the whole riddle of the world. This alone belongs to and speaks intelligibly to all alike, the learned and the ignorant, if but the heart listens. For alike present in all, it may be awakened, but it cannot be given. But let it not be supposed, that it is a sort of *knowledge*. For it is an immutable truth, that WHAT COMES FROM THE HEART, THAT ALONE GOES TO THE HEART: WHAT PROCEEDS FROM A DIVINE IMPULSE, THAT THE GODLIKE ALONE CAN AWAKEN.[24]

The three-volume *Friend* was one of his major statements in preparation for the *Opus Maximum*. Vigus, who regards his fragmentary remains

---

[23] See CNB 29 ff 4–4ᵛ (cf. *CN* IV 4512).   [24] *CF* (1818) (cf. *CFriend* I 524).

towards the latter work as embodying the final statements of his thinking, reads them as constituting an extended piece of propositional writing, arguing that all their necessary positions can be demonstrated to be dependent on his foremost, unconditioned belief in the primacy of conscience.

Some of the evangelical urgency that had characterized writings such as *The Friend* is set aside in favour of a patient if esoteric mode of discourse, based on his realization that ultimate truth, in the form that he apprehends it, is not to be found in verbal propositions but in what is ultimately unspeakable. The true master of such awareness would not therefore be a philosopher in the mould of Kant, but one after the order of Plato; and it was in pursuing the tradition that some of Plato's deepest thoughts were concealed in his esoteric doctrines that his ultimate value would be found.

In the same way Vigus argues that the core of an understanding of the *Opus Maximum* will be found not by a painstaking reading of its extended text, but by studying the interplay of his philosophic ideas with his marginal comments on Tenneman—originally intended, no doubt, to be understood by an esoteric reader such as Green. Some of his promises, however, such as the casual assurance in the *Opus Maximum* that an account of the points where he disagrees with Kant—namely, those in which Kant differs from the Christian code—and the philosophical grounds of his disagreement 'will appear in its own place in another part of this work'[25] were never in the event fulfilled.

This offering of an attractive but illusory promise happens often enough in Coleridge's writing to be seen as a habitual trope, helping to account for the sense of disillusionment that some of his readers experience. It is perhaps some recompense, however limited, to suggest that such rewards as exist are in fact permanently available for those who find a way of responding to his mental energies with similar ones of their own.

[25] *COM* 75–6.

14

Interinvolving Guilt and Innocence

At the end of 1813 Coleridge suffered a week of severe illness, in which (to quote his own account) 'tho' driven up and down for seven dreadful Days by restless Pain, like a Leopard in a Den, yet the anguish & remorse of Mind was worse than the pain of the whole Body. —O I have had a new world opened to me, in the infinity of my own Spirit!'[1] To another correspondent he described that new world in greater detail:

You have no conception of what my sufferings have been, forced to struggle and struggle in order not to desire a death for which I am not prepared.—I have scarcely known what sleep is, but like a leopard in its den have been drawn up and down the room by extreme pain, and restlessness, worse than pain itself. O how I have prayed even to loud agony only to be able to pray! O how I have felt the impossibility of any real *good will* not born anew from the Word and the Spirit! O I have seen far, far deeper and clearer than I ever saw before the ground of pernicious errors! O I have seen, I have felt that the worst offences are those against our own souls! That our souls are infinite in depth, and therefore our sins are infinite, and redeemable only by an infinitely higher infinity; that of the Love of God in Christ Jesus. I have called my soul infinite, but O infinite in the depth of darkness, an infinite craving, an infinite capacity of pain and weakness, and excellent only as being passively capacious of the light from above. Should I recover I will—no—no may God grant me power to struggle to become *not another* but a *better man*—O that I had been a partaker with you of the discourse of Mr Robt Hall! But it pleased the Redeemer to appoint for me a sterner, fearfuller, and even more eloquent preacher, if to be impressive is to be eloquent. O God save me—save me from myself....[2]

The spiritual crisis that engulfed Coleridge after his break with the Wordsworth household led him to retrace familiar paths. It is instructive

[1] To Mrs J. J. Morgan, *CL* III 463–4.   [2] To Thomas Roberts, *CL* III 463.

to read a letter from Hannah More when she encountered him about this time. On 13 Apr 1814 she wrote to William Wilberforce,

nothing has surprised me more than Coleridge the poet of the Lakes, whom I have carefully avoided so many years on every Account as at once the Trumpet of disaffection and Socinianism. Of this last he was a very powerful Abettor—insomuch that Etrurian Wedgewood pensioned him with £150 p^r. Ann. to give Lectures in favour of those doctrines—The other day I recd. a most respectful message desiring leave to visit us—As that piddling monosyllable No is the hardest word I ever learnt to pronounce—I gave him leave. I found him very eloquent, entertaining and brimfull of knowledge. Added to this he seemed to have great reverence for Evangelical religion and considerable acquaintance with it. His friend who brought him told that he had just got a letter, which he shewed me, from Dr. Estlin the great Apostle of Socinianism in Bristol, his friend for 20 years, forbidding him his house, for having spoken in his Evenings Lecture with great horror of Socinianism. Wedgwood has also withdrawn his pension, so that he is a sort of Martyr to his new faith. I hope he is sincere; he talked very solemnly. Another thing pleased me, there is at Bristol a very accomplished man a Mr. Elwyn who has been very wild and an infidel. Colridge told me he had sat up till 4 that morning reading ArchBp Leighton which M^r. Elwin whose favorite Author he is become, lent him![3]

In the copy of Leighton's writings that Mr Elwyn had lent him, Coleridge wrote:

Surely if ever Work not in the sacred Canon might suggest a belief of inspiration, of something more than human, this it is. When Mr E[lwyn] made this assertion, I took it as an hyperbole of affection, but now I subscribe to it seriously & bless the Hour that introduced me to the knowledge of the evangelical apostolic Archbishop Leighton.[4]

In later notes he was to develop an image of Leighton's commentary on the first epistle of Peter as a true reverberation from the inspiration of the gospels—'Next to the inspired Scriptures, yea, and as the *vibration* of that once struck hour remaining on the Air....'[5] If this sense of a timeless truth speaking to him was comforting it was also alarming. When Leighton writes, 'If any one's Head or Tongue should grow apace, and all the rest stand at a Stay, it would certainly make him a

[3] Transcript reproduced by courtesy of the Department of Manuscripts, Perkins Library, Duke University. I owe this quotation to Professor Heather Jackson.

[4] Flyleaf comment, in a copy of Robert Leighton, *Expository Works* (Edinburgh, 1748): *CM* III 508.

[5] *CN* IV 4867; cf. *CL* V 198.

Monster', Coleridge recognises the picture guiltily and writes down repeated cries for mercy. When Leighton writes of a sick man that 'the Kindness and Love of God is then as seasonable and refreshing to him, as in Health, and possibly more', he writes in the margin, 'To the regenerate; but to the conscious Sinner a Source of Terrors insupportable'—and then, perhaps aware that he has just written a capital S and a capital T he continues, 'S. T. C. i.e. Sinful, Tormented Culprit'.[6] Yet he is also sustained by Leighton's assurances concerning the grace of God. On a passage concluding, 'though I saw, as it were, his Hand lifted up to destroy me, yet from that same Hand would I expect Salvation', he writes, 'Bless God O my soul! for this sweet and strong Comforter. The Honey in the Lion.'[7] On the sentence, '. . . such an Assent as this, is the peculiar Work of the Spirit of God, and is certainly saving Faith', he comments, 'Lord I believe! help thou my unbelief. My natural reason acquiesces. I believe enough to *fear*—& grant me the Belief that brings sweet *Hope*.'[8]

The crisis had persisted throughout the spring of 1814, when Coleridge visited Bristol and was stung to respond to a letter from Joseph Cottle, who had just discovered the extent of Coleridge's drug addiction and urged him to rouse himself. Coleridge replied that this was like asking a man paralysed in both arms to rub them briskly together. Cottle replied immediately urging him to pray, upon which he wrote,

O I do pray inwardly to be able to *pray;* but indeed to pray, to pray with the faith to which Blessing is promised, this is the reward of Faith, this is the Gift of God to the Elect. O if to feel how infinitely worthless I am, how poor a wretch, with just free will enough to be deserving of wrath, & of my own contempt, & of none to merit a moment's peace, can make a part of a Christian's creed; so far I am a Christian—[9]

In another letter to Cottle at this time, however, he discussed the question of prayer in a less agonised manner, declaring that Christians expected 'no outward or sensible Miracles' from Prayer; 'it's effects and it's fruitions are spiritual, and accompanied (to use the words of that true *Divine*, Archbishop Leighton) "not by Reasons and Arguments; but by an inexpressible Kind of Evidence, which only they know who have it"'.[10]

The mention of Leighton in that letter indicates again the extent to which his writings were assisting Coleridge's fight for spiritual survival.

---

[6] *CM* III 512. [7] *CM* III 508. [8] *CM* III 509.
[9] *CL* III 478. [10] *CL* III 478–9.

For years afterwards he would be fond of recommending the exemplary innocence of this man, who, he felt, offered him something of the redemption he was seeking, particularly through his championing of the First Epistle of Peter. (In this he was to be followed by Thomas Arnold the Younger, who in going to New Zealand found himself drawn by the authority which this biblical text seemed to exude: 'The words of Peter sounded to me rather as a command than as a theme for discussion, and made a direct appeal to the practical reason and the will.'[11]) Coleridge's enthusiasm was one more sign of his turning away from Unitarianism and his growing respect for Evangelical religion, as shown in Hannah More's letter.

The full nature of his religious beliefs in later life is not easy to establish, however. At first, in the post-Revolutionary period, Unitarianism had seemed an obvious answer to the problem of religion, combining the humanity of Christ with a reverence for morality. From the first decade of the century, however, he had come to accept that logically such a belief could lead only to some form of pantheism.

The doctrine of the Trinity, on the other hand, seemed like a confidence trick, organized by priests to their advantage. If an attempt were made by a Trinitarian believer to justify it on the ground that God, as the personification of Love, Intelligence and Life, was properly to be regarded as threefold, this, Coleridge pointed out, was still, and necessarily, a humanist solution—to be compared with the old joke of making 'Flint Broth':

This is the mysterious cookery of the Orthodox—which promises to make Broth out of a Flint, but when you are congratulating yourself on the cheapness of your Diet, requires as necessary ingredients, Beef, Salt and Turnips! But the Layman might say—I can make Broth out of Beef, Salt and Turnips myself. Most true! but the Cook would have no plea for demanding his wages were it not for his merit in dropping in the Flint.[12]

Once he had become convinced that Unitarianism was incompatible with the New Testament and that Christianity must be identified to some degree with Trinitarianism, moreover, it remained a puzzle just how this could be explicated. To think of God as united with his Son, the Logos, in such a manner as to make them a twofold divinity was

---

[11] Thomas Arnold, note of October 1854, cited in his *Passages in a Wandering Life* (London, 1900), p. 153.
[12] *CLects (1795)* 206.

possible enough; but to subsequently enrol the Holy Spirit as a third participant was a tougher proposition. Yet in a notebook entry of 1805 he recorded a moment of inspiration. Whereas seven or eight years before he had toyed with proving the proposition 'No Christ, no God', he now felt, if anything more strongly, 'No Trinity, no God'. He was still evidently uneasy, however, expressing a need for this last conviction to 'work upon' him.[13]

During subsequent years he tried to expand on this perception, but constantly had to acknowledge the limits of what could be done, using phrases such as 'Datur, non intelligitur' (it is given, not understood').[14] To Cottle in 1814 he wrote, invoking his favourite hero of the time, 'The Trinity, as Bishop Leighton has well remarked, is "a doctrine of faith, not of demonstration".'[15] Despite various attempts at further explication, the production of a convincing doctrine of the Trinity continued to elude him.

On becoming acquainted with Southey's *Life of Wesley*, published in 1820, which he read and annotated over several years,[16] he welcomed its stress on the centrality of Reason. It must have been early in his reading, and soon after receiving the book, that he entered an approving annotation on one of its passages, affirming that forgiveness was a free gift of God, bestowed on the worthy and unworthy alike:

I venture to avow it as my conviction, that either Christian Faith is what Wesley here describes, or there is no proper meaning in the word. It is either the Identity of the Reason and the Will (the proper spiritual part of man) in the full energy of each consequent on a divine re-kindling: or it is not [at] all. Faith is as *real* as Life: as actual as *Force*; as effectual as *Volition*. It is the Physics of the Moral Being no less than it is the *Morale* of the zoo-physical.[17]

A note on a subsequent page reinforces this sense of the supremacy of Reason in distinguishing the nature of humans as opposed to that of brutes:

Self-consciousness is or implies Reason: for it implies the power of contemplating the Self, as an *Idea,* & loosened from the sensation of ~~any~~ one's own Self as the I Am,)(I, James or I, John—consequently, the power of determining an ultimate End—which if Brutes possess they are no longer Brutes...[18]

---

[13]   CNB 17 f 22ᵛ–23 (cf. *CN* II 2448).
[14]   Letter to George Fricker, *CL* II 1193.
[15]   Letter of 1814: CL III 480–6.
[16]   Some of his annotations are dated 1820, 1822, and 1825.
[17]   *CM* V 176.   [18]   Ibid., 177. The symbol means 'in contrast to'.

The nature of his continuing underlying preoccupation was, however, evident in a further annotation, where he attempted to utilize factors of his old idea of animal magnetism towards a spiritual end:

Wherein differs Reason from the Spirit, in and to a man if (as I believe) Reason be the Presence of the Holy Spirit to a finite Understanding—at once the Light and inward Eye?—I answer—even as the Sense of Light in the absence of the Sense of Touch and its accompanying sensation or feeling would differ from the joint impression from the Eye and the single & double Touch.—[19]

The exact form in which he understood the divine nature remained a matter for continuous thought. In 1829, for instance, he drew up a version setting out a view of the divine which was not Trinitarian but fourfold; to the familiar Trinity of Father, Son, and Spirit he adds a preceding item, that of the Absolute subject—as if God the Father himself represents a second stage in the divine. According to J. R. Barth, his early editor W. G. T. Shedd questioned this on the grounds that it assumed 'an aboriginal Unity existing primarily by itself, and in the order of nature before a Trinity . . . which is not in its own nature either triune or personal, but is merely the impersonal base from which the Trinity proper is evolved'.[20]

As mentioned above, his earliest acceptance of Trinitarianism had been associated with his interest in Plato, and, in particular, his enthusiasm for the writings of the Neoplatonists. Whatever the attractiveness of the speculations he had indulged in during his youth, however, he had come to conclude that in terms of his own personal life his beliefs were inadequate. There were spheres, it seemed, where the human will, however keenly exercised, was incapable of resisting physical cravings, and in such a world the only hope was to look for a redeemer—a consideration which lay well beyond the scope of Socinian Christianity. His enslavement to opium enforced a more traditional posture of humility, though still leaving room for wonder and a stance of adoration, well represented in the concluding words of *Biographia Literaria.* There he maintains that his aim has always been to show that

the scheme of Christianity, as taught in the liturgy and homilies of our Church, though not discoverable by human reason, is yet in accordance with it; that link follows link by necessary consequence; that Religion passes out of the ken of

[19] *CM* V, 191–2.
[20] Quoted in J. R. Barth, *Coleridge and Christian Doctrine* (Cambridge, Mass.: Harvard University Press, 1969), p. 94.

Reason only where the eye of Reason has reached its own horizon; and that Faith is then but its continuation: even as the day softens away into the sweet twilight, and twilight, hushed and breathless, steals into the darkness. It is night, sacred night! the upraised eye views only the starry heaven which manifests itself alone: and the outward beholding is fixed on the sparks twinkling in the awful depth, though suns of other worlds, only to preserve the soul steady and collected in its pure act of inward adoration to the great I AM, and to the filial WORD that re-affirmeth it from eternity to eternity, whose choral echo is the universe.[21]

At one point, nevertheless, he was careful to insert a paragraph stressing the tentative status of all his speculations:

If I should die without having destroyed this & my other Memorandum Books, I trust, that these Hints & first thoughts, often too cogitabilia rather than actual cogitata a me, may not be understood as my fixed opinions—but merely as the suggestions of the disquisition; & acts of obedience to the apostolic command of Try all things: hold fast that which is good.[22]

His favoured approach was evidently heuristic, appealing for open-mindedness yet constructed on an assurance that any disinterested reader was bound to reach the values he himself embraced, and to recognize the appeal of a man such as Robert Leighton.

As he moved towards the making of his 'Assertion of Religion', he was struck by the need to produce an appropriate work in the short term, drawing on his recent assurances. It was not surprising, therefore, that he found himself drawn to share his most recent enthusiasm by producing a work that would offer current readers the chance to appreciate Leighton's thought. The prospect of doing so was all the more attractive in that he could work in one of his favoured modes: annotating some of the best passages and then publishing both text and annotations as a kind of dual offering. This first approach worked well as a kind of 'pump-priming' enterprise, but Coleridge's mind was too active to allow him to stay long in this subordinate position. The book was already assuming a life of its own. Even while it was still in the introductory stage, 'The Beauties of Leighton' became 'Aids to Reflection'.

As he began work on the project, moreover, his own habits of analysis and organization came to the fore. For some time he was able to follow his projected plan closely, sending passages from a volume of Leighton's work to the printer to be set up as type. An introductory section devoted

---

[21] Chapter 14 end: *CBL* II.
[22] Notebook 18 f 41(cf. *CN* III 3881). For 'Try...' the Authorized Version reads 'Prove...' (I Thess. 5:21).

largely to his own work was followed by about a hundred pages more of aphorisms that could be gathered together, first as 'Prudential', then as 'Moral and Philosophical'. He also marked a number of passages to be used for the 'Spiritual' Aphorisms, but presumably could not work on them while the first volumes were at the printers. In any case, however, his own mind was refusing to be as passive to Leighton's as his initial attitude had demanded, so that he found himself calling on other divines as well—now no longer taking what they had to say simply as subjects for acceptance and approving comment, but as legitimate objects for critical comment. At first, he concerned himself with the close relationship that must be assumed between the human Spirit and the human Will; and for the purpose of producing suitable passages turned not to Leighton but to Henry More and Bishop Hacket. Secondly, he turned to the need to discuss 'that which is indeed Spiritual Religion'. In doing so he specifically excluded subjects such as the Trinity and the origin of Evil, which were not, he claimed, proper topics for reflection. The latter could be located rather in particular issues: of distinguishing between the Reason and the Understanding in the human mind; of Evil and of Original Sin. In the case of the first, statements by Leighton could be included, even if Coleridge could lament that he had not fully made out the necessary distinction involved, and could record with gratification that it had recently been adopted in his lectures by the current Professor of Anatomy.[23] While being guilty of a little disingenuousness in this, not revealing that his recent association with Joseph Henry Green had been as close as it had in fact been, he felt authorized to present evidence of his own concerning the mental abilities of animals, and their limitations. The matter of original sin, on the other hand, he approached by way of a quotation from Jeremy Taylor with which he had already taken issue in *The Friend*. Taylor had founded his case on the statement that 'Adam had turned his back on the Sun, and dwelt in the Dark and the Shadow':

He sinned, and brought evil into his Supernatural endowments, and lost the Sacrament and instrument of Immortality, the Tree of Life in the centre of the Garden.

The passage that Coleridge had picked on particularly in his earlier discussion, however, was Taylor's view of the later fate of mankind:

---

[23] See *CAR* 242–3 and nn.

'God on Adam's Account *was so exasperated with Mankind, that being angry* he would still continue the punishment!'[24] This lack of common justice on the part of the punishing divinity struck him as unacceptable—indeed it is hard to understand how he reconciled it with his unqualified praise of Taylor's wisdom elsewhere. His own view was that to think of sin as being inherited in such a sense involved mistaking the nature of time and causation. Once it was grasped that Adam's sin was an *eternal* fact, springing from his own inherent human nature, there was no need to think in terms of heritage and later responsibility, or indeed of innocence as such, since however regarded, it meant that the capability of sinning was planted in humanity for all generations. Its 'origin', in this sense, was a fact outside chronological time altogether.

The existence of sin and the need for a redeemer he nevertheless took to be incontestable facts—even if at the same time he found orthodox accounts and explanations deficient. In attempting an adequate account of his own he was forced to fall back on the conception of human evil as mysterious, and to recognize the mystery as one that he had wrestled with for many years. In literary terms it had created a difficulty in completing *Christabel*, particularly as it involved the question of Geraldine and her significance. Was she an incarnation of evil and its versatility, or would it be truer to think of her as embodying the very ambiguity of human energy? Her behaviour in Part One of the poem, notably the moment when after the drinking of Christabel's mother's wine and the glittering of her eyes,

> The lofty lady stood upright:
> She was most beautiful to see,
> Like a lady of a far countrée

could be read as a tribute to the beauty of energy; yet her behaviour next day was more questionable. Years later, when he produced a prose gloss like that accompanying the 1817 version of the *Mariner*, he was careful to bring out Geraldine's evil. It would be tempting to regard the prose version as presenting an authoritative interpretation, with Coleridge's own *imprimatur*, but it is equally possible to suppose that Geraldine stood for a crucial ambiguity in his thought, which never left him.

If evil constituted a mystery, then, it could be resolved only by way of another mystery, that of faith, which in turn rested on yet another, that

---

[24] *CAR* 280 (cf. *Friend* I 433).

of Reason, the God-given endowment of human beings which was to be distinguished from the Understanding, a power shared by humans with the animal and even the vegetable creation. It was this Reason alone which could respond intuitively to the divine Grace and Truth—which were in turn agents of the divine redemption.

Guilt, meanwhile, had assumed a more sinister form. Instead of the venial dissipations of his younger days, he was now in the imprisoning clutches of opium, against which his human will power struggled in vain. (Indeed, the nature of withdrawal symptoms was not recognized or understood at that time, so that his very efforts to fight against his cravings could actually increase their painfulness.) Innocence, on the other hand, induced 'Reflection', now one of Coleridge's most fruitful words—even if also one of his most ambiguous. If it stressed the need to think deeply, in a manner that did not always come readily to human beings, it also involved, through the imagery of light, the assumption that opening one's mind must produce illumination from within, and that that illumination must necessarily correspond to religious truth: St John's 'light that lighteth every man that cometh into the world'.

This ambiguity haunts *Aids to Reflection* throughout. The first point is emphasized in the closing paragraphs, where Coleridge rounds on a supposed reader who claims that he is 'content to think, with the *great* Dr Paley, and the learned Archbishop of Dublin ...' with the accusation 'You do not *think* at all!' The second meaning is apparent, meanwhile, in his characterizations of an 'enthusiastic Mystic', such as Boehme, and a Mystic of the 'second and higher order', such as Fénelon, along with the affirmation that 'the delightful Dream, which the latter tells, is a Dream of Truth; and that even in the bewildered Tale of the former there is Truth mingled with the Dream'. These, for Coleridge, are states to which all true reflection might respond.

There were other issues to be addressed, which for various reasons could not be brought under 'Aids to Reflection'. The most notable was the discussion contained in his letters 'On the right and the Superstitious Use of the Sacred Scriptures', offered to a publisher in 1825, but not actually published under its eventual title, 'Confessions of an Inquiring Spirit', during his lifetime. The reason for the delay may have been his fear of a hostile reception—a fear that was seen to be not unjustified when, despite the enthusiasm shown by figures such as John Sterling and Thomas Arnold, their posthumous publication in 1848 occasioned part of an article in the *English Review* entitled

'On Tendencies towards the Subversion of Faith'.[25] The other disquisitions mentioned in *Aids to Reflection* were on Faith, the Eucharist, Prayer, the Hebrew Prophets, and the Church; the last one (the only one that could be said to have reached something like fruition) became the pamphlet known as *On the Constitution of the Church and State*; fragments of others that he planned would survive among his unpublished manuscripts.

On the Constitution of the Church and State was in fact to be one of his most successful achievements. Yet no less than others of his later years, it bore marks of the internal conflict that still remained as a result of his lasting tendency to think in terms of the processes of life. At its best this could show itself as a fine mode of reconciliation, as in one of his most successful pieces of imagery for the relationship between the different powers in the state:

As the olive tree is said in its growth to fertilize the surrounding soil; to invigorate the roots of the vines in its immediate neighbourhood, and to improve the strength and flavour of the wines—such is the relation of the Christian and the National Church. But as the olive is not the same plant with the vine, or with the elm or poplar (*i.e.* the State) with which the vine is wedded; and as the vine with its prop may exist, though in less perfection, without the olive, or prior to its implantation—even so is Christianity, and a fortiori any particular scheme of Theology derived and supposed (by its partizans) to be *deduced* from Christianity, no essential part of the *Being* of the *National* Church...[26]

Although he could successfully incorporate a piece of natural lore into his argument, however, he was acutely aware of potential objections from contemporary readers. Accordingly, he subjoined an appendix to the work, consisting of a dialogue between his own 'unworldly' self, as an 'Allocosmite', and a fancied supporter of the contemporary world, 'Demosius of Toutoscosmos'. Under this guise he could set forth the more esoteric elements of his creed, which laid particular stress on the element of apparent design in the instinctual order, as when the larva of the Stag-beetle was found to occupy a space corresponding to the length it would need for itself when fully grown.

Such design could then be seen as serving the divine moral purpose. The play of Coleridge's mind, which had first taken him from an

[25] See *CSWF* (CC) II 1114–5 and *The English Review*, X (1848) 399–444.
[26] *CSS* 56, discussed further on p. 232 below.

acknowledgement of the charms of natural religion to a Berkeleyan belief in nature as the book in which God had written his revelation, had now led him to a belief in the sublime not as something readily available to the eye of the natural observer but as, ultimately, a gift of religious faith. This progression was most fully expressed many years later in the *Opus Maximum* manuscripts, where he discussed the proper religious approach to nature, finding it neither in the eighteenth-century empirical approach nor in the Berkeleyan, but in a mode transcending both. Having asked 'What...can be more delightful, more suited to our nature, than the argument from the order and harmony of the visible World, from the general adaptation of means to ends, and of an infinity and intrication of means and proximate ends, to the one ultimate end of beauty in all, and enjoyment in all, that live?', he gave his backing to the 'great Truth that there is a divine Author of an order so excellent... We feel the full force, we acknowledge the complete justice of the analogy so beautifully display'd by Bishop Berkeley between the world and a book, and find it as impossible to contemplate the one as to read the other without involving the conception of an intelligent Author.' Both arguments were, however, he now maintained, inadequate:

The difference is found not in any diversity of kind in the languages of the one or the other, but in the transcendent perfection only of that Divine eloquence in which the Heavens declare the Glory of God and the Firmament sheweth his handiwork.[27]

Having quoted more of the psalm, Coleridge went on to assert:

This method of proof, judged by its practical value and in reference to the ultimate purpose of all proofs, namely that we should all have a firm and lively faith in the existence of God, not that all men should be enabled to give a philosophic demonstration of existence, deserves and will ever retain its superiority over all other grounds of conviction.

At a literary level, this re-established the supremacy of Milton, who was to come under the hostile gaze of much twentieth-century criticism for his supposed insensitivity to the potentialities of the English language. 'Milton's celestial and infernal regions,' wrote T. S. Eliot, 'are large but insufficiently furnished apartments filled by heavy conversation.'[28] F. R. Leavis, likewise, felt that Milton's writing in his later verse lacked the Shakespearean life that had allowed him even in *Comus* to write of the

---

[27] *OM* 108–9. [28] *Selected Essays* (London: Faber and Faber, 1933), p. 321.

Millions of spinning Worms
That in their green shops weave the smooth-haired silk...[29]

Coleridge felt differently. The one word which summed up Milton, in his view, was 'ideality'.[30] If he did not resort to sensuous detail it was the result of a determined attempt to move beyond a state that might glorify the sensuous to the point where it risked lapsing into the sensual.[31] Coleridge particularly valued his unwillingness to make the impulse to grandeur an excuse for indulging in mere expansion. In his view it was a defect of poetry such as Klopstock's that sublimity was treated there quantitatively, rather than qualitatively: thus when the German poet likened God to a gardener who goes forth and scatters seeds, he could continue: '...so does the Creator scatter worlds with his right hand'. This comparison with smallness, he complained, did no more than make the Creator seem incredibly large.[32] In the same way he rejected the attempt by the translator of the Bhagavad-Gita to liken its imagery to Milton:

For if there be one character of genius predominant in Milton it is this, that he never passes off bigness for greatness. Children never can make things big enough, and exactly so is it with the poets of India.[33]

Early and late, in other words, Coleridge needed to stress the fact that the sublime was not a matter of size. A true poet would appreciate this: the thoughts of such a writer were 'like *fire-flies* at night, in a wood, rising and declining—appearing and disappearing—beautiful only in the inconstancy of the effect'.[34] If the Divine Ideas were far removed from the apprehensions of human sense this did not mean that they lacked sublimity.

---

[29] F. R. Leavis, *Revaluation* (London: Chatto & Windus; Toronto: Macmillan, 1936), pp. 47–8.

[30] See Prince Hoare's account in the entry for 16 May 1808: *The Farington Diary*, ed. James Greig (8 vols., London: Hutchinson, 1922–8) V 62.

[31] Coleridge thought that *Paradise Regained*'s status as a didactic work made it, at least in kind, superior to *Paradise Lost*: see his marginalia to Hayley's *Life of Milton, CM* II 968–9, and Crabb Robinson's Diary for 23 December 1810: I 311–12.

[32] This extract from table talk recollected by John Taylor Coleridge in 1811, evidently embodies a reminiscence from his meeting with Klopstock at the turn of the century: *CTT* I 6–7.

[33] *COM* 281.

[34] From a lecture of 20 January 1812, reported in *The Rifleman* of 26 January; cf. *CLects (1809–1819)* I 401–3.

Coleridge's final assertions had led him back eventually to the faith he had first glimpsed in his childhood and youth. The realization that had gradually dawned on him was of its self-reinforcing power, once taken as a guiding principle. He repeatedly quoted St Augustine's 'crede ut intelligas' ('believe in order that you may understand')[35] and in *Aids to Reflection* urged his readers to 'try' Christianity, asserting that if their assumptions were based on limited, eighteenth-century 'reasoning' they should be subjugated to the kind of 'Reason' that acceptance of Christian faith would liberate in them.

The play of his own mind by no means ceased. A number of the poems which he wrote and published in subsequent years included elements resulting from meditations on the coming of age and, more particularly, his failure to find true and lasting domestic love (a feature of his career that he felt linked him to the older Milton).[36] 'The Improvisator' was one example; another was given the simple subtitle 'Allegory'. In time he found reviving in him the spirit of Romance, as in 'The Garden of Boccaccio'. The setting he imagines, or describes, is that of sitting in despondency, and finding that even evocation of late events in his life does not have the power to lift his gloom, until a companion (presumably Anne Gillman) quietly slips an illustration of Boccaccio on to his desk. The result is that memories of his past life are transfigured and illuminated as he is now encouraged to view them in a magical light; best of all, he experiences a sense of warmth, and a reviving of the childhood imaginative state by which one is not only enchanted by an imagined scene but enabled actually to re-enter it—an analogue of Lewis Carroll's Wonderland. Through the operating of this looking-glass effect, Coleridge experiences a reversal of the very paradigm on which 'The Eolian Harp' had been based. Now the virtuous beloved is no longer his young bride, disastrously projected as reproving his romantic speculations, but a Boccaccian heroine, who, having learned to read 'Ovid's holy book of love's sweet smart', can afford to forget her 'Dian vest' and the 'vestal fires, of which her lover grieves', in favour of 'that sly satyr peeping through the leaves!' Something of the same limited indulgence is at work in the poem, subtitled 'A Ballad', which was given the title 'Alice du Clos: or the Forked Tongue': the story of a young woman who, while sitting engrossed in 'Dan Ovid's

---

[35] See e.g. *CM* I 605n and *CAR* 9 and n.
[36] Cf. the conclusion to a lecture of about 1818, recorded in his *Literary Remains* of 1836–9 (I 172–8) and in *CLects (1808–19)* II 425–9.

mazy tale of loves', is asked to hasten and join her betrothed lover on a hunting expedition. She tells the false and predatory knight who brings the message to take back her reply:

> 'Go tell thy Lord, that slow is sure:
>   Fair speed his shafts to-day!
> I follow here a stronger lure,
>   And chase a gentler prey.'

The knight does so but also reports his observation that as she spoke she had an eye fixed on 'her wanton page'—whereupon Lord Julian, when she arrives at last, accompanied by her page, is convinced of her infidelity and kills her.

The point of the poem evidently lies in the ambiguity of the word 'page', but reflection prompts further questions. A twenty-first century moralist could argue that her preference of reading a book to participation in a blood sport confirms her innocence, but a strict moralist of Coleridge's own day might well question the morality of taking delight in Ovid's writings—and would no doubt have been supported in this by Coleridge himself, at least in certain of his moods. That he was willing to write so indulgently of Alice's taste suggests, however, that he was not too disturbed by it and more exercised by the problem of textual ambiguity, with its possible effects. Such concern would square with his care for precision, not only in the wording of his poems but in the formulations of his philosophy.

It is also taken for granted that Lord Julian's reaction of killing his betrothed is natural, jealousy justifying murderous rage. Throughout the poem, nevertheless, the stress is on her essential innocence:

> As spotless fair, as airy light
>   As that moon-shiny doe,
> The gold star on its brow, her sire's ancestral crest! . . .
> Her face half drooping from the sight,
>   A snow-drop on a tuft of snow!

Her page (who does not, it must be noted, suffer from Lord Julian's jealous revenge) is also innocent:

> Florian was a stripling squire,
>   A gallant boy of Spain,
> That toss'd his head in joy and pride,
> Behind his Lady fair to ride,
>   But blush'd to hold her train.

Coleridge's horror, as when he saddled the Mariner with guilt after the casual action of killing a bird, is at the mindless destruction of a living creature at play. Ovid's 'mazy tale', meanwhile, need not be condemned as pornography for it had the saving grace of imaginative romance, which, in Coleridge's eyes, established Alice's essential innocence: 'Guilt was a thing impossible to her.'[37] Innocence, like all forms of imaginative activity, was, in the nature of things, playful.

---

[37] See his characterizations both of Joan of Arc: *CPW* (EHC) I 137; and of Dorothy Wordsworth: *CL* I 330.

15

Lucency and Florescences

From time to time, Coleridge was overtaken by depression. In spite of his ebullient spirits when in the company of the Wordsworths or attending Humphry Davy's lectures, the nightmare that the world might after all be an impersonal machine, set up in a hidden creative operation, would come back all too readily. He wrote in one of his notebooks,

Of the sentimental cantilena respecting the benignity and loveliness of NATURE—how does it not sink before the contemplation of a pravity of nature, on whose reluctance and inaptness a form is forced (the mere reflex of that form which is itself absolute Substance!) and which it struggles against, bears but for a while and then sinks with alacrity of self-seeking into dust or sanies, falls abroad into endless nothings or creeps and cowers in poison or explodes in havock— What is the beginning? What the end?—And how evident an alien is the supernatant in the brief interval?—[1]

Over the years it seemed to him increasingly that the course of human life could be viewed as a perpetual struggle between the human mind and the dull facts of Nature. He expressed the point memorably in a letter to one of the people who looked after him in his last years, James Gillman—though there he could not resist the temptation to treat nature as personalized:

the more we have seen, the less we have to say. In Youth and early Manhood the Mind and Nature are, as it were, two rival Artists, both potent Magicians, and engaged, like the King's Daughter and the rebel Genie in the Arabian Nights' Entertainments, in sharp conflict of conjuration, each having for it's object to turn the other into Canvas to paint on, Clay to mould, or cabinet to contain. For a while the mind seems to have the better in the contest, and makes of Nature what it likes; takes her Lichens and Weather-stains for Types and Printer's Ink, and prints Maps and facsimiles of Arabic and Sanscrit MSS, on her rocks; composes Country-Dances on her moonshiny ripples, Fandangos on her Waves, and Waltzes on Her Eddy-pools, transforms her Summer Gales into

---

[1] CNB 21$^{1/2}$ f 40 (cf. *CN* IV 4602 var).

Harps and Harpers, Lovers' Sighs and Sighing Lovers, and her Winter Blasts into Pindaric Odes, Christabels, and Ancient Mariners set to music by Beethoven, and in the insolence of triumph conjures her clouds into Whales and Walruses with Palanquins on their backs, and chases the dodging Stars in a sky-hunt! But alas! alas! that Nature is a wary wily long-breathed old Witch, tough-lived as a turtle and divisible as the Polyp, repullulative in a thousand snips and cuttings, integra et in toto! She is sure to get the better of Lady Mind in the long run and to take her revenge too; transforms our today into a canvass dead-colored to receive the dull featureless portrait of yesterday: not alone turns the mimic Mind, the ci-devant Sculptress with all her kaleidoscopic freaks and symmetries! into clay, but leaves it such a clay, to cast dumps or bullets in; and lastly (to end with that which suggested the beginning) she mocks the mind with its own metaphors, metamorphosing the Memory into a lignum vitae Escritoire to keep unpaid Bills and Dun's letters in, with outlines that had never been filled up, MSS. that never went further than the Title-pages, and Proof-sheets, and foul copies of Watchmen, Friends, Aids to Reflection and other stationary wares that have kissed the Publishers' Shelf with Gluey Lips with all the tender intimacy of inosculation![2]

Coleridge's difficulty in finding a satisfactory solution to the problem of evil was reflected in a further feature of his work as discerned by Vigus: elaborate promises, frequent enough in his writing, tended to be accompanied by inability to produce a completely positive verbal conclusion.

For major Romantic writers of the time this was not untypical. However powerful their initial insights, they were forced eventually to recognize that their view of human life must involve a recognition of paradox in its essential nature. As Blake put it at one point in his mid-career,

> Do what you will, this Life's a Fiction
> And is made up of Contradiction[3]

For Coleridge, the only possible resolution of the problem lay in the possibility of overcoming death. He concluded his poem 'Human Life, On the Denial of Immortality' with the lines:

> Be sad! Be glad! Be neither! seek, or shun!
> Thou hast no reason why! Thou canst have none!
> Thy being's being is contradiction.

---

[2] Letter to Gillman, 9 October 1825, *CL* V 496–7.   [3] *BK* 751.

Wordsworth, considering the beauty of women, came to accept that happiness in the marriage to the woman he loved must involve reconciling the welcome, but necessarily occasional, visitations of celestial light that he saw in her with the fact of her everyday domestic homeliness. Coleridge, on the other hand, already caught into an unsuitable marriage, committed himself to the 'eternal' aspect he perceived in Sara's similar radiance, paying scant attention to any other social needs she might have. In the same way, he moved away from his early Unitarianism, hoping to discover a version of Christianity more fitted to his needs—though he did not find traditional Anglicanism altogether satisfactory, either.

One pattern above all emerges from the play of his mind as it tried to make sense of the universe: it was the gravest of mistakes to imagine that truth would eventually be discovered in some version of stability, or stabilities. Ultimate truth must rather be found, if at all, behind the dialectical play of stability and movement. In this respect the Mariner's dawn vision—a central sun in perpetual interplay with energies which it both emitted and received back—remained utterly central, while the attempt to anchor himself in his vision of Sara Hutchinson's 'eternal Self' was doomed to failure. His larger perception was crucial to his favourite imagery of reflection, for example, calling for an unusual kind of mental agility which would be in itself a kind of play—the ability to indulge in processes which allowed the mind at once to objectivize phenomena into determinate forms or delight in their own movement. Early on in *Aids to Reflection* this was expressed in a footnote, in which he looked back to his earlier appreciation of Horne Tooke's work Ἔπεα Πτερόεντα, meaning literally 'Winged Words'. There he states that his own impulse would have been to found the subject of his discourse not in 'ἔπεα' but 'λόγοι'—immediately tempering the point, however, by indicating another word that might be used for the translation: 'ῥῆμα'—meaning, literally, a flowing.[4] In this necessary dialectic between stability and flowing he thus envisaged a master-strategy for understanding the universe. But in the absence of any language that might encapsulate such a complicated mental process, the only resort was to adopt the word 'logos', and by adding the adjective 'living' express its dynamic aspect. If this dualism were to be expressed verbally, it would be necessary to find some mediating concept—which he in

---

[4] *CAR* 7n. This point was made only in the 1825 edition. For a full discussion see *CAR* 551.

fact reached towards in his image of the moon. It could be argued that such an insight had already existed in the ancient mythology which had rejected the sun as a straightforward image by reason of its essential nature of destructiveness, yet could not remain content with resigning itself to lifeless earthly or earthy matter; the moon was a necessary mediating image, reflecting the light of the sun without transmitting its destructive energy.

The problem for Coleridge was that when brought against the demands of the material world his thinking might only be regarded as a kind of moonshine: bewitching in its charm, and particularly in its resource for poetic imagery, perhaps, but desperately impractical as a way of coping with the 'real world'. It was not surprising if, greeting the need to earn his keep and bring up a family, and living in a society which had been deeply challenged by the implications of the French Revolution, Coleridge felt the need to offer some programme or message of hope to his fellows; but this, unfortunately, was not where his best gifts lay. He felt an immediate sympathy with those of his young contemporaries who, like Wordsworth, had 'yielded up moral questions in despair', yet when he tried to cope with the situation by straightforward political writings, it was to discover that his seed fell on stony ground.

Other problems were deeply personal—particularly his recognition of the treachery of nature involved in the trust he placed in opium, and even in the writings of Jacob Boehme, whose apparent attempts to reconcile an instinctive feeling for nature with Christian philosophy he had championed at an early age. Had his delight in eliciting from Boehme's discourse philosophical insight been in the end no more than a kind of conjuring?

The belief that the deepest truths could not be put into words, only intimated, that was central to much of his developed religious thinking, had been expressed many years before in *The Rime of the Ancient Mariner,* where he had evoked a kind of vision that might bring together music and light.

> Around, around, flew each sweet sound,
> Then darted to the sun;
> Slowly the sounds came back again,
> Now mixed, now one by one.

There were also, he believed, experiences available in nature which though not to be relied on as themselves providing permanent vision, combined light and glory in a manner that could be thought of as embodying truth symbolically. In 'The Three Graves', for instance, the two young female characters, Ellen and Mary, are struck at one point by the extraordinary beauty of what they see:

'The sun peeps through the close thick leaves,
    See, dearest Ellen! see!
'Tis in the leaves, a little sun,
    No bigger than your ee;

A tiny sun, and it has got
    A perfect glory too;
Ten thousand threads and hairs of light,
Make up a glory gay and bright
Round that small orb, so blue.'

This kind of visionary moment in the midst of nature then recurs many years later in the ballad 'Alice du Clos'—another poem which is destined for melodrama, but in which there is a glimpse of the visionary in nature as Alice dresses for the hunt:

There stands the flow'ring may-thorn tree!
From thro' the veiling mist you see
    The black and shadowy stem:—
Smit by the sun the mist in glee
Dissolves to lightsome jewelry—
    Each blossom hath its gem!

At this point, when the flowering may-thorn is transfigured by the advent of the sun, the imagery of light is caught up into that of vegetating nature.

The phenomenon of light, most particularly the illumination emitted by human beings, fascinated Coleridge all his life. After the tonic writings of 1802, with Coleridge foreshadowing many of his later critical ideas, a modulation in his mind occurred, largely to do with his intensified love for Sara Hutchinson. But already, he judged literature—even more, perhaps, art—by the element of illumination it included. Speaking affectionately to Godwin about Charles Lamb in the spring of 1800,[5] he contrasted him with the men of mere talents:

Conversation with the latter tribe is like the use of leaden bells—one warms by *exercise*—Lamb every now and then *eradiates*, and the beam, though single and fine as a hair, is yet rich with colours, and I both see and feel it.—

[5] *CL* I 588.

For him such illumination was a quality to be associated with the nature of true being. In a letter of December 1796, concluding a long discussion of the problem of life, in which he cites a number of opinions concerning its nature, he had remarked

And I, the last not least, I do not know what to think about it—on the whole, I have rather made up my mind that I am a mere apparition—a naked Spirit!— And that Life is I myself I! which is a mighty clear account of it.[6]

As in Coleridge's more tantalizing statements, he clearly means more than he allows himself to say, seeming to indicate, as far as the passing clues may be followed, an identification between the essential nature of life and the central sense of identity—even if use of the words 'a mere apparition' and 'naked Spirit' results in an effect of caricature.

When the phrase 'I myself I' turns up once more in Coleridge's writings, oblique light is perhaps thrown on the statement under discussion. Some years later he wrote a poem entitled 'A Soliloquy of the Full Moon, she being in a mad Passion', which he sent to Sara Hutchinson. It is a light-hearted piece, describing the exasperation of the moon at being compared by poets to such objects as a sickle, a canoe, a half-cheese, a Barley-mow or an ostrich's egg. The moon concludes,

> But now Heaven be praised in contempt of the Loon,
> I am I myself I, the jolly full Moon.

Remembering Coleridge's habit of interchanging his serious ideas with those in his light verse, we may ask whether the connection between 'I myself I' and the moon may not cover a deeper concern, exercised quite differently in other contexts. Could it be that Coleridge thinks of the naked spirit, the 'apparition' of a personal identity, as something which irradiates from within a person, just as the moon may appear, say, behind a cloud? Such a reading could not be derived other than tortuously from the poem, yet the suspicion that Coleridge was exchanging light-hearted whimsy with speculation of another kind may be reinforced from his occasional habit of commenting on other people in these terms. To his praising phrase 'Lamb sometimes *eradiates*,' may be added the image, even more to the point, used for his own son Hartley:

An utter visionary! like the Moon among thin Clouds, he moves in a circle of Light of his own making—he alone, in a Light of his own.

---

[6] *CL* I 295.

When these statements are set alongside his description of Hartley as 'an apparition of Love' the suspicion grows that a view of personal identity as associated with an inner physical irradiation was gaining on him in these years, this in its turn being intimately related to the operation of love.

This may be the reason why Coleridge was fascinated by the natural phenomenon known as the 'glory'—a phenomenon which, in his own words,

occurs occasionally when the Air is filled with fine particles of frozen Snow, constituting an almost invisibly subtle Snow-mist, and a person is walking with the Sun behind his Back. His Shadow is projected, and he sees a figure moving before him with a glory round his Head. I have myself seen it twice, and it is described in the 1st or 2d Volume of the Manchester Philosophical Transactions.[7]

The article he mentions is the one from which he himself had transcribed a passage into an early notebook. In it, John Haygarth describes how, returning to Chester at sunset, he 'was struck with the peculiar appearance of a very white shining cloud, that lay remarkably close to the ground':

I walked up to the cloud, and my shadow was projected into it; the head of my shadow was surrounded at some distance by a circle of various colours whose centre appeared to be near the situation of the eye, and whose circumference extended to the Shoulders. The circle was complete except where the shadow of my body intercepted it—it exhibited the most vivid colors red being outermost—all the colors appeared in the same order & proportion that the rainbow presents to our view.[8]

This is a slightly different image from that of the moon. In the latter case it is an irradiation within the individual himself which is stressed; here it is what the light behind him does to an image, projected away from himself, that is in question. But since Haygarth's account of the Glory appears in the same volume of the *Manchester Memoirs* as an article on the vital principle from which Coleridge seems to have culled much of the knowledge of theories of life which precede his own statement, it seems possible that his speculations on irradiating identity and the nature of the Glory took place at the same time.

---

[7] From an annotated copy of *Aids to Reflection: CAR* 227n.

[8] *Memoirs of the Literary and Philosophical Society of Manchester* III 463, quoted by Coleridge in CNBG f 73ᵛ (cf. *CN* I 258). See also *RX* 29 and n.

Was the soul itself, then, to be regarded as material or immaterial? Either way, problems arose. Coleridge was drawn to Descartes, the leading philosopher on the subject, and in his Lectures quoted the view that if God had pleased, 'twice two should not have been four, nor the three angles of a plain triangle equal to two right ones, and the like', a view which helped to establish the sense of an indwelling, God-given reason. This view he seems to have derived not from Descartes directly, but from Cudworth, who quoted it. But it is also clear that he read Descartes himself, for two Latin quotations in his notebooks have been traced to the *Meditations*. Translated, they read as follows:

Just as a slave, who in his sleep enjoys an imaginary liberty, fears to wake as soon as he begins to suspect that his liberty is but a dream, and acquiesces in these agreeable illusions . . .

and

. . . fallen into very deep water, I can neither find foothold at the bottom, nor swim to keep myself at the top.

Just why Coleridge transcribed these particular passages we cannot know: very often at this time he seems to have used his notebook to store up phrases for later rhetorical use. It is noticeable, however, that both refer, directly or indirectly, to dream-states. And in taking the trouble to read Descartes in the original Latin he was engaging himself with one of the most subtle discussions of the problem of knowledge in the history of thought. If he extended his reading to the *Discourse on Method*, he would also have come across the celebrated passage recording his adoption of the maxim 'I think therefore I am', followed by the reflection that

. . . this I, that is to say, the soul by which I am what I am, is entirely distinct from the body, and even easier to know than the body, and although the body were not, the soul would not cease to be all that it is.[9]

—a statement which might have helped Coleridge formulate the phrase 'I myself I'. In the *Meditations*, however, he would certainly have found much discussion of the nature of knowledge, including an acknowledgement of the possibility of delusion, as much in waking life as in sleeping life, along with the assertion that nevertheless we possess the

---

[9] *Discourse on Method*, in *Discourse on Method and Related Writings* (1637), trans. Desmond M. Clarke (Harmondsworth: Penguin, 1999), Part 5, 40.

ability to distinguish between delusory and true experiences. Other relevant ideas in Descartes include his reflection that when he discovers certain properties of a triangle they seem to 'call to remembrance something that I knew before', his statement, 'I am lodged in my body like a pilot in his boat', and (most pregnant of all, perhaps) his assertion of a relationship between the infinity in God and the infinity in human beings.

Coleridge always spoke of Descartes with respect, and used some of his ideas in writings such as *The Friend*; but we need not suppose that he took over the Cartesian positions without amendment. If they are set in the context of other intellectual concerns of the time indeed, such as Priestley's belief in the material nature of the soul and his own 'Eolian harp' lines, one can see that it would have been more natural for him to be working towards a view of the 'I myself I' which would give it a firmer physiological basis.

The theory to be advanced here is that during the summer of 1795, particularly, Coleridge explored further some of the territory mapped out by Descartes, hoping to throw light on the manner in which the infinity in human beings might correspond to the infinity in God.

In the *Discourse on Method*, Descartes argues that the essential qualities which distinguish a human being from an animal which might be created mechanically in the same mould are twofold:

The first is, that they could never make use of words, or of other signs of the mind, as we do to declare our thoughts to each other . . .

And the second is, that although they might do many things as well as any of us, or perhaps better, they would infallibly be wanting in others, by which we should see that they did not act by knowledge, but merely after the disposition of their organs . . .[10]

What then is it that initiates the communicative power in words and the enlightening power in knowledge? If, with Descartes, we believe it to be the soul, is it possible to identify its powers any further?

During 1795 Coleridge would appear to have been seeking out possible analogies and images (the beanfield that starts up in paradisal scents to the touch of the breeze, the harp that is stirred by it into music), which might suggest intimately the relation between the power of God and the individual soul.

---

[10] Ibid.

He sometimes returned to the point in his later writing. He used the image of the glory both in *Aids to Reflection* and in his poem 'Constancy to an Ideal object'; the word 'apparition' is employed in another poem, 'Love's Apparition and Evanishment'. For reasons to be examined later, however, his use in the later works is a trifle stilted and restrained; the remarkable point in the early period is to see how images which a few months before would have been used under tight restraint are beginning to assume a presence of their own, the moral and natural worlds assimilating themselves to one another from Coleridge's renewed interest in the sense of an 'inward light', which treats it not just as a religious metaphor but a phenomenon to be observed in the faces of actual living people. It is responsible for the experience of seeing the natural world transformed not by its own workings but by the lucific power of human emotions and vision.

A crucial development in his thinking on the subject came as a result of the acquaintance that he formed in Rome during 1805 with the painter Washington Allston. There was evidently a good deal of cross-influence, and for Coleridge, at least, the period was to remain one of happy memories. Allston himself remembered Coleridge for his moments in 'the poetic state', 'when the divine afflatus of the poet possessed him':

When in that state, no face that I ever saw was like his; it seemed almost spirit made visible without a shadow of the physical upon it. Could I then have fixed it upon canvas!'

In his paintings of him he tried to render something of that quality—'but it was beyond the reach of my art'.[11] There are signs that Coleridge found him an easier artistic companion than Wordsworth and even tended to transfer some allegiance. This was particularly so in the period around 1813, when he showed himself extremely active on Allston's part, hurrying to go to Bristol when he was ill so that he could consult a physician, Dr George Leman Tuthill, who had treated Mary Lamb and whom he had consulted about his own opium problem.[12] It is no

---

[11] *CT* 107–9 (with memorial poem 'On Coleridge') and Seamus Perry, *S. T. Coleridge: Interviews and Recollections* (London: Palgrave, 2000), pp. 102–4, quoting J. B. Flagg, *Life and Letters of Washington Allston* (New York, 1892; London: R. Bentley and Son, 1893 (printed New York)), p.104.

[12] *CL* III 490n. In the event, being too ill to proceed to Clifton, Allston was forced to stop at Salt Hill, where he was joined by Coleridge and Tuthill. During his Bristol convalescence he painted the portrait of Coleridge now in the National Gallery.

accident, perhaps, that some of Coleridge most 'illuminist' public criticism came in the course of lectures that he gave subsequently in Bristol to assist Allston, who was by then exhibiting in the city at the Merchant Taylors' Hall.

It is rare to find his veneration of light expressed in a pure form. For poetic purposes, at least, it was most likely to occur in conjunction with his delight in the vegetative—particularly flowers—or even more, in birds. One of his finest lyrics, based roughly on a text by Tieck, was 'Glycine's Song' in *Zapolya*:

> A Sunny shaft did I behold,
>   From sky to earth it slanted:
> And poised therein a bird so bold—
>   Sweet bird, thou wert enchanted!
>
> He sank, he rose, he twinkled, he troll'd
>   Within that shaft of sunny mist;
> His eyes of fire, his beak of gold,
>   All else of amethyst!
>
> And thus he sang: 'Adieu! adieu!
> Love's dreams prove seldom true.
> The blossoms, they make no delay:
> The sparking dew-drops will not stay.
>   Sweet month of May,
>   We must away;
>   Far, far away!
>   To-day! to-day!'

In notes for a later lecture, on the other hand, can be found a restored search for correspondence:

Every step antecedent to consciousness found in Nature—so to place them as for some one effect, totalized, and fitted to the limits of a human Mind, as to elicit and as it were superinduce *into* the forms the reflection, to which they approximate—this is the Mystery of Genius in the Fine Arts—Dare I say that the Genius must act on the feeling, that *Body* is but a striving to become Mind—that it is *mind*, in its essence—?[13]

These notes became the posthumous essay produced for his *Literary Remains* entitled 'On Poesy or Art', in which (even if the words are not all indisputably Coleridge's) his best-known formulation is to be found:

[13] CNB 22 f 51 (cf. *CN* III 4397, repeated in *CLects* (1808–18) II 221).

In the objects of nature are presented, as in a mirror, all the possible elements, steps, and processes of intellect antecedent to consciousness, and therefore to the full development of the intelligential act; and man's mind is the very focus of all the rays of intellect which are scattered throughout the images of nature. Now so to place these images, totalized, and fitted to the limits of the human mind, as to elicit from, and to superinduce upon, the forms themselves the moral reflexions to which they approximate, to make the external internal, the internal external, to make nature thought and thought nature,—this is the Mystery of genius in the Fine Arts. Dare I say that the genius must act on the feeling, that body is but a striving to become mind,—that it is mind in its essence![14]

By the time of this statement he had also begun to set out the conception of symbolism quoted earlier, which included the formulation

a Symbol . . . is characterized by a translucence of the Special in the Individual or of the General in the Especial or of the Universal in the General. Above all by the translucence of the Eternal through and in the Temporal. It always partakes of the reality which it renders intelligible . . . .[15]

Here again, the paramountcy of light is reaffirmed in the word 'translucence'. There is also an autobiographical flavour to the picture of human life at the end of the 1818 lecture-note that became 'On Poesy or Art', distinguishing

The seeming Identity of Body and Mind in infants, and thence the loveliness of the former—the commencing separation in Boyhood, and the struggle of equilibrium in youth—from thence onward the Body first indifferent; then demanding the translucency of the mind not to be worse than indifferent—finally all that presents the Body as Body almost of a recremental ($\epsilon\xi$) nature.—[16]

The phrase 'translucency of the mind' is notable, as is also the tendency to make the 'body as body' excremental in nature. A similar image is used in some important—if pedestrian—lines written in old age:

> Whene'er the mist that stands between God and thee
> Defaecates to a pure transparency
> There Reason is and there begins her reign!

In this last phase, Coleridge's concern with the workings of energy seems to have waned, as he concentrated rather on the phenomena of light—still clinging to the idea, it seems, that the symbolism discernible in its power might turn out to spring from an actual power in nature.

---

[14] *CLR* I 222–3, reprinted in *CBL* (1907) II 257–8.
[15] See above p. 174, quoting *CSM* 30–1.   [16] *CLects (1808–19)* II 224–5.

The search for correspondence led him also to music, and especially any music apparently produced in nature. He reflected on the latter in a notebook entry of 10 September 1823:

An *Air* that whizzed δία ἐγκεφάλου (right across the diameter of my Brain) exactly like a Hummel Bee, <u>alias</u> Dumbeldore, the gentleman with Rappee Spenser, with bands of Red, and Orange Plush Breeches, close by my ear, at once sharp and *burry*, right over the summit of Quantock, at earliest Dawn, just between the Nightingale that I stopt to hear in the Copse at the Foot of Quantock, and the first Sky-Lark that was a Song-Fountain, dashing up and sparkling to the Ear's eye, in full Column, or ornamented Shaft of Sound in the Order of Gothic Extravaganza, out of Sight, over the Cornfields on the Descent of the Mountain on the other side—out of Sight, tho' twice I beheld its *mute* shoot downward in the sunshine like a falling Star of melted Silver:—

The 'Air' itself begins—

> Flowers are lovely, Love is flower-like,
> Friendship is a shelt'ring tree—[17]

As has already been mentioned, Coleridge's devotion to light was complemented by a corresponding delight in flowers and blossoms, one of the most striking features of his later life being an increasingly strong feeling for them. One reason was no doubt his settling down to life in a leafy suburb such as Highgate; another, the role of the flower in his mental lore as a symbol of the need of human beings for light and life. From the point when he could ask in *The Friend* 'Hast thou ever said to thyself thoughtfully, IT IS! heedless in that moment, whether it were a man before thee, or a flower, or a grain of sand?' the image of the flower was for him among the supreme instances of exemplary existence.

In his own career, a shift of emphasis is indicated by the movement between a note of April 1816, which he introduced as 'Reflections on my four gaudy flower-pots, compared with the former Flower-poems',[18] and in which the flowers discussed turn out to be simply pegs on which to hang a discussion of shifts in poetic fashion, and a note written just ten years later, which was devoted to the flowers themselves:

Spring Flowers, I have observed,—look best in the Day, and by Sunshine; but Summer or Autumnal Flower-pots by Lamp or Candle-light. I have now before

---

[17] CNB 3^{1/2} ff 117–17^v (cf. *CN* IV 4994 and *CPW* (EHC) II 1084–5).
[18] CNB 18 f 150^v (cf. *CN* III 4313).

me a Flower-pot of Cherry-blossoms, Polyanthuses double Violets, Periwinkle, Wall-flowers &c—but how dim & dusky they look![19]

His fondness was illustrated in the light-hearted verses of 1825 entitled 'The Reproof and Reply', excusing his 'theft' of some flowers from the garden of a neighbour, Mrs Chisholm. It was also no doubt responsible, two years later, for a gift from Mrs Gillman of his favourite plant, the myrtle. He wrote immediately a letter of appreciative gratitude:

My dear Friend

I received and acknowlege your this morning's Present, both as Plant and Symbol, each with appropriate thanks and correspondent feeling. The Rose is the Pride of Summer, the Delight and Beauty of our Gardens; the Eglantine, the Honey-suckle and the Jasmine, if not so bright or so ambrosial, are less transient, creep nearer to us, clothe our walls, twine over our porch, and haply peep in at our Chamber window, with the nested Wren or Linnet within the tufts warbling good morning to us.—Lastly, the Geranium passes the door, and in it's hundred varieties, imitating now this now that Leaf, Odor, Blossom of the Garden still steadily retains its own staid character, it's own sober and refreshing Hue and Fragrance. It deserves to be the Inmate of the House, and with due attention and tenderness will live thro' the winter, grave yet chearful, as an old family Friend that makes up for the departure of gayer Visitors in the leafless Season. But none of these are the MYRTLE! In none of these, nor in all collectively, will the MYRTLE find a Substitute.—All together, and joining with them all the aroma, the spices and the balsams of the Hot-house, yet should they be a sad exchange for the MYRTLE! O precious in it's sweetness is the rich innocence of its snow-white Blossoms! And dear are they in the remembrance—but these may pass with the Season, and while the Myrtle Plant, our own myrtle-plant remains unchanged, it's Blossoms are remembered the more to endear the faithful Bearer; yea, they survive invisibly in every more than fragrant Leaf. As the flashing Strains of the Nightingale to the yearning Murmur of the Dove, so the Myrtle to the Rose—He who has once possessed and prized a genuine Myrtle will rather remember it under the Cypress Tree, than seek to forget it among the Rose-bushes of a Paradise.

God bless you, my dearest Friend! and be assured that if Death do not suspend Memory and Consciousness, Death itself will not deprive you of a faithful Participator in all your hopes and fears, affections and solicitudes.[20]

---

[19] Note of 18 April 1826: CNB 23 f 46ᵛ (cf. ibid., IV 5356).
[20] Letter of May 3 1827: *CL* VI 678.

In these years, the importance of light had not diminished. His son-in-law vividly remembered his behaviour on an evening of June 1827:

How well I remember this Midsummer-day! I shall never pass such another. The sun was setting behind Caen Wood, and the calm of the evening was so exceedingly deep that it arrested Mr. Coleridge's attention. We were alone together in Mr. Gillman's drawing-room, and Mr. C. left off talking, and fell into an almost trance-like state for ten minutes whilst contemplating the beautiful prospect before us. His eyes swam in tears, his head inclined a little forward, and there was a slight uplifting of the fingers, which seemed to tell me that he was in prayer. I was awestricken, and remained absorbed in looking at the man, in forgetfulness of external nature, when he recovered himself, and after a word or two fell by some secret link of association upon Spenser's poetry.[21]

The strength of his response to the light of a sunset did not mean that it could for him be expressed in poetry. As he put it in a manuscript note of the same year, scribbled in the margins of a letter from Lady Beaumont:

Lady B. in this letter urges me to resume Poetry.—Alas! how can I?—Is the power extinct? No! No! As in a still Summer Noon, when the lulled Air at irregular intervals wakes up with a startled Hush-st, that seems to re-demand the silence which it breaks, or heaves a long profound Sigh in it's Sleep, and an Aeolian Harp has been left in the chink of the not quite shut Casement—even so—how often!—scarce a week of my Life shuffles by, that does not at some moment feel the spur of the old genial impulse—even so do there fall on my inward Ear swells, and broken snatches of sweet Melody, reminding me that I still have that within me which is both Harp and Breeze. But in the same moment awakes the Sense of Change without—Life unendeared. The tenderest Strings no longer thrill'd.

In order to poetic composition I need the varied feeling—Thought charmed to sleep; and the too great continuity of mind broken up, to begin anew, with new power seeking & finding new themes.[22]

Despite the touch of pessimism in this note, the mode of expression suggested that he was constantly returning to his vegetation/animation distinction:

A late Physiologist represents the nervous system as a Plant, of which the spinal Cord is the Stem and the Brain the compound Flower—and if you have ever watched a Humble-bee at a Fox-glove or a Monkshood, visiting one Bell after

---

[21] See HNC's note to Table Talk of 24 June 1827 (cf. *CTT* II 60).
[22] Comment in margin of letter from Lady Beaumont of 16 May 1828: see *CL* VI 731n.

another, and bustling and humming in each, you will have no bad likeness of the dips and dives I have been making into the several cells and campanulae of my Brain.[23]

In 1795, despite the check which restrained him as he wrote 'The Eolian Harp' (a check not unrelated to a foreboding of the moral defects just noted), he had possessed a mind that delighted in its own exercise, and which shortly afterwards received a new access of strength from frequent discussions with Wordsworth, who for a time found his powers indispensably complementary to his own.

It was natural for Coleridge, therefore, that any withdrawal from his strongest hopes should rekindle his delight in the vegetable world. His model for a human being would henceforward be that of the plant unfolding in accordance with its own law, allowing itself to be visited by energies but not normally allowing them free play. In a manuscript note making the old distinction in this new form, which suggested his growing suspicion of all free animation, he saw the Flower as the 'Crown of mature vegetative life' and its fragrance as the sign of its sacrificial nature:

All offering that is truly sacrificial, i.e. hallowing, sanctifying, proceeds from & is preceded by, and the act of a *Yearning*, desiderium, πόθος [pothos], στοργή [storge]—what will not the mother sacrifice when her bowels are yearning for her Child.—And this constitutes the diversity of Yearning and desire . . . Yearning offers up, resigns itself—passes wholly into another. Desire seizes hold of, draws to itself, devours, ravishes—and in its fiercest form (ex. gr. See a hornet devouring a peach thro' a magnifying glass) *ravages*, Hence in all ages, incense, fragrant steams, have been the accompaniments of sacrifice. Likewise of gentle Love.[24]

This love of flowers prompted small presents of them from his neighbour Eliza Nixon. When she sent a small bunch of celandines (a small scentless flower blooming in the early spring) he adapted an epigram by Claudian in thanks:

> Whate'er thou giv'st must still prove sweet to me:
> For still I find it redolent of thee.[25]

[23] *CL* V 464.
[24] BM MS Egerton 2800 f 155: cf *CSWF* II 1454–5. Coleridge goes on to recall Song of Solomon 1: 12–14—and 2: 1, 'I am the Rose of Sharon, and the Lily of the Valley', along with the perfume of the lover: III 6.
[25] *CPW* (CC) I (2) 1040.

A month before his death he wrote again about their fragrance and form:

That my Sense is from illness become obtuse to the fragrance of Flowers, I but little regret, but O! Let my eyes be closed when their Beauty is no longer revealed to me—& finds no counterpart in my mind—[26]

In contrast to the plant's symbolism of love, yearning, and sacrifice, the insect is seen as

the Symbol of Appetite, Desire—Lust hard by hate, Manifold motions making little speed And to deform and kill the things whereon they feed.[27]

Blake had a similar feeling for flowers, with their fragrance and intimations of eternity, but had a much more jaded view of vegetation as such, seeing any leaning towards the vegetated state among human beings as a fall. He showed in 'The Sick Rose', moreover, that he shared Coleridge's awareness of the manner in which an energy in nature might work against a beautiful vegetative form. Yet while Blake became disillusioned concerning the possibilities of free energy, his political enthusiasm in some of the early prophetic books being short-lived, he never lost his faith that through continual creative use of his energies man was enabled to keep alive the divine image in himself. Indeed, he used the very same word that Coleridge had employed ('storge', the yearning of a parent for its young) to express something which he saw as dangerous: His state of Ulro was seen at one point as inhabited by certain females who span it from their bowels

> with songs of amorous delight
> And melting cadences that lure the Sleepers of Beulah down
> The River Storge (which is Arnon) into the Dead Sea...[28]

More than one critic, noticing how Coleridge used the terms death-in-life and life-in-death in his *Epitaph*, has seen in this a continuing identification of his own career with that of his own Mariner. Any very ready interpretation on these lines, however, is defeated by the fact that whereas he speaks of his own 'death in life' the Mariner's fate was very explicitly that of 'life in death'.

The relationship between epitaph and ballad is, I suggest, a shade subtler. Coleridge, it may be argued, became aware over the years (even if he had not felt before) that he as a human being was at once Mariner

[26] *CL* VI 984.   [27] *CSWF* II 1454–5.   [28] *Milton* 34: 28–30 (*BK* 524).

and shipmate. He, as much as anyone else, had to bear the burden of mechanical living and the weight of custom. But he also responded to the pulse of inner consciousness which continues to speak of other awarenesses, other modes. As a human being he knew the burden of daily living, as a poet the haunting divergence between external and internal perceivings. When he reached Malta and stepped ashore after many trials and tribulations, his self-identification next day was with the Mariner:

> Found myself light as a blessed Ghost—[29]

But when he had been there for some time, knowing the burden of hopelessness and its effect upon his work, his imagining mind was dominated by the plight of the shipmates:

I work hard, I do the duties of common Life from morn to night/ but verily—I raise my limbs, 'like lifeless Tools'—The organs of motion & outward action perform their functions at the stimulus of a galvanic fluid applied by the *Will*, not by the Spirit of Life that makes Soul and Body one.[30]

In the *Epitaph* Coleridge was not simply making straightforward use of his poem; the ideas that had organized it were evidently still present in his mind.

In his last days, visitations from previous imaginings were not un-common. 'I am dying,' he said, 'but without expectation of a speedy release.' Words and phrases which he had used in writing to his son Derwent some years before were now included in a statement that would be used by Henry Nelson Coleridge to conclude a record of his Table Talk:

Is it not strange that very recently bygone images and scenes of early life have stolen into my mind, like Breezes blown from the spice-islands of Youth and Hope—those twin realities of this phantom world! I do not add Love; for what is Love but Youth and Hope embracing, and so seen as one? I say realities: for reality is a thing of degrees, from the Iliad to a dream . . .[31]

The phenomenon brought into play here fits Coleridge's old pattern of ideas. For if, as he had suggested many years before, death belonged strictly to the sphere of the organic, it was not at all out of place that in

---

[29] CNB 10 f 2 (cf. *CN* II 2100).
[30] Note of April 1805, CNB 17 f 76 (cf. *CN* II 2557).
[31] See the 1835 edition: *CTT* II 296.

the decline of vitality the organic, and the memory which belonged to it, should release memories from its past, or that the bulk of the dying body should greet them as fallen Satan had glimpsed paradise itself:

> As when to them who sail
> Beyond the Cape of Hope, and now are past
> Mozambic, off at sea north-east winds blow
> Sabean odours from the spicy shore
> Of Arabie the blest.

The ability of youth, with hope clinging round it like the climbing vine, to transfigure the world, had been lost, until a vegetative and odoriferous paradise had become the true reality in what was more like a phantom world. 'Yet, in a strict sense,' Coleridge said just afterwards, 'reality is not predictable at all of aught below Heaven.' Even when he came to say of himself, in 1815, that 'in all but the Brain I am an old man'[32] the exception deserves to be noted. Certainly the play of his mind, including the double strategy of 'The Improvisatore', continued unabated, The old ambiguities persisted—to be resolved, he no doubt hoped, in death itself. The same riddle haunts the *Epitaph* itself, composed some time earlier:

> Stop, Christian passer-by: Stop, child of God,
> And read, with gentle breast. Beneath this sod
> A poet lies, or that which once seem'd he—
> O, lift one thought in prayer for S. T. C.—
> That he who many a year with toil of breath
> Found death in life, may here find life in death:
> Mercy for praise—to be forgiven for fame—
> He ask'd, and hoped through Christ. Do thou the same.[33]

These lines, revolving the old paradox of life and death, are complemented by the four-line stanza 'Desire':

> Where true Love burns, Desire is Love's pure flame;
> It is the reflex of our earthly frame,
> That takes its meaning from the nobler part,
> And but translates the language of the heart.

Between them, the two statements take under their wing both the humility of a writer who can produce an epitaph that is little more

---

[32] *CL* IV 607.
[33] 'Epitaph': *CPW* (EHC) I 491–2. Cf. *CPW* (CC) I (2)1146. The word 'for' here means 'instead of'.

than a plea for divine mercy, and the concept of an ideal relationship, where the energy of desire validates the illumined form of love, presenting back to him the true 'language of the heart'—even if the realization of that ideal has always eluded him.

The most persisting theme was that of light. Three weeks before his death he wrote to a Mrs Dashwood who had just offered him a small annuity,

I was under no danger of finding a temptation to self-glorying in your too favorable expressions, your too exalted estimate of my moral and intellectual Being in your kind letter to Mrs Gillman. I was assured, that they proceeded from your love and inward honouring of a Light not mine, but of which you believed yourself to see the translucence thro' the earthly Vessel, the fragile and clouded Lamp vase, thro' which the Light gleamed.[34]

Nevertheless, his accompanying delight in vegetative growth did not leave him. Even the most hard-bitten sceptic must acknowledge the imaginative appropriateness of the story that was told in the Gillman household after his death:

'The myrtle was a special favorite of Mr Coleridge. He tended it himself and only a few hours before his death after he had bidden all his friends farewell, and asked them to leave the room, he requested that it might be brought near him. It was on the eve of blooming, and the dying Poet watched it long and wistfully. Scarcely had he ceased to breathe when the myrtle burst forth into bloom, and filled the chamber with its fragrance.'[35]

---

[34]   *CL* VI 987.
[35]   Anecdote told by Mrs Gillman to Dr Prentiss and retailed by her grand-daughter Lucy Watson in *Coleridge at Highgate* (London: Longmans, Green and Company, 1925), p. 135. Mrs Watson maintained that since her grandmother was not with Coleridge at his death the story must have originated from his nurse, Harriet Macklin.

16

Questioning Closure

Highgate, where Coleridge took up residence for the last eighteen years of his life, was a place embodying its own, suitable contradictions: in his time it was still connected loosely with the neighbouring metropolis of London, yet it also survived as a village in its own right. There was a further appositeness in the fact that this place, which kept its inhabitants in touch with the City, was uphill from it. Highgate Hill, which had almost succeeded in taking Dick Whittington away from London on a famous earlier occasion, was steep enough to be chosen later by Andrew Smith Hallidie, the pioneer responsible for the cable-hauled tram-cars in San Francisco, to make a similar experiment in Britain.[1] For the purposes of Coleridgean narrative, however, the main feature was simply that it made Highgate seem to stand above the city. Several writers of the period wrote of the poet as if he were now in a lofty position, happily exalted above them

Thomas Carlyle used the same point of outlook to initiate a more sardonic view:

Coleridge sat on the brow of Highgate Hill, in those years, looking down on London and its smoke-tumult, like a sage escaped from the inanity of life's battle...

The visitor might have been admitted to his own room, with its rearward view, which was 'the chief view of all':

Nowhere, of its kind, could you see a grander prospect on a bright summer day, with the set of the air going southward,—southward, and so draping with the city-smoke not you but the city...[2]

---

[1] It was opened in 1884 and ran, apart from one long interruption following an accident, until 1909.
[2] *Life of John Sterling* (1850), chapter 7.

It comes as a surprise to realize that he himself could never have seen this view, in the form that he describes it, from Coleridge's window. By the time he visited the poet in 1823, the Gillmans had moved into The Grove, which at its back commands a pastoral scene, leading in the direction of Hampstead Heath. Only by craning with immense difficulty could he have seen more. There *was* such a direct view of London from a house where Coleridge lived, but that was earlier, at Moreton House across the road, which the Gillmans had left the year before, and where Coleridge's earlier decision to take up residence had marked the major turning point in his later career. Before that, visits to London had taken place with hotels and landladies and were often the scene of depression concerning his prospects and his opium-taking. In 1816, however, things had taken a notable turn, with Byron sufficiently enchanted by his poetry to recommend to his publisher John Murray that he publish the unfinished 'Christabel' and 'Kubla Khan'.

This turn for the better also held good at Highgate. Coleridge became prolific in publication, sometimes, in addition, turning his attention to practical affairs. His work on children's labour[3] was complemented by an increasing devotion of energies to local matters, such as the future of Highgate School.

One of the difficulties involved in painting a picture of Coleridge's life in his new habitat is indeed that it may appear too untroubled. There are only a few occasions when Coleridge slips a little from his normal adulation of the Gillmans, as when he complained that in his attempts to complete *Aids to Reflection* he was 'almost incapacitated from thinking of and doing anything as it ought to be done' by Mrs Gillman's 'restless and interrogatory anxieties', which meant that he must either 'enter into the mock-indifference of a Quarrel' or suffer himself to be 'fidget-watched and "are you going on?—what are you doing now? Is this for the book?" &c &c, precisely as if I were Henry at his lesson'.[4]

As one might expect, Charles Lamb could comment mischievously on this new state of affairs—all the more predictably since James Gillman at first took his responsibilities very seriously and must have seen in Lamb, with his irreverence, someone who might undermine the discipline he was prescribing (with the patient's concurrence) for his opium addiction. Richard Holmes, among others, tells how Crabb

---

[3] See *CET* II and III and *CSWF* I 714–51.   [4] *CL* V 411.

Robinson, visiting Coleridge in July there and joined after a time by Lamb, who was no doubt hoping to pick up his friendship on much of its previous terms, found that after half an hour Gillman came into the room 'very much with the air of a man who meant we should understand him to mean: "Gentlemen it is time for you to go!" We took the hint and Lamb said that he would never call again.' On the same occasion, however, Robinson remarked that 'he seems to have profited already by the abstinence from opium etc. on which he lately lived, for I never saw him look so well'.[5] The new regime was evidently working well, and he was to remain free from the worst effects of his addiction for the rest of his life.

Lamb relented in the course of time, and so no doubt did Gillman, relaxing his attitude to those who had known his patient longer. Coleridge, we know, obtained supplies of laudanum from Thomas Dunn, a local chemist: several notes ordering more and one or two letters about the account that was being run up were to survive and be included in the *Letters*.[6] That Coleridge retained his addiction is attested in an anecdote by Wilkie Collins, who was himself to become a notable addict of the drug, and who remembered from his boyhood an occasion when Coleridge, visiting his family and probably suffering from withdrawal symptoms, had broken down in front of them:

His grief was excessive. He even shed tears. At last my mother addressed him, saying 'Mr Coleridge, do not cry: if the opium really does you any good, and you *must* have it, why do you not go and get it?' At this the poet ceased to weep, recovered his composure, and turning to my father, said with an air of much relief and deep conviction: 'Collins, your wife is an exceedingly sensible woman!'.[7]

In spite of unsuccessful efforts to break himself totally of his craving Coleridge was nevertheless now indulging in a dosage smaller than that which he had taken at the height of his addiction. His was not, after all, an isolated case, moreover: the much-respected William Wilberforce continued to take the drug through a long lifetime. It is also worth mentioning that during his last illness Gillman administered laudanum as an analgesic by hypodermic injection, a method which, according to Richard Holmes,[8] was still a rare procedure

---

[5] *HCR* I 185.   [6] See e.g. a letter dated tentatively May 1824: *CL* V 362.
[7] See William Malpas Clarke, *The Secret Life of Wilkie Collins* (Stroud: Alan Sutton, 1996; London: Allison & Busby, 1988), p. 20.
[8] Richard Holmes, *Coleridge: Darker Reflections* (London: HarperCollins, 1998), p. 559.

When he went to Highgate he was still recovering from his love for Sara Hutchinson and the deadening realization that their love was over; subsequent poems had dwelt on the death of love and the aftermath. 'The Pang more sharp than All' refers to 'sad compassion and atoning zeal!' It concludes,

> O worse than all! O pang all pangs above
> Is Kindness counterfeiting absent Love!

It sounds like a sad critique. Even in the summer before he died, he could still include the image of a 'sod-built seat of camomile', which he had earlier associated with her, in a poem entitled 'Love's Apparition and Evanishment'. Although published so late, Coleridge had been working for some years at the poem, which seems to have had its origin in conjunction with lines that in a note book of 1824 he claimed to have been produced extempore:

> Idly we supplicate the Powers above!
> There is no Resurrection for a Love
> That, unperturb'd, unshadowed, wanes away
> In the chill'd heart by inward self-decay.
> Poor Mimic of the Past! The Love is o'er
> That must *resolve* to do what did itself of yore.[9]

In those years, mortifyingly, he not only acknowledged her lack of reciprocation but recognized the death of his own love. The sense of loss was haunting. Lamb kept up with Sara as an occasional correspondent and even hatched a plan that included bringing her and Coleridge together for a Ramsgate visit, but he wrote to her sadly in 1823, 'Time—as was said of one of us—toils after us in vain. I am afraid that our co-visit with Coleridge was a dream. I shall not get away before the end (or middle) of June, and then you will be frog-hopping at Boulogne. And besides' (he added mischievously) 'I think the Gilmans would scarce trust him with us, I have a malicious knack at cutting of apron strings.'[10]

For his own part Coleridge was to direct in his will that a small, plain gold mourning ring should be left to her—the only woman among four of his friends selected for such a gift. There is also a touching note in the comment on the post-mortem that followed her mention of his death to

---

[9] CNB 28 f f68ᵛ (cf. *CN* IV 5146).　　　[10] *LL* (Lucas) II 382.

a friend in 1834: 'poor dear Coleridge is gone. He was opened—the disease was at his heart.'

Coleridge seems always to have needed to have an emotional relationship of some kind with any affectionate woman with whom he had extended dealings, and there was certainly a sentimental attachment to Anne Gillman. This comes out in the manuscript of the poem 'Work without Hope', which in his notebook forms part of a letter evidently addressed to Anne in 1825. It was headed 'THE ALONE MOST DEAR a complaint of Jacob to Rachel as in the tenth year of his Service he saw in her, or fancied that he saw Symptoms of Alienation'. Against this Mrs Gillman later wrote, 'It was fancy'.[11] Meanwhile Lamb was both shocked and amused to hear it rumoured that Coleridge was living in open adultery with her in Ramsgate, where they had been seen on holiday.

Coleridge did not, so far as we know, walk with her in Highgate, where he was often to be seen strolling in places such as the local poplar avenue.[12] He might be followed there by the local children, for whose benefit he was well known to carry a supply of sweets,[13] filling them sometimes with terror and amusement as they bowled their hoops;[14] he was also fond of haranguing any listener whom he could captivate, such as the baker's boy—to whom he was heard on one occasion asserting, 'I never knew a man good because he was religious, but I have known one religious because was good.'[15] Seymour Porter, Dunn's assistant, was delighted to have encountered Coleridge outside the shop as Lord Byron's cortège passed up the hill in 1824 and to have heard the 'strain of marvellous eloquence' in which he pronounced a spontaneous funeral oration.[16]

In these years, his reputation—particularly as maintained by Julius Hare, the tutor at Trinity College in Cambridge—and his air of having solved questions that troubled the age had led to a cultivation of his work among young men, and particularly members of the Cambridge

[11] CNB 29 f 83 (cf. *CN* IV 5192 and n). For Coleridge, the love of Jacob for Rachel (Genesis 29) was love in its ideal form (see *CN* IV 4848, 5184 and n).

[12] A. G. L'Estrange, *The Literary Life of William Harness* (1871), pp. 143–4, collected in Seamus Perry (ed.), *S. T. Coleridge: Interviews and Recollections* (Basingstoke: Palgrave Macmillan 2000), 184–5. The trees immediately outside The Grove appear to have been chestnuts.

[13] Lucy Watson, *Coleridge at Highgate* (1925), p. 53.

[14] A. G. L'Estrange, *The Literary Life of William Harness*, pp. 143–4.

[15] L'Estrange, *loc. cit.*

[16] Seamus Perry, *S. T. Coleridge: Interviews and Recollections*, pp.186–7.

Conversazione Club (the Apostles), who continued their enthusiasm after graduation by visiting him in Highgate and carrying out his injunction that they should become members of the 'clerisy', as advocated in his prose writings. Among these John Sterling (particularly prominent, and later a pall-bearer at his funeral) was sufficiently swayed by Coleridge's teaching to be ordained, and even to serve as curate at Herstmonceux under Hare. Sterling was also, however, disillusioned in later years, as came out in letters to his son Edward—constructed, it must be noted, to inculcate the superior virtue of steady work:

I have his figure now at my elbow broad short & dressed in black very neatly— the smooth silvery hair gray eyes & fleshy ruddy cheeks but with a mouth so loose & weak in its expression that one could only be thunderstruck by the Eloquence that broke from it, & not surprised at any weakness of conduct in the man. He was most sweet-voiced, most kindly gentle, & loving, almost incapable of ill will, taking acts of friendship with the open laughing cordiality of a child, sometimes perhaps forgetting them as readily. His soul was full of all things lovely & sublime, and had hardly a sense for what was otherwise. And yet one vice Indolence marred all this & made the man of the greatest mind in England for his whole life an object of compassion and often shame to all who knew him.[17]

Sterling was particularly dismayed to discover that his hero might 'retail perhaps for a whole hour & with all the pomp of an original discovery what in after years I found had been plundered wholesale from some German book'. The point which evidently puzzled him most was to understand how a man could combine in his personality such an apparent tendency towards delinquency with his notable openness of innocence—a chief characteristic of Sterling himself, and no doubt a quality that endeared him particularly to Carlyle, who met him in 1835.[18]

De Quincey, an early investigator of the problem, expressed equal bafflement at the complexity of personality indicated:

With the riches of El Dorado lying about him, he would condescend to filch a handful of gold from any man whose purse he fancied: and in fact reproduced in a new form, applying itself to intellectual wealth, that maniacal propensity

---

[17] See A. K. Tuell, *John Sterling: A Representative Victorian* (New York: Macmillan, 1941), pp. 261–3.
[18] Carlyle was probably responsible for sowing some of the doubts concerning his originality that came to trouble him.

which is sometimes well known to attack enormous proprietors and million-aires for acts of petty larceny.[19]

The contradictoriness prompts questions concerning his religious prac-tice, or non-practice, at Highgate. For some years he had been deeply absorbed in a study of Swedenborgianism, as a number of letters to his friend, the MP C. A. Tulk, make clear, and he showed a lively interest in other sects, particularly when their concerns touched his. So far as Anglicanism was concerned, however, the person he knew best was the Reverend Samuel Mence, master of Cholmeley's Free Grammar School and local parish clergyman. In a notebook entry Coleridge discusses the views of 'two neighbor Ministers', one of whom was probably Mence. Neither, he thought, had fully considered the difference between the National Church and the Ecclesia, or Spiritual community.[20]

His hosts the Gillmans appear to have been in the main conventional, God-fearing people who probably went to Church every Sunday (what-ever James's private views may have been), but whether or not Coleridge normally accompanied them is far from clear. Throughout the period he was thinking increasingly about religion, yet unless he was quietly going to church regularly in a way that seemed so natural that even the sermon was not thought worth commenting on (uncharacteristic beha-viour, one might have thought) he practised his religion mainly by thinking and writing rather than through observance of official rites. The main exceptions are furnished by his strong interest in Edward Irving, whom Gillman drove him to hear preach at the Scotch Chapel in Hatton Garden in 1823, and his praise of a sermon ('the very best sermon the best delivered, I ever heard') in 1829 by Edward Bather, whom he probably heard at Highgate, since he was a friend of Mence.[21]

On one occasion, at least, however, he emerged into the open as a revived member of the Anglican Church, writing in 1827 of his re-engagement:

Christmas day. Received the Sacrament—for the first time since my first year at Jesus College/ Christ is gracious even to the Laborer that cometh to his

---

[19] Thomas De Quincey, *Recollections of the Lakes and the Lake Poets*, ed. David Wright (Harmondsworth: Penguin Books, 1970), p. 40.

[20] See CNB 26 f 77ᵛ (cf. *CN* IV 5398), where he discusses the opinions of his 'two neighbor Ministers L. and N'. (In her note the editor identifies these two as Samuel Mence and the Reverend E. Lewis of the Baptist Church in Southwood Lane; the second identifi-cation is not certain, however, since in neither case do the sentiments cited read as those of a dissenting clergyman.) For further discussion of the 'ecclesiastical' point, see p. 233 below.

[21] *CL* V 280, VI 816.

Vineyard at the eleventh hour—33 years absent from my Master's Table /—Yet I humbly hope that spiritually I have fed on the Flesh & Blood the Strength and the life of the Son of God in his divine Humanity, during the latter years—. The administration & Communion Service of our Church is solemn & affecting.[22]

His growing reconciliation with the Anglican church culminated in the publication in 1829 of one of his most successful works, the short treatise *On the Constitution of the Church and State*, which enabled him to ruminate on some of the most complex issues of his time but also brought into final prominence intricate problems of his career. To deal with them he needed to solve the great dilemma that had always beset his writing, that of knitting together competing modes of discourse.

Torn between such possibilities, Coleridge, literary in a traditional sense and impressed deeply by his great predecessors Shakespeare and Milton, had sensed instinctively (while mourning his lack of mathematical skills) that the new world of science would be damagingly inadequate for the emerging world. It is small wonder that he often felt overwhelmed by his inability to resolve the conflict of discourses with which he believed his civilization to be beset—which enables one to view in a different light the figure who was to Carlyle no more than 'a mass of richest spices putrefied into a dunghill'.[23] His apparent torpor and sluggishness may be seen not as an effect of indolence or inertia but as embodying an *aporia*, a deadlock between equally demanding, yet essentially irreconcilable, forces, which at their worst cancelled out one another.

The need to play between such discourses, accompanied by a sense of impotence through surfeit of beguiling pressures, came to a head in this attempt to solve the problem of Church and State. Years before, preaching to a Unitarian congregation that had included the young William Hazlitt, he had had little difficulty in setting out his positions

upon Church and State —not their alliance, but their separation—on the spirit of the world and the spirit of Christianity, not as the same, but as opposed to one another.[24]

---

[22] CNB 36 ff 32ᵛ (cf. *CN* V 5637). Quoted in part by J. R. Barth, *Coleridge and Christian Doctrine* (Cambridge, Mass.: Harvard University Press, 1969), pp. 178–9 nn.

[23] Letter to his brother John Carlyle, 22 January 1825, *The Collected Letters of Thomas and Jane Welsh Carlyle*, general ed. Charles Richard Sanders (34 vols., Durham, N.C.: Duke University Press, 1970–), I 238.

[24] *HW* XVII 108.

Shortly afterwards, however, his thinking had been jolted by two events: the Act of Unity between Britain and Ireland, which brought into prominence the problem of arranging how Catholics and Protestants might live side by side in a single state, and the *Concordat* between Napoleon and the Vatican.

In these circumstances, what he had to say about the question of Church and State in the 1820s came after lengthy consideration. Though characterized by Julius Hare as 'written in the fullest maturity of his judgment' it is not a monumental piece of reasoning, but has to be viewed, rather, by way of appreciating the intensity and intricacy of play between diverse elements in his mind. Like some of Coleridge's other works (and as is clear from some of the passages themselves) this one was compiled by a process of accretion, passages being added in turn as points occurred to the author, and regardless of what might already have gone to press. Even the conclusion was inadequate, or—to use the phrase of the *Collected Works* editor—'disastrously ragged'.[25]

The reasons for that raggedness are worth teasing out further. A major feature of Coleridge's attempt to propose an adequate account of the State was his insistence that it involved positing a proper balance between two forces, those of permanence and progression. For the first, one looked to the landowners, who could be relied on to further the interests of stability, and for the second the commercial and mercantile classes, whose function it was to answer the need for innovation and development. The monarch, meanwhile, must constantly hold a balance between the two.

The question of the State's constitution, then, was a matter of devising the right balancing act. But that of the Church was another matter, involving further problems. How far should it be thought of as an *enclesia*, evolving according to its own pattern, how far an *ecclesia*, itself developing into a National Church (as he thought it was in fact beginning to do in the United States of America)?

Balance, certainly, was one of the key concepts in the work; another, endearing him to many of a conservative cast of mind, was that of establishment. One of the most eloquent passages, first drafted in the *Biographia*, was devoted to its praise:

That the maxims of a pure morality, and those sublime truths of the divine unity and attributes, which a Plato found hard to learn, and more difficult to

[25] *COM* lvii.

reveal; that these should have become the almost hereditary property of childhood and poverty, of the hovel and the workshop; that even to the unlettered
they sound as *common place*; this is a phenomenon which must withhold all but
minds of the most vulgar cast from undervaluing the services even of the pulpit
and the reading desk. Yet who should *confine* the efficiency of an Established
Church to these, can hardly be placed in a much higher rank of intellect. That
to every parish throughout the kingdom there is transplanted a germ of
civilization; that in the remotest villages there is a nucleus, round which the
capabilities of the place may crystallize and brighten; a model sufficiently superior
to excite, yet sufficiently near to encourage and facilitate, imitation; *this*
unobtrusive, continuous agency of a Protestant Church Establishment, *this* it
is, which the patriot and the philanthropist, who would fain unite the love of
peace with the faith in the progressive amelioration of mankind, cannot
estimate at too high a price.[26]

In spite of the conservative nature of such comments, Coleridge
remained, as noted earlier, strikingly liberal in his sentiments, fully
alive to the injustices abounding in society at large. When he tried to
elaborate on his conception of the Church for the benefit of his own
society, setting forth the desirability of nourishing a 'clerisy', the members of which would be devoted to furthering a Christian society's ends
while themselves remaining in their own professions, his ideas were
taken up eagerly by contemporaries—particularly the young.

An even more fruitful conception was that of the organic, present
already in the word 'germ', and to be drawn memorably into full
maturity when Coleridge turned to show how Church and State might
activate one another (in a passage quoted more fully on p. 197 above):

As the olive tree is said in its growth to fertilize the surrounding soil; to
invigorate the roots of the vine in its immediate neighbourhood; and to
improve the strength and flavour of the wines—such is the relation of the
Christian and the National Church. But as the olive is not the same plant with
the vine, or with the elm or poplar (i.e. the State) with which the vine is
wedded; and as the vine with its prop may exist, though in less perfection,
without the olive, or prior to its implantation—even so is Christianity.

This was one of the most refreshing preoccupations in the whole
work. Although Coleridge was often laudably judicious in his conclusions, his main concern, evidently, was to combat the constant presence
of the mechanical by invoking the organic. The preoccupation recurs

[26] *CCS* 75.

most notably when his discussion of corporate bodies draws on his knowledge of the physiology of the individual human being.

This was accompanied by another welcome feature. In an atmosphere where it was all too easy to descend to personalities, given the petty interests involved in religious matters, Coleridge's contribution was distinguished by a refusal to follow such a path, concentrating instead on matters of principle. His further concern remained: support for the National Church should be supplemented by awareness of the distinctions, not only between that and the State but, within the Church, between the *ecclesia,* the body which gathered together Christians, and the *enclesia*—the body which separated itself from the world. But this distinction, not easy to separate from that between the Church visible and invisible, could not easily be worked out in detail. Faced with the difficulty of establishing it he tried another tack: ending with a dialogue between the worldly and the unworldly in which he introduced rhetorically the persuasiveness of a philosophy that interpreted the lower in terms of the higher—concluding in a familiar image, already cited:[27]

> Whene'er the mist, that stands 'twixt God and thee
> Defecates to a pure transparency.
> There Reason is, and there begins her reign!

In the end ratiocination must be superseded by submission to the light of the Absolute Will. Any other consideration was simply a distraction, amounting to an intervening stain.

Thinking over his past life he was struck by the abiding depth of his love for the Anglican Church—so much so that he had felt the need, as here, not only to defend it, but to explain and justify its status and significance: its unique and peculiar relation to the earthly kingdom in which he had grown up. Yet, as already noted, he was not notable for church attendance, and it seems that in some other part of himself he found the existing churches unsatisfactory, being conscious of needs, intellectual and emotional, that remained unsatisfied. Despite his constant questing he had not found a community in which he could feel properly at home. Once again, he had recourse to his notebook:

Am I or is the non-existence of a Christian Community, in fault—God knows how much I feel the want of Church Fellowship! But where can I find it? Among the *Methodists?* *Vide* the Cuts & Frontispieces to the Methodist,

---

[27] See above, p. 214.

Arminian Evangelical &c Magazines. The *Quakers?*—I want the heart of Oak—& here is *the Rind* & Bark in wondrous preservation, counterfeiting *a tree* to the very life/—. *The C. of Eng?*—the Churches, and Chapels? O yes, I can go to a Church, & so I can to a theatre—& go out again—& know as much as my fellow-goers in the one as in the other— —the Moravians?—if any where, among them. YET—but I will talk to Dr Oakley. But I fear, that every fancy is tolerated among them but the fancy of free enquiry and the free use of the Understanding on subjects that belong to the Understanding—I fear, a wilful Stupor with the sacrifice of Reason under the name of Faith, instead of a Faith higher than Reason because it includes it as one of it's Co-partners—I fear the Tyranny of *Dogmas.*[28]

The longing for something he could properly call 'fellowship' remained as strong as it had ever been; equally potent was the need for the activity of the 'Inquiring Spirit'—the phrase that he had sometimes used in connection with his own concerns—so that it remained doubtful whether any institutionalized religion could ever be adequate to his needs. The Gillmans might be friends of the Mences and part of the Highgate élite, but with the development of medical science James, as a surgeon, knew well enough the human demands, physical and mental, that were becoming steadily less satisfied during these years.

Meanwhile, the great aspiration of his life, to create a great work in which he might resolve major religious and intellectual issues, still escaped him. Some parts of a solution seemed to have been achieved already, at least provisionally. His lectures on the history of philosophy, his *Aids to Reflection*, along with the treatise on a right attitude to the Scriptures that would be published as *Confessions of an Inquiring Spirit*, and his writing on Church and State, all seemed indications of a larger achievement, already in progress. Yet the crowning key remained. He still needed to establish once and for all the central truth for which he had struggled all his life: that in God could be found united both moral responsibility and intellectual clarity; that consciousness and conscience would eventually be united. Great tracts of this *opus maximum*, dictated to and discussed with his friend and disciple J. H. Green, were committed to manuscript; yet they lacked the intellectual finality that would sanction their being offered to a publisher, despite the power of their affirmation that, to quote his own words, 'in the absolute Will, which

---

[28] CNB 35 ff 34–34^v (cf. *CN* V 5636). In connection with his possible exemption of Moravianism, cf. his brother James's response to someone who had accused him of being a Jacobin: 'No! Samuel is not a Jacobin—he is a hot-headed Moravian!', *CTT* I 310.

abideth in the Father, the Word and the Spirit, totally and absolutely in each, one and the same in all, the ground of all reality is contained'.[29]

The realization that he had not succeeded in finally proving this proposition by no means inhibited him from considering points that might yet assist him, or indeed, of course, from indulging in the continuing play of his mind. For many years he had followed the discussion of relevant questions avidly, and the possibility of resolving the problem of the relationship between the physically organic and the ethically moral that was, in his time, assuming centre stage, remained one of his hopes. In a note to Mence, asking him to assist with the problems of one of the local parishioners, he recorded his faith: 'The facts both of Physiology and Pathology lead to one and the same conclusion—viz. that in some way or other the Will is the obscure Radical of the Vital Power.'[30] As the century drew on, bringing with it more and more challenges from science, the need to establish such correspondences would become central. If, on the other hand, the will itself was regarded as enslaved to organic needs, religion itself would be in danger of losing authority. Apart from his Christian concerns at Highgate, therefore, these longer-standing questions continued to dog him. He remained confident that the human will, belief in which he shared with Immanuel Kant, would see mankind through, however weak his own had sometimes proved to be. The necessary knowledge could be discovered and preserved—so long as thinkers were sufficiently enlightened and intellectually strenuous.

Coleridge nevertheless insisted that his work was systematic, writing in 1831,

My system is the only attempt that I know of ever made to reduce all knowledges into harmony; it opposes no other system, but shows what was true in each, and how that which was true in the particular in each of them became error because it was only half the truth. I have endeavored to unite the insulated fragments of truth and frame a perfect mirror. I show to each system that I fully understand and rightfully appreciate what that system means; but then I lift up that system to a higher point of view from which I enable it to see its former position where it was indeed, but under another light and with different relations; so that the fragment of truth is not only acknowledged, but explained. So the old astronomers discovered and maintained much that was true, but because they were placed on a false ground, and looked from the wrong point of view, they never did—they never could—discover *the* truth—that is the whole

---

[29] *COM* 222.   [30] *CL* V 406.

truth. As soon as they left the earth—their false centre—and took their stand in the Sun—immediately they saw the whole system in the true light—and their former station remaining—but remaining a part of the prospect. I wish in short, to connect by a moral copula Natural History with Political History—or in other words, to make History scientific, and Science historical—to take from History its accidentality—and from Science its fatalism.[31]

What remained from all his intellectual struggles, in addition, his conviction of the value of consciousness itself, was of equally long standing. Murray Evans has quoted relevantly from an earlier lecture, where he discusses the

principle which probably is the condition of all consciousness, without which we should feel & imagine only by discontinuous Moments, & be plants or animals instead of men—I mean, that ever-varying Balance—or Balancing—of Images, Notions, or Feelings... conceived as in opposition to each other—in short, the perception of Identity & Contrariety—the least degree of which constitutes *Likeness*—the greatest, absolute Difference—but the infinite gradations between these two form all the Play & all the Interest of our Intellectual & Moral Being.[32]

It was appropriate, therefore, that when death finally approached, he should make time for both conscience and consciousness. At first he asked to be left alone for 'meditations on his Redeemer',[33] in tune with the first imperative; but within a day or two the second sense was pressed with equal urgency: the need that his followers and friends should share his mature insights, striving above all things to sustain the crucial distinctions that played an essential part in his religious conviction.

He had written little on the question of immortality—mainly, perhaps, because he never really questioned its validity. 'All intense passions', he wrote in 1811, 'have faith in their own eternity, & thence in the eternity of their objects'[34] and what he believed to be true of the passions was even more true of the sense of Being that underlay all such emotions. The point, made directly in a late note on immortality, remained vividly a point of his philosophy to the end. His last message was given to J. H. Green the night before his death: 'he articulated with difficulty, but his mind was clear and powerful'. He affirmed once again his belief in the absolute quality of the 'I am', both as a divine and

---

[31] *TT* (CC) I 247–8.
[32] *CLects (1808–1819)* 83–4; see Murray's contribution to J. W. Barbeau, *Coleridge's Assertion of Religion* (Leuven: Peeters, 2006), pp. 94–5.
[33] *CL* VI 991.   [34] CNB 18 f 144ᵛ (cf. *CN* III 4056).

human statement, as well as to the equally vital need for communication of all such Beings with each other—and with the Divine:

first of all is the Absolute Good whose self-affirmation is the 'I am,' as the eternal reality in itself and the ground and source of all other reality.

And next, that in this idea nevertheless a distinctivity is to be carefully preserved, as manifested in the person of the Logos by whom that reality is communicated to all other beings.[35]

His urgent sense of the necessity to keep alive, at one and the same time, existential self-affirmation and readiness of communication, was not only a distillation of what he had learned over the years, but implicitly embedded the need, absorbed from his eighteenth-century predecessors, to maintain a balanced view. A similar concession to preceding commonsense attitudes may be traced in his final insistence that in spite of his sufferings his mind was still essentially clear.

However distinct its clarity, nevertheless, it could not finally resolve the problem that had dogged him all his life: whether that self-affirmation of the 'Ground of all Being' was ultimately personal, or simply shaded off into impersonality. That uncertainty still remained within the play of his mind, along with an inevitable under-questioning whether he had carried far enough his investigations into the potentialities of life and human consciousness. Had he ever properly probed the implications of his insights into the potentialities of language? Had he ever, for that matter, used language to the full?

An unregenerate Romantic liveliness leavened his final conclusions, therefore. There may even have been a touch of sad retrospect at his failure quite to fulfil the promise hoped for by those who had once discerned in him the quality of a 'young Mirandula', previously manifest in the juvenile John Donne.[36] His final recorded words were

'I could even be witty.'[37]

[35] Quoted by Lucy Watson, *Coleridge at Highgate*, p. 158, from J. A. Heraud's posthumous oration.

[36] See above, p. 158.   [37] *CL* VI 992.

17

'Obstinate in Resurrection'

After Coleridge's death the literary world was divided between those who thought, like Wordsworth, that the most appropriate word to characterize him was 'wonderful' and those who remained sceptical.

Carlyle, for example, who must have been particularly impressed in his youth by Coleridge's reputation and would during recent years have been immersing himself in works such as *The Friend* and the *Lay Sermons*, was evidently struck by Coleridge's failure to be the figure that the age called for, writing of his disappointment to his brother in June 1825:

Figure a fat flabby incurvated personage at once short, rotund and relaxed, with a watery mouth, a snuffy nose, a pair of strange brown timid yet earnest-looking eyes, a high tapering brow, and a great bush of grey hair—; you will have some faint idea of Coleridge...

His main criticism had less to do with his appearance, however:

His cardinal sin is that he wants *will*; he has no resolution, he shrinks from pain or labour in any of its shapes. His very attitude bespeaks this...[1]

A few years later Arthur Hugh Clough, noted among his contemporaries for his strong grasp of the actual, wrote:

I should like much to have heard Carlyle's complaints against Coleridge. I keep wavering between admiration of his exceedingly great perceptive and analytical power and other wonderful points and inclination to turn away altogether from a man who has so great a lack of all reality and actuality.[2]

---

[1] Letter to his brother John of 24 June 1825: *CCL* III 90.
[2] Letter to J. N. Simpkinson, 18 February 1841: *Correspondence*, ed. F. L. Mulhauser (2 vols., Oxford: Clarendon Press, 1957), I 106.

The nature of those 'complaints' (however they had come to Clough's attention) is evident from the comments cited above, the main one being that Coleridge had not fulfilled his destiny as a hero. It became possible for Clough and other contemporaries to read them at length and in polished form, moreover, in 1850, when the *Life of John Sterling* was published. Carlyle's impatience at Coleridge's physical feebleness, particularly by comparison with the robustness of German contemporaries such as Schelling and Goethe, whom he had recently come to admire, had been evident at the time of their meeting. He himself was increasingly enamoured of German writers, and in particular of their reverence for the human Will, so that Coleridge's career seemed to him to have been correspondingly pathetic. Carlyle himself, by contrast, came to be seen by his readers as a great prophet, so that he was taken to be the proper model for an aspiring young man. When George Eliot, discussing such matters earnestly with Frederic Myers, spoke of the three great inspiring trumpet-calls of men, God, Immortality, and Duty, asserting how inconceivable was the first, how unbelievable the second, and yet how peremptory and absolute the third, the teaching of Carlyle must have been foremost in her mind; just as she found in his stricture that Coleridge had lacked the courage to press resolutely across the 'howling deserts of infidelity' to 'the new firm grounds of Faith beyond' a vital summary, insisting that 'the emphasis of quotation [could] not be too often given' to this 'pregnant paragraph', which, she felt, reflected current concerns.[3]

The establishment of such attitudes was assisted a few years later, in 1859, by the publication of Darwin's *Origin of Species*, which initiated a wave of thought demanding new intellectual and moral stringency as the forcefulness of earlier arguments concerning religion and morality declined. The possibility of defending Christianity by retreating to permanent elements that would survive the assaults currently being mounted—a hope which Coleridge's work had seemed to support—faded; instead, the need for honesty in dealing with Darwin's theories introduced an unprecedented scepticism into the examination of arguments and evidences. In the new climate Coleridge's argument that

---

[3] *Westminster Review* (Jan 1852), n.s. I 249–50. It was, above all, the Will that gave Coleridge most trouble, since his affirmation of the concept was not matched by exercise in action. The supreme master of the subject seemed to be Immanuel Kant, whose work he read repeatedly, and it was Kant's thought which dominated contemporary Germany, to the admiration of Thomas Carlyle. For Carlyle, his friend John Sterling's devotion to Coleridge was a lamentable lapse.

Christianity conformed to individual religious experience might appear less persuasive than an encouragement of wishful thinking; while Mill's identification of him as one who taught people not to dismiss, as meaningless, phenomena that had persisted through time seemed less relevant as significance drained from the post-Darwinian universe. In particular, Coleridge's insistence that the idea of human beings as having descended from the animal creation was totally unacceptable was increasingly rejected as untenable. Nevertheless, George Eliot's own remark about Darwin was to prove uncannily prescient:

to me the Development theory and all other explanations of processes by which things came to be, produce a feeble impression compared with the mystery that lies under the processes.[4]

Despite the invalidity of his immediate claims, Coleridge could still be regarded as a prime investigator of 'the mystery underlying the processes'. In accordance with the dismissing of his attacks on evolutionary theory positive mentions of his thought by leading intellectuals became rarer; though aspects of his thought continued to appeal to a more general level of readers. When new editions of his prose works ceased to appear they were reprinted in the popular format of Bohn's Library; enthusiasm for his writings shifted to valuation of the sensibility revealed by publication of his letters and notebooks, while, as before, there was continuing appreciation of his poetry—particularly the informality of what came to be known as his conversational poems.

In the nineteenth century attitudes to Coleridge, however much his best poetry might be admired, were dominated by a sense of disappointment at his failure to produce some unequivocal body of achievement in prose. With the twentieth century, moreover, the kind of sensibility that the Victorians had particularly appreciated became increasingly suspect when matched against the horrors of two world wars. At the same time there arose a questioning of the ideal of 'the survival of the fittest' which, in the form of 'Social Darwinism', was seen to favour unbridled competitiveness and to license solution by warfare. As Jacques Lacan was to put it,

Darwin's success seems to derive from the fact that he projected the predations of Victorian society and the economic euphoria that sanctioned for that society the social devastation that it initiated on a planetary scale, and...that it

---

[4] Letter to Barbara Bodichon, 5 December 1859: *GEL* III 227.

justified its predations by the image of a laissez-faire of the strongest predators in competition for their natural prey.[5]

Lacan focused thus on elements in 'Darwinism' that could be seen to run with the advance of developments identifiable with material gain. The early years of the twentieth century were marked by the rise of attitudes more favourable to other aspects of it, especially those which reflected Darwin's wonder at the processes of life. D. H. Lawrence, a notable supporter, developed a life-philosophy of his own, corresponding to that cultivated by the early Romantics as discussed earlier.[6] He alluded approvingly to Coleridge's work on so many occasions that it is not surprising to find him writing to Amy Lowell in 1914, 'I'd like to know Coleridge, when Charon has rowed me over'.[7] At the same time he was not attracted to Coleridge's moral preoccupations, which warred against one of his favourite assertions: 'With "should" and "ought" I have nothing to do.' But thinkers such as Lawrence and I. A. Richards were all attracted to the evident intelligence displayed throughout his writings— particularly the early ones.

It is less common to find response at a deeper level, despite the attention Coleridge gave to the matter of 'being'. He himself had been attracted by the idea that his initials STC could be transliterated into Greek as $\epsilon\sigma\tau\eta\sigma\epsilon$ (esteese), meaning 'he hath stood'; but those who have considered the point seriously have been forced to point out that $\epsilon\sigma\tau\eta\sigma\epsilon$ does not actually mean 'he hath stood', which would require the form $\epsilon\sigma\tau\eta\kappa\epsilon$; it can, however, be taken to mean 'caused to stand'. Ironically, Coleridge's flawed interpretation has a truth of its own: he was always better at stimulating others to be themselves.

This indeed was how some recalled him. Hazlitt, for example, despite his pervasive disappointment at Coleridge's failure to fulfil his promise, still thought of him as 'the only person I ever knew who answered to the idea of the man of genius... the only person from whom I ever learnt anything'. One has only to look at his work, or at that of de Quincey or Lamb, to see how pervasively Coleridge could prompt achievement in others. At the same time, he can hardly be thought of as a figure standing in his own right. Instead, it is more natural to think of him,

---

[5] Jacques Lacan, *Écrits: A Selection* (New York: W. W. Norton, 1977), p. 20.

[6] See e.g. my *Romantic Influences: Contemporary, Victorian, Modern* (London: Macmillan, 1993).

[7] *Letters*, eds. G. J. Zytaruk and J. T. Boulton (Cambridge: Cambridge University Press, 1981), II 223.

politically at least, in relation to, say, twentieth-century figures who
could be thought of as notable for standing fast. The phrase 'he hath
stood' has been true, for example, of Vaclav Havel —and of him to an
extent that Coleridge could never match—if only because of his quiet
stand through the years of repression. It is not that Havel was particularly strident in opposition; he was simply firm. As someone said of him
he managed always to speak as if censorship did not exist. And various of
his writings during the period, gathered in the volume *Living in Truth*,
bore witness to his acuteness in observing how the party operated during
this period to keep a whole country under domination. There were also
further factors, the love of good argument and the respect for artistic
and intellectual values that are characteristic of Czechoslovakians. It did
not appear at all a bizarre gesture that he should be honoured in time
with election to their presidency.

Apart from *Living in Truth*, the collection *Letters to Olga* contains
various letters that Havel wrote to his wife during the years when he was
in prison from 1979 to 1982. These have a particular element which
helps to bring out their relevance to Coleridge's career. In 1977 an
incident took place which had a very important effect upon his thinking
for years afterwards. He was under detention by the authorities and
undergoing interrogations that were leading nowhere. It occurred to
him one evening to put in a request for release which he thought he had
worded very cleverly. He managed to word it while saying nothing that
he did not believe or that was not true. He sent it off and for some time
nothing happened; but then to his surprise he was told that in all
probability he would be released and that 'political use' would be
made of his request. At that moment he realized that he had in fact
been guilty of an act of self-betrayal: however cleverly he had phrased his
request it would be seen as a sign that he had reneged on his former
principles and said what the authorities wanted to hear in order to get
out of jail. The crisis that he suffered as a result involved him in asking
more urgently questions that had already been present in some of his
plays, about the nature of individual existence and where it is to be
located. This enquiry lasted all through the second period of imprisonment and was the subject of many of his letters. For anyone reading
them now, there is the moving spectacle of a human being trying to
interpret his or her existence under conditions of stress. Unexpectedly,
however, he also turns out to be exploring many of the same issues that
Coleridge faced during the years of his major creative thinking. Coleridge was not, of course, under the same pressure and his general position

was more optimistic. But the paradox within which both men were working was that their need to find a grounded position was accompanied by the equally powerful conviction that that 'being', when found, could not be finite but must be infinite. 'And who shall bind the infinite?' Blake once asked; it was the contradiction within which any humane philosophy must be formed, according to both Coleridge and Havel.

The resemblances are particularly marked during Coleridge's early years, for at that time he was still working through the idea that there might be something to be learned from all religions, those which seemed to be founded on pantheism as well as those which were founded upon a transcendent deity. Havel, similarly, dwelt on the fact that although his own sympathies tended to lie with the Judaeo-Christian order of belief they were not limited by that:

To be more specific it seems to me foolish, impossible and utterly pointless, for instance, to try to reconcile Darwin with Christ, or Marx with Heidegger, or Plato with Buddha. Each of them represents a certain level of being and human experience and each bears witness to the world in his own particular way; each of them, to some extent and in some way, speaks to me, explains many things to me, and even helps me to live, and I simply don't see why, for the sake of one, I should be denied an authentic experience of whatever another can show me, even more so because we are not talking here about different opinions on the same thing, but different ways of talking about very different things.[8]

Both men were conscious of similar dangers. Havel had a long passage, for example, concerning the way in which an authentic philosophy grounded in Being could easily slide into a sense of conviction to be described as fanaticism. This he believed was the trap awaiting those who

cannot resist the attractive force of self-deception, the kind that hides self-surrender to existence-in-the-world beneath the illusion that it is a particularly radical form of orientation toward being. The essence of this idea is the notion that transferring primordial self-transcendence from the boundlessness of the dream to the reality of human actions is a one-shot affair, that all you have to do is to 'come up with an idea' and then blindly serve it—that is, create some intellectual project that permanently fixes and fulfils the original intention—to be relieved of the duty and effort of constantly aspiring toward being: for in its place there is a handy substitute—the relatively undemanding duty of devoted service to a given project.[9]

---

[8] *Letters to Olga* (London: Faber, 1990), p. 191.   [9] Ibid., 363.

And that of course is the root of fanaticism, a condition which Coleridge discusses in more psychological terms by describing its attractions as those of a combined, reinforcing, warmth like that of bees working together in a hive—though having rejected its manifestation in revolutionary France.

The exploration of this idea of being, coupled as it was with the determination not to be limited by the tradition to which he felt himself most readily drawn, resulted in Havel being drawn into mental countries like those that the earlier Coleridge had also travelled. He was fascinated by the idea of the 'collective spirit' of humanity:

none of us knows what is lodged in our subconscious, what archetypal experiences we've inherited from thousands of years of human existence, what tortuous ways they follow before finally surfacing in our 'existential praxis'. Even less do we understand the mysteries of the 'psychic field': what if individual existences are really only nodes in a single gigantic intersubjective network?[10]

Or, as Coleridge put it in an early poem,

> . . . what if all of animated nature
> Be but organic harps diversly fram'd,
> That tremble into thought, as o'er them sweeps
> Plastic and vast, one intellectual breeze,
> At once the Soul of each, and God of all?

In the same way Havel spent a sequence of letters meditating on the relationship between what he called the 'order of life' and the 'order of death'. Coleridge and Wordsworth, as was pointed out earlier, had been thinking in very much the same way in 1798 as they looked at nature and asked themselves what elements in it ministered to the life-sense and what to the death-sense. The results of this thinking were apparent in their writing of the time. There was yet another such convergence of concern when Havel asserted that 'the meaning of life was 'not only unlike information or a commodity that can be freely passed on, it is not even "objectively" knowable or graspable as a concept'. He continued:

Though we cannot 'respond' to it in the traditional sense of the word, nevertheless, by longing for it and seeking after it, we in fact indirectly confront it over and over again. In this regard, we are a little like a blind man touching the woman he loves, whom he has never seen and never will.[11]

---

[10] *Letters to Olga* (London: Faber, 1990), 272.   [11] Ibid., 225.

When Coleridge was describing in 1802 the 'tact' required of a poet, one of the instances he gave was 'the Touch of a Blind Man feeling the face of a darling Child'.[12]

Coleridge and Havel were not, of course, pursuing identical trains of ideas. The thoughts that Coleridge was pursuing in the years from 1797 to 1805 were heavily coloured by his friendship with Wordsworth and the underlying idea that the inner being of humans might be in correspondence with the inner being of nature—and both of the divine, if they could only tease out the subtle relationship between them. A similar preoccupation is not evident in Havel's mind, nor does he show interest, like Coleridge, in a dualism in consciousness. He is also a more rigorous judge of himself by comparison with Coleridge, who wavered constantly between shrewd self-examination and extraordinary abilities of self-deception. What they have in common, however, and it is an insight perhaps more likely to be afforded to those who have lived through cataclysmic upheavals in their time, is a sense that modern civilization is always in danger of reducing human beings to a finite scheme, whether the imposed pattern is socialist or consumerist, and that those who do not accept this but believe in a concept of the human transcending any pattern that may be put on it will find themselves hard put to express what they are trying to say, given the kinds of language that have been endorsed by their culture.

Wider implications are involved. As particular religions and national literatures are dominated by global concerns, existential matters, questions about what it is to be human, come to the fore. And wherever this means falling back on general play of the human mind, issues that concerned Coleridge will be seen to be relevant. His spirit rises from the past, a forerunner of those who have probed most deeply into matters concerning human civilization. Questions about possible failures in his personality are replaced by recognition that in his many readings and questionings he was always dealing with basic human issues.

One effect of uncertainty about the nature of 'being', for example, has been to bring to the fore the need for all civilizations to acquire an adequate mythology. Wordsworth blamed the 'hackneyed and lifeless use' of classical mythology towards the close of the seventeenth century for its decline in his time, but still dwelt on the difficulty of finding a

---

[12] *CL* II 810. See above, pp. 86–7.

mythology adequate to the creation of a major poem.[13] Coleridge saw
that the deep and serious issues involved were bound up with the recent
fate of poetic language. Translating Schiller's *Piccolomini* in 1800 he
found the matter so compelling that he introduced a passage of his own,
suggesting that the human needs which mythology served to answer
could never pass away:

> The intelligible forms of ancient poets,
> The fair humanities of old religion,
> The power, the beauty, and the majesty,
> That had her haunts in dale, or piny mountain,
> Or forest by slow stream, or pebbly spring,
> Or chasms, and watery depths, all these have vanished.
> They live no longer in the faith of reason!
> But still the heart doth need a language, still
> Doth the old instinct bring back the old names.[14]

Some recent writers, disturbed by tendencies in their surrounding
culture, have stressed the vital part in the development of poetic vision
played by the existence of a mythology shared between writer and
audience—a factor much more important in earlier centuries. As Ted
Hughes was to write,

By modern secular definition, myth is something not to be taken seriously. This
is so rooted in the popular point of view, and this point of view has so
thoroughly naturalized Shakespeare as a secular author, that it is almost impossible for a modern reader to consider the myth of Venus and Adonis, as
Shakespeare adapts it, as anything but a picturesque fable, a Renaissance
ornamental fantasy, sensationalized to amuse an idle lord.[15]

Hughes's point about the value for poets when added significance was
afforded their work by the possession of a shared mythology needs to be
taken seriously. Among his own contemporaries the literary fashion was
setting hard against any such ideas, the scene being dominated by
writers such as Philip Larkin, who deplored the predilection of writers
for a practice he described as dipping into the 'myth-kitty', and Kingsley

---

[13] See his *Prose Works* edited by A. B. Grosart (3 vols., London: Moxon, 1876) III
168; and discussions of the problem in *Prel* (1805) i 157–221 and *The Excursion* vi
539–52 (*WPW* V 203–4).
[14] Excerpt from *Piccolomini*, II, 4, v 110–38 (14–22) (9 lines).
[15] *Shakespeare and the Goddess of Complete Being* (London: Faber, 1992), p. 56.

Amis, who informed poets that they should 'shut up about Orpheus'.[16] In one sense of course they were right: since the world of mythology, and still more of mythological reference, had disappeared from ordinary life and was no longer available to writers who wanted to reflect their contemporary culture, it became simply pretentious for them to go on writing as if it had not. But it remained legitimate to ask what was lost when a meaningful mythology died, and even to attempt the more worthwhile, if Quixotic, venture of trying to create a mythology fitted to the modern world that might restore to human beings a sense of the sacredness of their own existence, as Blake, and, to a certain degree, Hughes, had attempted. In Hughes's world, as to a limited extent in Coleridge's, the importance of mythology, given the alienation of the modern poet from society, was twofold. On the one hand it offered a way of interpreting one's own personal identity, since the poet might see himself or herself as a being set apart from society, with a special calling, in which case it was possible to draw on all the mythological figures who corresponded to that sense of self. But it was also possible to look at all mythologies for their common elements and to infer from them the existence of an original shared mythology that had once been common to all. In Coleridge's time this had been more possible than it has ever been since, particularly given the undeveloped state of etymology, which made it possible to explore the possibility that there had once been a universal language from which all subsequent languages derived. Afterwards that possibility more or less disappeared, with the scientific study of etymology and the understanding both that languages were more numerous and widespread than had been supposed and that the civilization in which they grew up was much older than the six thousand years that the biblical chronologies had allowed for. At the end of the older road lay the monitory figure of George Eliot's Mr Casaubon, still toiling away at the task of bringing the work of the eighteenth-century mythologists to fruition and not noticing that the world had changed. But of course Mr Casaubon's presence was deadly in a very particular sense, since he had already decided in advance what the conclusion of his researches would be. At the end of the road, he was certain, it would be finally established that all mythologies were distortions of the original account of things in the Jewish and Christian sacred writings. Coleridge's early version, by contrast, was more liberal: it would rather open

[16] Quoted by Frank Kermode, *Puzzles and Epiphanies* (London: Routledge, 1962), p. 35.

out mythologies to reveal an ancient wisdom that transcended particular religions and might also include the discoveries and theories of recent science.[17] In its boldest form this dream did not survive his expedition to Germany, though it is also doubtful whether he ever quite abandoned it. If it was in many ways a doomed enterprise, particularly when he relied on the Bible for confirmation, it was by no means as deathly as Casaubon's, given the open and exploratory nature of his mind. Even now, if one begins looking at ancient mythologies for the correspondences between them, it is striking to see how many links can be divined, existing across a wide range of cultures. One of the rival systems, just before Casaubon's time, attempted to establish the origin of all mythologies in sun-worship,[18] while even Sir James Fraser's later work *The Golden Bough* still offered a 'key to all mythologies', this time to be looked for in ancient fertility cults. Coleridge's attempts to sketch out a universal mythology had its own particular attraction, even though its chief fruit was to become abbreviated and scrambled into the dream-work of *Kubla Khan*, where, as I have tried to show in various studies, its chief lines of argument were still boldly visible; in composing that poem he also demonstrated how the line of such a project, if seen as emblematic of genius and its fate, could become at its deepest level bound up with the question of the poet's own personality, so that in the concluding stanza the tyrannical genius of the Tartar emperor presented at the beginning of the poem would turn almost effortlessly into the first-person identity of the poet himself.

By the time that Hughes came on the scene the world had altered in many respects from that in which Coleridge made his mark, but his interest in mythologies and their significance was not dissimilar. The general narrative that he tried to establish changed its character over the years, but at its centre was a sense of the crucial connection between human beings and nature, evidenced among other things in the part played by animals and other living creatures in religious rituals. This preoccupation meant that in addition to writing the brilliant poems about animals that all readers could respond to, Hughes developed his subject matter to take in these links, devoting himself more intensely to

---

[17] This venture, which I discussed in *Coleridge the Visionary* (London: Chatto & Windus, 1959), has since been explored further by Ian Wylie in *Young Coleridge and the Philosophers of Nature* (Oxford: Clarendon Press, 1989).

[18] For C. F. Dupuis and his *Origine de Tous les Cultes* see my *Coleridge the Visionary*, pp. 109, 213.

elements in poetic imagery drawn from immediate observations of animals and related natural organisms.

As already mentioned, the mythological interests of the eighteenth century had been rather different. At that earlier stage of knowledge it had been possible to look at traditional myths and images in the hope of interpreting them as a whole: the Egyptian myths of Isis and Osiris, for example, might show the permanence of sun and moon as human symbols. In particular, comparative linguistic studies had not been developed far enough to make clear the difficulty of supposing that originally there had been a single language for all mankind. Since Coleridge as a young man was living at the last point when such investigations seemed worth pursuing, such speculations cast a glow over the whole of knowledge. The child Coleridge, walking with his father under the stars, was unimpressed by the lore he was expounding because he had already been made aware of cosmic wonder in the oriental myths he had read; the poet Coleridge, walking with the Wordsworths under the moon, could likewise convey a possible sense of its direct human influence. When such bodies appeared in his poems of the supernatural the sense of magic could be enlisted.

When in later years Hughes's mythological thinking developed on a wider front, this actually included a reading of Coleridge's poetic work, notably that of his great creative period. He gradually began to slot the pieces he found into a mythological pattern produced from his own ideas, and even to do a little research on his own account. Any references to plants and animals were immediately seized on—particularly if they were made more than once by the poet, since then it was possible to believe that they had strong symbolic significance. Bartram's account of the great 'alligator hole', for example, in his *Travels through North and South Carolina*, had so struck Coleridge in the 1790s that he copied it into his notebook and introduced it as a detail into the prose draft for his 'Wanderings of Cain'. What he copied shows that he was particularly struck by the description of the 'old Champion' who, when in rut, gave an extraordinary display of roaring and twirling. He

darts forth from the reedy coverts all at once on the surface of the water, in a right line; at first, seemingly as rapid as lightning, but gradually more slowly until he arrives at the center of the lake, where he stops; he now swells himself by drawing in wind & water thro' his mouth, which causes a loud sonorous rattling in the throat for near a minute; but it is immediately forced out again thro' his mouth & nostrils with a loud noise, brandishing his tail in the air, & the vapor ascending from his nostrils like smoke. At other times when swollen to an extent ready to burst, his head & tail lifted up, he twirls round on the surface of the water. He retires—& others, who dare, continue the exhibition— all to gain the attention of the favorite Female—

The distant thunder sounds heavily—the crocodiles answer it like an echo—[19]

It is not surprising that Hughes should have been seized by so marvellously vivid an account of animal behaviour, or that he should have seen it as a key to understanding Coleridge's poetic development. He would come to find in it a crucial clue to 'Kubla Khan', giving a context of animal, orgasmic violence to the woman wailing for her daemon lover and—above all—to the mighty, destructive fountain of the poem, erupting from a tremendous force below. To this primaeval sexual roaring and powerful, fountainous eruption he then brought Coleridge's contemporaneous lines (first in the notebook, then in the poem) about the nightingale that precipitates 'with fast thick warble' the 'delicious notes' of his love-chant, and noted the resemblance to the 'fast thick pants' of the earth's breathing in Coleridge's poem. 'A song of some kind is twisting into existence,' he wrote, 'a "mingled measure" like the braids of current in the Alph itself.'[20] With such deft touches he created something like a poetic canvas of his own, centred in the orgasmic, even orgiastic, energy of the scene at the centre of the second stanza, which he regarded as having given Coleridge an opportunity to vent fully what was repressed within himself. When he came back to read *The Rime of the Ancient Mariner* in these terms, similarly, he discerned a clear parallel between the voyage, desolation, and restoration of the Mariner and the process of stripping and recreation in the shamanic dream-flight.

Coleridge, on Hughes's reading, had lost his way at an early stage. Accordingly, there were to be traced in him two selves: the Christian self, brought up as son to the Vicar of Ottery St Mary and forever afterwards trying to find his way back to a fulfilment of his earliest religious identity, a self which militated against his potentialities as a poet; and the primitive self, suppressed from earliest childhood when his mother ceased to give him proper attention and so left him always in flight from his deepest feelings. On this view, his ill-fated marriage to a young woman from an orthodoxly religious family having been contracted under pressure, he only began to discover his primitive self

[19] CNB G ff 31ᵛ–33 (cf. *CN* I 218, 221).
[20] Ted Hughes, *Winter Pollen: Occasional Prose*, ed. William Scammell (London: Faber, 1994), pp. 394–6.

briefly during his walks with the wild young woman Dorothy Wordsworth on the Quantock hills in 1797 and 1798—which was when he
also wrote his great visionary poems. During this period he was seen as
having come closer to acknowledgement of the other, truer side of his
identity, figured particularly in two images: those of the 'snake' and the
'oak'. On Hughes's account of the matter Coleridge's failure to fulfil his
poetic potentiality meant that he did not have the strength of identity
that he found figured in the oak tree. Instead, he was a weak figure,
captive to the Puritan ideal of Christianity that had ensnared him from
birth. Hughes found a telling illustration of this in one of Coleridge's
later notebooks, already quoted, where he wrote of the 'cold hollow
spot' that had thwarted even his childhood prayers, 'as if a snake had
wreathed around my heart'. It was characteristic of Hughes's concerns
that the central image he seized on was that of the snake, coiled round
the heart and waiting to dart its poison on any generous impulse. What
was less predictable was that he should also have fastened on Coleridge's
reference to the 'unleavened self' as a key to his personality. This is all
the stranger since it does not quite correspond to Coleridge's biblical
reference. St Paul urged his recipients in Corinth to put aside the 'leaven
of malice and wickedness' and to keep the feast with the 'unleavened
bread of sincerity and truth'.[21] Coleridge uses the metaphor rather
differently, figuring human nature as something which can normally
be leavened by true Christianity but which may still retain an unleavened element of self-centredness. Hughes gave the metaphor a further
twist, assuming that Coleridge's despised unleavened self was in fact the
true one, struggling to waken into activity and to be leavened by the
sincerity and truth of his animal nature. That this further development
of the sense is what is in his mind becomes clear from subsequent
references to Coleridge's 'Unleavened Self '; but it is not what Coleridge
himself had in mind. The existence of a division of some kind within
Coleridge's personality is hard to deny. Many pieces of evidence can be
brought together to support the sense of a Christian, preaching self
constantly undermined by the work of an imagination that attracted
him into other paths of discourse—only to retreat unceremoniously
if their fuller implications loomed. And Hughes's own imaginative
powers gave him an unusually privileged entrée to this sphere. They
are most fruitfully at work when he can enter the dance of imagery and

---

[21] I Cor. 5: 5–8.

create his own pattern; they also encourage him to concentrate on little-regarded aspects of the previous poetry, notably the contributions to Southey's *Joan of Arc* later used for the unfinished 'Destiny of Nations', which displayed his strong contemporary interest in myths, notably those of the northern nations, and in myth-making. It may well be, as Hughes suggests, that Coleridge would have been a better poet if he had given more rein to that side of himself. But many of the details that he conjures—for example in projecting an 'unleavened self' of sincerity and truth that Coleridge consciously rejected—are harder to accept.

Nonetheless, there are points at which Coleridge's feeling for natural energies chimed notably with Hughes's. At the turn of the century, the dialectic between Wordsworth and Coleridge had fruitfully reflected their respective conceptions of the 'one Life'. For Coleridge this sense had focused itself in various scenes, as for example his contemplation of the sunset in North Somerset, gazing 'till all doth seem | Less gross than bodily . . .' and blessing the single homeward-flying rook, which, with the creaking of its wing, seemed a potent, isolated manifestation of the one Life. Just over a year later, on his way to Germany, he wrote to his wife:

About 4 o'clock I saw a wild duck swimming on the waves—a single solitary wild duck—You cannot conceive how interesting a thing it looked in that round objectless desart of waters . . .[22]

Between the two—the single rook and the single wild duck—there had appeared the most striking of his creations: the single albatross that attached itself to the human beings on the ship bearing the Ancient Mariner. But in addition to the isolation of these living beings Coleridge had evoked in that poem a different vision of the one Life, in the shape of the water-snakes:

> They moved in tracks of shining white,
> And when they reared, the elfish light
> Fell off in hoary flakes.
>
> Blue, glossy green, and velvet black,
> They coiled and swam; and every track
> Was a flash of golden fire.

It was the point, perhaps, when he came closest to expressing his vision of the one Life in terms of its energies. In his poem 'That

---

[22] *CL* I 426.

Morning', similarly, describing an experience in Alaska when he and their son were pursuing the son's work in the fisheries there and saw an overwhelming number of salmon moving together in a stream, in accordance with the laws of their nature, Hughes's vision of existence reached a moment of clarification. For him the closest parallel to that experience had been a sight of Lancaster bombers once seen moving majestically in formation over Yorkshire, presumably usurping the sky with their mechanical menace, just as the salmon now overwhelmed his sense of the whole landscape with a vision of apparently unceasing life:

> There the body
> Separated, golden and imperishable,
> From its doubting thought – a spirit-beacon
> Lit by the power of the salmon
> That came on, and came on, and kept on coming
> As if we flew slowly, their formations
> Lifting us toward some dazzle of blessing
> One wrong thought might darken.

In one of Shakespeare's darkest moments 'Light thickens | And the crow makes wing to the rooky wood'. It looks like a comment on the manner in which even the more questionable beings in nature need companionship (just as Macbeth was to be distressed by the absence of 'troops of friends'). For Hughes his vision of the salmon was evidently an experience akin to Coleridge's view of the sunset in North Somerset, gazing 'till all doth seem | Less gross than bodily...' and blessing the homeward flying rook, with the comment that 'no sound is dissonant that tells of life'—a reflection which in turn prefigured the moment of unconscious blessing in *The Ancient Mariner*; Hughes, similarly, finds himself blessing—almost unconsciously—the abounding salmon. In 1798 there had been nothing to link such moments with any particular religion, even if they might be taken up later into a Christian interpretation: the blessing was presented as an existential act from deep within the Mariner's being, a simple affirmation directed towards the luminous energies of the water-snakes as they 'coil'd and swam'. Potent beyond all particular manifestations, the same joy would be recreated in Coleridge's psyche when he looked at all the luminous activity in the shadow of the boat at sea a few years later on his way to Malta and saw the energies at work there as 'Spirals, coiling, uncoiling, *being*.'[23] At such

---

[23] CNB 15b f 30; *CN* II 2070.

moments the Coleridge whose Mariner blessed the water-snakes and the Hughes who found himself blessing the myriad salmon seem to encounter most surely, as if in a stance of mutual recognition.

The fact of this guarded similarity between the reverence for life expressed by Hughes and Coleridge inevitably invites some comparison of the latter's poetry with that of Sylvia Plath, who was, like him, a poet of highly developed consciousness, yet, also like him, unballasted by any strong sense of inner being. I have elsewhere argued that there is an important parallel to be drawn between the ranging consciousnesses of Plath and Coleridge on the one hand and, on the other, the monolithic, self-confirming identity characteristic of Hughes and Wordsworth. The latter pair, I have suggested, were nevertheless fascinated by their counterparts, needing their mercurial stimulus.[24] The pattern of behaviour involved corresponds, in fact, to the two types of genius as described by Coleridge: the one, the Shakespearean, that darts itself forth, passing into all the forms of human character and passion, 'the one Proteus of the fire and flood'; the other, the Wordsworthian and Miltonic version, attracting all forms and things to itself, 'into the unity of its own IDEAL'.[25] In her journals Plath returns more than once to her sense that she had no identity, suggesting even less self-confidence than Coleridge's. Her personality, on this reading, was taking his problems a stage further, involving an identity which was by no means non-existent but rather constantly shifting, in correspondence with the energies at work on any one occasion. As it happened, she actually represented this state of things in a poem—'Snakecharmer'—which was strangely self-referring. 'As the gods began one world, and man another', the poem begins, 'So the snakecharmer begins a snaky sphere'. And by the time he has finished 'nothing but snakes is visible':

> The snake-scales have become
> Leaf, become eyelid; snake-bodies, bough, breast
> Of tree and human. And he within this snakedom
> Rules the writhings which make manifest
> His snakehood and his might with pliant tunes
> From his thin pipe[26]

---

[24] See the last chapter of my *Post-Romantic Consciousness: Dickens to Plath* (London: Palgrave, 2003).

[25] *CBL* II 27–8.

[26] Sylvia Plath, *Collected Poems* (London: Faber, and Faber, 1981), p. 79.

'Moon-eye, mouth-pipe': the whole poem relies on the interplay between the two as he produces a snake-play so powerful that the scene, and the verse describing it, are one in their intricate interweaving of sinuosities. As he tires, what has been created subsides into its constituent elements: the interweaving snake forms become straightforward warp and weft, which in turn are seen as cloth, dissolving then into green waters, until only the charmer himself is left, silent and unseeing.

The fit of energies and form is superb throughout: no further meaning need intrude beyond the story of the charmer's enterprise and his eventual tiring, which precipitates the relapse of the snakes and the closing of his moony eye. Technically, Plath has touched perfection. And the tight intricacy of the threefold pattern, music, interplaying energies, and moonlight, reveals itself as one of the most important paradigms in her visionary imagery.

At the conclusion the only fixed identity is that of the charmer—and he has fallen asleep. The preceding mutations and metamorphoses in fact help to explain why Plath's own identity is often found so hard to appreciate by those who look for settled form in poetry: it shifts and changes its point of focus even as one looks. It was for the same reason, no doubt, that those who dealt with her personally found her equally elusive. Although Coleridge's poetry succeeded better in its formal content there is something of the same evasiveness in his tendency to escape any particular net one tries to throw around him.

Although Coleridge's path was beset by dangers, he proved in the end to be essentially a survivor. Sylvia Plath, by contrast, like the bird in Joseph Wright's painting, suffered the fate of unballasted energy. Whereas, though lacking the support of an adequate love, Coleridge had been sustained throughout a lifetime by the counterweight of his moral nature and a conventional (if longsuffering) family, she, deprived of the oxygen that would have been furnished by duration of the single love that she had found, could only drop out of the world and die— leaving those who still remained in other relationships to her in varying attitudes of appalled wonder and distress.

Bibliography

Rosemary Ashton, *The Life of Samuel Taylor Coleridge: A Critical Biography* (Oxford: Blackwell 1996).

Jeffrey W. Barbeau (ed.), *Coleridge's Assertion of Religion: Essays on the Opus Maximum* (Leuven: Peeters 2006).

Owen Barfield, *What Coleridge Thought* (London: Oxford University Press, 1972).

J. Robert Barth SJ, *The Symbolic Imagination: Coleridge and the Romantic Tradition* (Princeton, N.J.: Princeton University Press, 1977).

—— *Romanticism and Transcendence: Wordsworth, Coleridge, and the Religious Imagination* (Columbia and London: University of Missouri Press, 2003).

Walter Jackson Bate, *Coleridge* (New York and London: Macmillan, 1968).

John Beer, *Coleridge the Visionary* (London: Chatto and Windus, 1959).

—— *Coleridge's Poetic Intelligence* (London and Basingstoke: Macmillan, 1977).

—— *Romanticism, Revolution and Language* (Cambridge: Cambridge University Press, 2009).

—— (ed.) *Coleridge's Variety* (London and Basingstoke: Macmillan, 1974).

Frederick Burwick (ed.), *Coleridge's* Biographia Literaria: *Text and Meaning* (Columbus: Ohio State University Press, 1989).

J. D. Campbell, *Samuel Taylor Coleridge: A Narrative of the Events of His Life* (London: Macmillan, 1896).

Maurice Carpenter, *The Indifferent Horseman: The Divine Comedy of Samuel Taylor Coleridge* (London: Elek Books, 1954).

E. K. Chambers, *Samuel Taylor Coleridge: A Biographical Study* (Oxford: Clarendon Press, 1938).

Jerome Christensen, *Coleridge's Blessed Machine of Language* (Ithaca, N.Y.: Cornell University Press, 1981).

Henry Nelson Coleridge (ed.), *Specimens of the Table Talk of the Late Samuel Taylor Coleridge* (2 vols., London: John Murray and New York: Harper & Brothers, 1835).

John Colmer, *Coleridge: Critic of Society* (Oxford: Clarendon Press, 1959).

John Cornwell, *Coleridge: Poet and Revolutionary 1772–1804* (London: Allen Lane, 1973).

Graham Davidson, *Coleridge's Career* (London and Basingstoke: Macmillan, 1990).

George Dekker, *Coleridge and the Literature of Sensibility* (New York: Barnes & Noble; London: Vision Press, 1978).

Oswald Doughty, *Perturbed Spirit: The Life and Personality of Samuel Taylor Coleridge* (Rutherford, N.J.: Fairleigh Dickinson University Press, 1981).

Norman Fruman, *Coleridge: The Damaged Archangel* (Scranton, Penn.: George Braziller, 1971).

Tim Fulford, *Coleridge's Figurative Language* (Basingstoke: Palgrave Macmillan, 1991).

Lawrence Hanson, *The Life of Samuel Taylor Coleridge: The Early Years* (London: George Allen & Unwin, 1938).

Richard Haven, *Patterns of Consciousness: An Essay on Coleridge* (Amherst: University of Massachusetts Press, 1969).

Douglas Hedley, *Coleridge, Philosophy and Religion: Aids to Reflection and the Mirror of the Spirit* (Cambridge: Cambridge University Press, 2000).

Richard Holmes, *Coleridge: Early Visions* (London: Hodder & Stoughton, 1989).

—— *Coleridge: Darker Reflections, 1804–1834* (London: HarperCollins, 1999).

Kathleen Jones, *A Passionate Sisterhood: Women of the Wordsworth Circle: The Sisters, Wives and Daughters of the Lake Poets* (New York: St. Martin's Press, 2000).

Edward Kessler, *Coleridge's Metaphors of Being* (Princeton, N.J.: Princeton University Press, 1979).

Michael John Kooy, *Coleridge, Schiller and Aesthetic Education* (Basingstoke: Palgrave Macmillan, 2002).

Nigel Leask, *The Politics of Imagination in Coleridge's Critical Thought* (Basingstoke: Macmillan, 1988).

Molly Lefebure, *Samuel Taylor Coleridge: A Bondage of Opium* (London: Gollancz and New York: Paragon House, 1974).

—— *The Bondage of Love: A Life of Mrs. Samuel Taylor Coleridge* (London: Victor Gollancz, 1986).

Trevor H. Levere, *Poetry Realized in Nature: Samuel Taylor Coleridge and Early Nineteenth-Century Science* (Cambridge: Cambridge University Press, 2002).

Laurence S. Lockridge, *Coleridge the Moralist* (Ithaca, N.Y., and London: Cornell University Press, 1977).

John Livingston Lowes, *The Road to Xanadu: A Study in the Ways of Imagination* (Boston and New York: Houghton Mifflin Company, 1927).

Paul Magnuson, *Coleridge and Wordsworth: A Lyrical Dialogue* (Princeton, N.J.: Princeton University Press, 1988).

Richard E. Matlak, *The Poetry of Relationship: The Wordsworths and Coleridge, 1797–1800* (Basingstoke: Palgrave Macmillan, 1997).

Thomas McFarland, *Coleridge and the Pantheist Tradition* (Oxford: Clarendon Press, 1969).

—— *Romanticism and the Forms of Ruin: Wordsworth, Coleridge and Modalities of Fragmentation* (Princeton, N.J.: Princeton University Press, 1981).

John Stuart Mill, *Mill on Bentham and Coleridge*, ed. F. R. Leavis (London: Chatto & Windus, 1950).

J. H. Muirhead, *Coleridge as Philosopher* (New York: Macmillan and London: George Allen and Unwin, 1930).

Lucy Newlyn, *The Cambridge Companion to Coleridge* (Cambridge: Cambridge University Press, 2002).

G. N. G. Orsini, *Coleridge and German Idealism* (Carbondale and Edwardsville: Southern Illinois University Press; London and Amsterdam: Feffer and Simons Inc., 1969).

Mary Anne Perkins, *Coleridge's Philosophy: The Logos as Unifying Principle* (Oxford: Clarendon Press, 1994).

Seamus Perry, *Coleridge and the Uses of Division* (Oxford: Clarendon Press, 1999).

—— (ed.) *S. T. Coleridge: Interviews and Recollections* (Basingstoke: Palgrave Macmillan, 2000).

Stephen Prickett, *Wordsworth and Coleridge: the Poetry of Growth* (Cambridge: Cambridge University Press, 1970).

—— *Romanticism and Religion: The Tradition of Coleridge and Wordsworth in the Victorian Church* (Cambridge: Cambridge University Press, 1976).

David Pym, *The Religious Thought of Samuel Taylor Coleridge* (Gerrards Cross: Colin Smythe, 1978).

I. A. Richards, *Coleridge on Imagination* (London: Kegan Paul, 1934).

Daniel Sanjiv Roberts, *Revisionary Gleam: De Quincey, Coleridge And the High Romantic Argument* (Liverpool: Liverpool University Press, 2000).

Nicholas Roe, *Wordsworth and Coleridge: The Radical Years* (Oxford: Clarendon Press, 1988).

—— (ed.), *Samuel Taylor Coleridge and the Sciences of Life* (Oxford: Oxford University Press, 2001).

Elinor S. Shaffer, *'Kubla Khan' and the Fall of Jerusalem: The Mythological School in Biblical Criticism and Secular Literature, 1770–1880* (Cambridge: Cambridge University Press, 1975).

Jack Stillinger, *Coleridge and Textual Instability* (New York and Oxford: Oxford University Press, 1994).

Donald Sultana, *Samuel Taylor Coleridge in Malta and Italy* (Oxford: Basil Blackwell; New York: Barnes & Noble, 1969).

Anya Taylor, *Coleridge's Defense of the Human* (Columbus: Ohio State University Press, 1986).

—— *Erotic Coleridge: Women, Love, and the Law against Divorce* (Basingstoke and NY: Palgrave Macmillan, 2005).

David Vallins, *Coleridge and the Psychology of Romanticism: Feeling and Thought* (Basingstoke: Palgrave Macmillan, 1999).

Neil Vickers, *Coleridge and the Doctors* (Oxford: Oxford University Press, 2004).

James Vigus, *Platonic Coleridge* (Leeds: Modern Humanities Research Association (Legenda) and Maney Publishing, 2009).

James Vigus and Jane Wright (eds), *Coleridge's Afterlives* (Basingstoke: Palgrave Macmillan, 2009).

Stephen M. Weissman, *His Brother's Keeper: a Psychobiography of Samuel Taylor Coleridge* (Madison, Conn.: International Universities Press, *c.* 1989).

R. J. White, *The Political Thought of Samuel Taylor Coleridge* (London: Jonathan Cape, 1938).

Basil Willey, *Samuel Taylor Coleridge* (London: Chatto and Windus, 1972).

John Worthen, *The Gang: Coleridge, the Hutchinsons, and the Wordsworths in 1802* (New Haven, Conn.: Yale University Press, 2001).

Index

The Winter's Tale 166
sonnet, sonnets 111, 162
Venus and Adonis 246
Sharp, Richard 41n, 49, 71, 74
Shedd, William Greenough
    Thayer 192
Sheridan, Richard 158
Sicily, 128
Sidney, Sir Philip 114
silence, silent 13, 31, 65
single and double touch 76, 79, 81
    and n., 167, 184 *see also* touch
Skeltoniad 39
sky-lark 215
Smith, Charlotte 29
Smith, John, *Select Discourses* 128
Smith, R. and Sydney 49
Smith, Thomas 125
snake(s) 95, 251, 254–5
    adder 59
    water-snakes 252
Social Darwinism 240
socialist 245
Sockburn 31, 32
Socinianism 188
Somerset 61, 95, 252
Sotheby, William 85 n. 5, 86, 87,
    88, 91, 101
soul 131, 170, 179, 210, 211
South Molton 1
Southcott, Joanna 176
Southey, Robert 18, 26, 30, 34, 40,
    51, 56, 71, 73, 74, 113, 115,
    117, 125, 127, 133, 179n, 191
    Joan of Arc 252
space 71, 76, 141 *see also* time,
    Mackintosh
Spectator, The 127
Spenser, Edmund 217
Spinoza, Baruch 23, 45, 85n
spirit 208, inquiring 234
Spleenwort 93
spring 60, 107, 135, 161, 170

springs and fountains 54, 60
spy 23 n. 6
St John 196
St Peter *see* Peter
Stäel, Madame de 42
starlings 99, 100
Statesman's Manual, The 104
Stephen, Leslie 37
Sterling, John 196, 228, 239n
    Edward (son) 228
    Life of John Sterling 239
Sterne, Laurence 156
Stewart, Dugald 76 and n
Stevens, Wallace 21
stock-doves 36
Stoics 180, 182
Stoke D'Abernon 70
stream 28, 54, 95, 97, 107
Stuart, Daniel 41, 42, 47, 90,
    103, 105
sun 128, 249
survival of the fittest 240 *see also*
    evolution
Swedenborgianism 229
Swift, Jonathan 82
Swiss cantons 102
Sykes Davies, Hugh 151 *see* Davies
symbol, 214, 249
symbolism, symbolic, symbolical
    129, 174, 214, 249
systole 147, 168

talent 49
Tatler, The 127
taxes, taxation 123
Taylor, Jeremy 194
Taylor, William 26, 71, 74, 75, 116
Temple Sowerby 79
Tennemann, Wilhelm Gottlieb 180,
    186
theism 29
Thelwall, John 14, 82
Thomson, Heidi 89, 90